OKWADIKE

Celebrating the 80ᵗʰ Birthday Anniversary of

Dr. Chukwuemeka Ezeife,

PhD Harvard, CON

First Executive Governor of Anambra State

THEME:

NIGERIA - DEMOCRACY & STATE OF THE ECONOMY

Edited by:
HUMPHREY KANAYO AKAOLISA
DR OBIANUJU M. CHIEKEZIE
& TAGBO OGUEJIOFOR

GiPi Publications, Abuja

Plot 701 Mabushi, Cadastral Zone B6, Abuja

+2348024478189

ISBN-13: 978-978-55820-7-9

QUOTE

"Since after the civil war, of the ethnic tripods, on which the country stands, only the Igbo have not supplied an elected Chief Executive Officer of the country. Again, of the six geo-political zones of the country, only the Southeast, home of most Igbo, has not supplied a President of Nigeria. The corruption that is fueled by Oil Money, combined with apparent death of conscience in Nigeria, has weakened values, especially the value of hard work. And so Nigeria grows backwards, remaining in the kindergarten, while those that started the development race with her, are far into the tertiary levels. It seems to be the case that as the Igbo remains down politically, so must Nigeria remain down economically." - Dr. Ezeife 2012

CONTENTS

Foreword   vii

Introduction: NIGERIA – DEMOCRACY & STATE OF   ix
THE ECONOMY – Dr Obianuju Mary Chiekezie &
Humphrey Kanayo Akaolisa

PART I   1
CELEBRATING OKWADIKE @80

1   A Brief Biography of Dr. Chukwuemeka Ezeife   3

2   The Man: Okwadike, Dr Chukwuemeka Ezeife   9

3   Sun Newspaper Interview in Commemoration of the 80th   22
    Birthday Annivasery

4   An Ode to Dike n' Agha Nd'Igbo: Celebrating Okwadike   30
    @80 – Tagbo Oguejiofor

5   Democracy and Development – Obiora Okonkwo PhD   32

PART II   41
SELECTED WORKS OF DR EZEIFE – DEMOCRACY

6   Nigeria: Her Manifest Destiny and Basis for Unity   43

7   Towards God's Own Nigeria   54

8   The Imperative and ABC of Restructuring Nigeria   96

9   The Imperative of a New Nigeria   106

10   Rigid Zoning and Rotation of Office of Governor in States   112

11   Engr. Charles Mbanefo Distinguished Lectures, 2017   117

12   What Federating Units – States or Zones/Regions   127

13   An Appeal to Fellow Nigerians   133

14   Why I Prefer Restructuring to Biafra   142

15   True Federalism, Citizen Rights and National Unity   156

16 Bayelsa State 17th Anniversary Public Lectures   165

17 Born to Rule – Phychosis Killing Nigeria   174

PART III   185
SELECTED WORKS OF DR EZEIFE – ECONOMY
18 The Strategy for Supply of Petroleum Products to the   187
    Domestic Market
19 Diversification of Nigerian Economy   192

PART IV   199
SELECTED WORKS OF DR EZEIFE – IGBO/BIAFRA
20 Igbo Leadership   201

21 Ndigbo and Their Role in Nation Building   205

22 2012 Ahiajoku Lectures, Owerri   211

23 Corporate Campaign Strategy for Igbo Nigeria President 215

24 Ndigbo: The Way Forward with One Nigeria   224

25 Biafra: Injustice can Make Igbo Republic Possible   234

26 Open Letter to Northern Elders   238

27 We Must Begin Again   245

PART V   249
CONTRIBUTIONS ON THE THEME: NIGERIA –
DEMOCRACY AND STATE OF THE ECONOMY
28 Democracy and Good Governance – Nwosu M. Eze   251

29 Building Democracy in the Context of Poverty – Louis   267
    Nwabueze Ezeilo PhD
30 Are more Tolerant Societies more Likely to Invest in   290
    Education – Willie Eyo
31 Democracy and Sustainable National development in   303
    Nigeria – Chukwudi Ucheagu
32 Is Nigeria Better United? – Eze Uzoamaka Jennifer   322

FOREWORD

Dr Chukwuemeka Ezeife, CON fondly called Okwadike is a giant that needs no introduction. For those meeting him for the first time through the medium of this work, this book will not suffice though it may give them a bird's eye view of him. For those who already knew him, this will not only be a renewal of the man they knew but also an insight into his intellectual world. More than this, a shocker might be in the offing for them, for there might be a few things they really never knew about his ideology and energy that powers it.

As a distinguished Economist and Harvard product, Okwadike has been a devout, consistent and prime player in the Nigeria political economy and democratic processes right from the second republic; a leader to his people. He has left the footprints of a sage in this regard. On this day of the 80th birthday anniversary of this Igbo and Nigerian icon, it is imperative that renowned Nigerians, scholars, academicians, intellectuals, politicians, technocrats and indeed, all Nigerians should reflect on his contributions to this process, the state of the nation today and the place of the Igbo people in contemporary Nigerian politics.

For more than two decades since leaving office as the first executive governor of Anambra state, Dr Ezeife has fearlessly and tirelessly fought for an open and decent society not just for his people; the Igbo, but for all Nigerians with the Igbo philosophy of 'let the kite perch and let the eagle perch: live and let live.' Ezeife has fought for fairness and equity for all Nigerians as well as the protection of lives and properties irrespective of ethnicity or religion. He has extended his mentorship to all leaders and politicians who cared.

Beyond being a political colossus of his time, a man among men, an iroko, Dr Ezeife as could be seen from this anthology of his journalistic writings, is clearly an intellectual giant whose ideals and bravado has continued to dazzle and flabbergast all including his closest associates. From these pieces, Ezeife has all that goes into the making of outstanding political intellectual: the courage, brilliant insight and mental energy. All these put together clearly set him apart.

In this 80th anniversary commemorative publication, we have tried to draw the attention of Nigerians to our current socio-economic and political state. This publication is designed essentially to bring to the larger audience, some of the ideas and vision which Okwadike has articulated on how to re-engineer, remake Nigeria and return her to God's original design for her, as a super power. The more people read these ideas, the greater the chance that someday, someone will emerge in the Nigeria's political scene and implement them, at least, some of the crucial ones for progress.

We must understand where the rains started beating us in order to know where we dried our bodies. Nigeria is in turmoil today because we refused to do the needful. Our economy is in shambles. Our roads are death traps. Our health care is heavily neglected. People are living in fear as lives and properties are not secured. Many are starving and dying. Parents are suffering untold hardship to make ends meet. The youths are without jobs. The people have lost trust in their leaders. The leaders are reluctant to engage in a political reconstruction. Ezeife has been consistently in the forefront of leaders calling for what has entered the Nigerian political dictionary as restructuring with the aim of moving a stagnant country ahead.

We can unequivocal say that Dr Ezeife, CON is a man and a prophet of his time who effectively deployed his intellectual prowess to fight for the emancipation of his people in their struggle for equity, fairness and justice. It is our conviction that a reading of these writings will offer a deeper insight into the working of his mind, his ideology, philosophy, courage and above all his commitment to justice for all.

Happy reading!

The Editors

An Introduction to the Theme:

NIGERIA – DEMOCRACY AND STATE OF THE ECONOMY

Dr. Obianuju Mary Chiekezie &
Humphrey Kanayo Akaolisa

Democracy is not a new term, it is as old as ancient Athens and Greek philosophical states. Democracy has also existed in Africa from antiquity as seen in the Igbo traditional system of leadership and the Kikuyu of Kenya. However, the concept of democratization is a relatively new ideology which developed in the 1980's and 1990's. Democratization, though broader than, is believed to be linked to the collapse of communism and the rediscovery of economics in the present era. (Fukuyama, 1989) Simply put, democratization is the political process of replacing dictatorial and autocratic governments with freely elected governments. This simple definition is complicated because there is no clear answer to the question, "when is a government democratic?" (Papp, 1997)

Despite the complexities and vagaries found in democracy, most analysts agree that the world had experienced growing trend towards democratization. This trend began in the 1980's in Latin America as countries moved away from authoritarian governments and instituted democratic governments. With the restoration of a freely elected government to power in Haiti in 1994, thirty-four (34) of the thirty-five (35) states in the Western Hemisphere were governed by freely elected government. This trend proceeded to Eastern Europe. In 1989 communist governments fell and in most instances were replaced by freely elected governments. The same trend extended to Soviet Union (USSR) in 1991, where one state became 15 states many of which embraced free elections. In Asia, Cambodia, South

Korea, Taiwan, Thailand and many others adopted the same process. Africa was not left out, countries such as Benin, Malawi, Mozambique, Namibia, Sao Tome and Principe, South Africa, Uganda, Liberia, Ghana and many others followed. In 1999, Nigeria, where autocratic regimes had reigned for 30 years out of 39 years of her independence, joined the race. (Diamond and Plattner, 1999)

The relationship between democracy and development has been one of the most vibrant and important debates within social science scholars; political philosophy, political science and development studies. Democracy has been linked to economic growth. But their relationship may have been overstated. Many countries do not have democratic government but had made significant or sometime enormous economic development. Democracy has been brutally suppressed in China in 1989, yet China is acclaimed today as one of the fastest growing economies in the world. Some other countries have experienced better economic growth under dictatorial regimes than under democratically elected governments. Countries like Libya in Africa recorded quite impressive economic growth under the dictator, Muammar Gaddafi. North Korea has become a significant global power with their recent developments of military arsenals. Whereas Venezuela, Greece and Nigeria where freely elected democratic governments have reigned for over decades, have recorded the worst economic recessions in recent history. Nigeria is currently ranked as having the highest poverty index in the world in spite of its high GDP (World Poverty Clock, 2018), while Venezuela could be rightly described today as a failed state. The fear is that Nigeria will join Venezuela soon. It is important to note that both Venezuela and Nigeria are oil producing states.

It is obvious that in spite of the fact that elections have been held in Nigeria, democracy hold is tenuous as economic problems, ethnic unrest, religious extremism, terrorism, civil strife, corruption, impunity, marginalization of disliked groups and extremist movements on political left and right, threaten to undermine her development and existence. This had raised quite important question on the indices that engender economic growth, is it political stability, good leadership or mere holding elections? Democratization is a face of liberalization which simply refers to political and social liberalization. It is thought that liberal governments are the best form of government, but on another hand, liberalism is thought to be the cause of political, ethnic and religious insurgences because of the concomitant freedom that goes with it. Nigeria became more polarized on religious, social and ethnic lines since the dawn of democratization.

Holden (1974) writing on the Necessary Conditions for Democracy opines that without the basic principles of democracy, that "democracy could not for long continue to exist." The universal principles of democracy are basically two – equality and freedom. However, they also include popular sovereignty, majority rules and minority rights, the rule of law and constitutional safeguard, which are corollaries of equality and freedom. Significantly, these basic universal principles are also the same very principles on which all religions are based. For this meeting point, therefore, it beats the imagination how religions cannot cohabit in a democracy, and why violence and insurgences are fundamentally linked to democratization in Nigeria.

The first question is whether democracies perform better when it comes to development. This is an old and rich question which considers many pressing issues of our time such as: Does political competition actually prevent governments from making important long-term decisions on a range of issues from climate change, investing in education to pension's reform? Are multi-ethnic and religiously divided African societies or states ready for democratization? Do new democracies enjoy higher economic growth than other states in a comparative socio-economic level? Does the cost of executing elections and change of government have any impact on the national economy? Can a democracy make developmental impacts without the right and qualified people in place to make and execute developmental policies?

The second important question that is raised by this process of democratization is the concept identified as "Government House Utilitarianism". Adoption of democracy from the west as the ultimate form of government and applying the principles, hook, line and sinker, without the Africans performing their own calculations seems to be the bane of democratization in Africa. This brings up the question whether higher levels of development are required for democracy to work. This is even an older and richer debate and one that taps into areas of continued academic and policy controversy. Does development promote democracy? Is it possible to build democracies in the context of poverty? Why might the level of national wealth, or development, shape the prospects for democratic consolidation?

The theme of this intellectual discourse was chosen based on the contributions of the man that is being celebrated by this work. Okwadike, Dr. Chukwuemeka Ezeife is a renowned Economist who has made and still makes his contributions to the development of Nigeria as a country and Ndi-Igbo as a nation. In this regard, he has left the footprints of a sage. Nigeria has all it takes to be a giant, not just of Africa, but in the world arena. In the area of human resources, Nigeria has produced some of the world best economists and intellectuals but it is surprising that there is nothing to show for it. It is not that these intellectuals kept quiet, as will be revealed in this book, Okwadike has been outspoken and had willingly made his marks and contributions. His rich ideas were made available to leaders and people in power to use.

In Nigeria, it is clear that the institutions for democracy are either ineffective or are completely alien to the culture of our society. The questions that boarder on the incentive for democratization in Nigeria, remains therefore, are these institutions, like the judiciary and the legislature strong enough and independent of the executive? In modern thoughts about democratization, scholars have wondered if the question should not be, how do people take up their own situation and build up their own democratic principles? China for instance, in resistance to America force on the spread of political values contend that free trade, free economy will eventually translate into political freedom. Former American President Bill Clinton had to join in the declaration that "democracy has no fixed model" as a result of his meeting with Ugandan President Yoweri Museveni at Entebbe during his first diplomatic visit to Africa in 2000. (Apesin, 2000)

Government House Utilitarianism is a model that has been recycled in Nigeria without any serious effort to study and analyze the impacts and effects this model has on Nigeria. Reading through Okwadike's thoughts, it is evident of his attempt to explicitly draw connections between practice and contemporary debates about democratic reforms in Nigeria. He solicits for far-reaching political reform in the economic, social and political arena. His papers have therefore suggested better models for democratizing Nigeria. Additionally, he has made suggestions towards improving economic developmental models and governing principles in sub-Saharan Africa, with Nigeria leading the Black Race.

Okwadike truly has a roadmap for the economic recovery for Nigeria. It is on record that he designed the roadmap for the emancipation of Anambra State, but unfortunately, his opportunity for the implementation was cut short. Subsequent leaders of the State who followed his roadmap had succeeded in transforming Anambra State. Okwadike's roadmap for the economic recovery of Nigeria is a sacrosanct for every Nigerian leader. The reader will be convinced. Democracy is a continuous process and does not just imply development; it requires knowledge, goodwill and consistency in the right actions. Good leadership is the key to the desired end of democratization. Gleaning from the works of Okwadike, it is glaring that this man meant well for Nigeria and for his people. He answered most of the questions raised above, but as usual, truth, goodwill and moral support are often relegate in our society.

Finally, Okwadike has made bold to say that "since after the civil war, of the ethnic tripods, on which the country stands, only the Igbo have not supplied an elected Chief Executive Officer of the country. Again, of the six geo-political zones of the country, only the Southeast, home of most Igbo, has not supplied a President of Nigeria. The corruption that is fueled by Oil Money, combined with apparent death of conscience in Nigeria, has weakened values, especially the value of hard work. And so Nigeria grows backwards, remaining in the kindergarten, while those that started the development race with her, are far into the tertiary levels. It seems to be the case that as the Igbo remains down politically, so must Nigeria remain down economically." (Dr. Ezeife 2012)

Presently, Nigeria is coming to terms with Okwadike's postulations, and this is hope for Nigeria.

References

Ake, Claude. 2001, *Democracy and Development in Africa*. Ibadan: Spectrum Books Limited.

Cunningham, Frank. 1987, *Democratic Theory of Socialism*. New York: Cambridge University Press.

Diamond, Larry and Plattner, Marc F. 1999, *The Global Resurgence of*

Democracy. New York: Cambridge University Press.

Ezeife, Chukwuemeka, in Akaolisa, Humphrey Kanayo. 2012, *Ten Reasons Igbo People are Rich and Successful Busisness People.* Nigeria: GiPi Publications.

Graham, Keith. *The Battle of Democracy Conflict, Consensus and Individual,* Great Britain: Wheatsheaf Books, 1986.

Held, David. 1987, *Models of Democracy.* Stanford California: Stamford University Press.

_____ 1993, *Prospects of Democracy.* Stanford California: Stanford University Press.

Holdens, Barry. 1974, *The Necessary Conditions for Democracy; The Nature of Democacy.* London: Nelson.

Michelini, Alberto. 2006, *The Challange of Democracy and Development in Africa: Interview with Olusegun Obasanjo, President of Nigeria.* Chiasso, Italy: Elvetica Edizioni.

Papp, Daniel S. 1997, *Contemporary International Relations (Framework for Understanding)* Fifth Edition, Georgia: Georgia Institute of Technology, Ellyn and Bacon.

Sidgwick Henry. 1999, *The Complete Works and Selected Correspondence of Sidgwick Henry,* Edited by Bart Schultz, 2nd Edition, InteLex Corp, Charlottesville, Va.

Stephen, Fish M. 1995, *Democracy from Scratch: Opposition and Regime in the New Russia.* Princeton, New Jersey: Princeton University Press.

Vanhanen, Tatu. 1997, *Prospects of Democracy: A Study of 172 Countries.* London and New York: Routledge.

JOURNALS

Apesin, Sam. 2000, *The Scorecard of Civil Rule*. News Africa, Vol. 1 No. 2 June 28.

Fukuyama, Francis. 1989, *The End of History*. National Interest pg 3-18

World Poverty Clock, 2018, Daily Trust Newspaper, Oct, 30 2018

PART I

CELEBRATING OKWADIKE @ 80

1

A BRIEF BIOGRAPHY OF
DR. CHUKWUEMEKA EZEIFE

A Narrative Summary Profile

Chukwuemeka Ezeife is the product of the fusion of two reputable families in Igbo-Ukwu, the famous ancient town and site of the earliest archeological finds in Igboland. His maternal grandfather is Ezeudegbunam (may fame not be my ruin), on the paternal side is Ezeifedikwo (there is wealth). Earlier (1953) "calculations and measurements" put Chukwuemeka's date of birth at 1939. Better information from mothers, who had babies the same year Chukwuemeka was born, confirm 1938 as the actual year of birth. Sleeping dogs must lie!

Chukwuemeka had a very solid, traditional Igbo village upbringing, with his parents playing their proper roles: father fierce and appearing hostile, especially, to boys; and mother kind and conciliatory. He tells stories of how, as children, they would mimic the funeral rites practiced by their elders. They would kill a lizard, bury it with all the ceremony observed for the dead. For dane guns they used bamboo barrels and sticks with one puffed end; and for gun powder, cassava buds and saliva.

3

Education (Academic)

Chukwuemeka Ezeife went to Primary school with his cohort (to the Salvation Army, Igbo-Ukwu, for infant 1 to standard 4, and the Holy Trinity Primary School Igbo-Ukwu, for standards 5 and 6). He completed the eight year primary education system in six years. Without the benefit of secondary school education but only two years of Grade Three teacher training, he prepared himself for University education, through correspondence courses and entered the university the same year with some of his primary school mates. His path to the University was: GCE Qualifying Test, January, 1959; GCE Ordinary Level, January, 1960; and GCE Advanced Level, January. 1961. That was the minimum period within which those examinations could be taken. This led him to the University College, Ibadan in October 1961. Chukwuemeka considers his best academic achievement to be his winning the Faculty Price, as the best student in the Faculty of Economic and Social Studies, 1962/63

Chukwuemeka's formal education ended with MA. PhD (Harvard) as a Rockefeller Foundation Scholar. 1969 - 1972.

Education (Professional)

His professional education took him to Tokyo International Centre, Tokyo, Japan (September to November 1965), and Arthur D Little Management Education Program, Cambridge Massachusetts (November 1966 to August (?) 1967). In both International professional programmes, attended by participants from various countries, Chukwuemeka Ezeife emerged with the best result.

Employment/Work Experience

From age 9, while still in primary school, Chukwuemeka engaged in petty trading, selling matches and soap bought for him by the mother. He pushed truck and did other menial jobs but not out of necessity. He was a **Pupil Teacher**, The Salvation Army Primary School, Igbo Ukwu (1954 – 1960), a **Headmaster** of a Junior Primary School the Salvation Army

4

Primary School, Osumenyi; After his graduation, he held the following posts: **Marketing Trainee,** Nigerian Breweries Ltd 1964 (where he achieved the distinction of beating old and new marketing officers in a sales competition); **Administrative Officer,** Federal Government, from 1965; **Lecturer in Economics, Makarere University College Kampala, Uganda,** a college of the University of East Africa from 1967 (he enjoyed the honour of joining to informally, advise President Milton Obote of Uganda); **Teaching Fellow in Economics, Harvard University** 1970 – 71. On return from the United States of America, Dr Ezeife held the following offices: from **Principal Planning Officer to Assistant Director, Central Planning Office, Ministry of National Planning; Director, National Transport Co-Coordinating Commission, Ministry of Transport 1978. Chairman, Productivity, Prices and Incomes Board 1982, Cabinet Office (Office of the President).** This was a Permanent Secretary grade assignment and was formally declared so when he left the position. In this position, he was drafted to process import licenses for "essential commodities" when the shortage of these commodities threatened the chances of the NPN in Election in 1983 and it was necessary to take the activity out of the responsible ministry to someone who would do it fast and not spend time bargaining for personal gain. He became a federal **Permanent Secretary** in 1983.

Dr Ezeife in Nigerian Politics

In politics, Dr. Ezeife participated in three key national bodies: the Constituent Assembly of 1988/89, the National Political Reform Conference 2005 and the 2014 National Conference. In politics also, he held positions as Executive Governor, Anambra State, 1992 - 93 and Special Adviser to the President (Political) 2001 - 2002. He was a founding member of Alliance for Democracy (AD) and held the post of National Vice Chairman of the party. He was founding member of the G34 (where on the death of Abacha, he advised the group to, in the interest of Nigeria, sponsor two political parties along ideological lines, and sustain the G34 as the Clearing House for politics in Nigeria). He initiated action on, and became a founding member of Peoples' Progressive Party (PPP), he held the post of National Secretary of the party. He aspired for the Presidency of Nigeria in 1998-9 (under Alliance for Democracy) and in 2002-3 (under United Nigeria People's Party). He was associated with the founding of a party which, because of its late formation, has joined the many un-known quantity parties in Nigeria. Today he finds no political party suitable for his membership.

Dr Ezeife in Business

In Business, Dr. Ezeife was at one point a major exporter/promoter of Nigerian produce (cocoa, coffee, palm kernels, timber, sesame seeds, tantalite etc.).He successfully ran a number of companies partly owned by him. Further, he was a founding National Secretary, Cocoa Association of Nigeria and founding National Vice Chairman, Finance Houses Association of Nigeria.

Local and International Honours

Dr Ezeife was honoured by the Senate of Atlanta, USA 1993, was adopted as honorary member of the City of Gary Indiana, USA, 1993. He was President, Nigerian Chess Federation, Chairman, Swimming/Chairman Premises, Ikoyi Club 1938, Lagos. He is Chairman Evergreen Habitat Organisation, an NGO; preterm Chairman, Senior Citizens and Elders' Forum of Nigeria etc. He belongs to the Boards of Trustees of a number of bodies (including Murtala Mohammed Foundation, Chief E K Clark Foundation etc). He is the patron of several organisations (including Yar'Adua/Jonathan Solidarity Forum, Council of Igbo-Ukwu Merit Chiefs etc.). Dr Ezeife has been conferred with many traditional titles among which are Okwadike Nd'Igbo, Garkuwan Fika, Akintolugboye of Egbaland.

Dr Ezeife has authored a major book: "Remaking Nigeria with Progressivism" 1977, and several booklets. He has written many professional papers and political commentaries. He wrote a column, "Political Currents", for the Punch Newspaper for about a year.

Dr Ezeife is married with many gifted upward-bound children one of whom has become the first person to make First Class Honours in the Department of Economics, Nnamdi Azikiwe University.

A Few of the Thoughts of Dr Chukwuemeka Ezeife

Ezeife's "Natural Law of Success" (developed before he was 20):

"Develop an objective that is good...and pray over it....have a craving as if your life depends on it and go after it with commitment, persistence and determination".

On "Osu".

The continued existence of Osu is a failure of society, and especially, of modern religions, Christianity and Islam.

"The basis for Osu no longer exists. Nobody, today, runs to any idol for protection and nobody who stupidly does so will get any protection or feeding which was the case in the past. The fire that runs out of wood supply must die. But those who are looking for whom to feel socially superior to are keeping the idea of Osu alive."

On The Basis of Unity in Nigeria

"Nigeria was purposefully created by God using British imperialism merely as a tool. God's purpose for creating Nigeria is the manifest destiny of (God's assignment to) the country."

"Nigeria is one Black African country which has all the potentials in population size, geographical extent, resources and history to develop into a World Super Power. It is the manifest destiny of Nigeria to develop into a Super Power and become the rallying point and big brother of Black and

African Peoples everywhere, raising their dignity and respect. If things can be made to work in Nigeria, no group can walk away from the Nigerian system feeling triumphantly. One Nigeria is in the interest of Nigerians, in the interest of Black and African Peoples, in the enlightened interest of the World."

On Politics as God's Vineyard

"The ignorant says there is no **morality** in politics and that politics is the zone of the filthy where anything goes, the abode of the demons! This just cannot be true. Politics is God's vineyard because politics deals with the affairs of men, the highest of God's creation. None can escape the judgment of God on things done in politics. Therefore onward godly soldiers, marching as to war, against the filth of Nigerian politics. Join hands! Let us Remake Nigeria, reform the minds of Nigerians. So that this country, Nigeria, will never be the same again."

On Political Leadership in Nigeria

Nigeria needs an integrator. The integrator must begin by appreciating, as blessings and assets, not as curses and liabilities, the so-called diversities in Nigeria. For God so loves Nigeria that He gave her, not only abundant material resources, good climate and stable earth (no volcanoes, no earthquakes), but also many peoples and cultures, many talents from many tribes. The integrator will fire the minds of Nigerians, focus them on the good great goal conceived by him, and tap the material resources to make Nigeria a Super Power. The search for such effective political leadership will not end until Nigeria gets God-centred principled leaders. A political leader of Nigeria has work to do, a burden to carry. He will need Knowledge, wisdom, vision and more. He must possess correct and sound principles of personal character....He must be sensitive. He must care genuinely. And he must lead by example. "Do as I do" should be his war cry" (**And the "I" is not narrowly defined**).

2

THE MAN: OKWADIKE, DR. CHUKWUEMEKA EZEIFE

(Garkuwan Fika, Dan Amar din Jama'a, Fiwajoye of Itori, Akin Tolugboye of Egbaland, Ochendo Umu- Akwukwo Okwadike Nd'igbo etc.)

Dr. Ezeife is the Alliance for Democracy Political Adviser to Chief Olusegun Obasanjo, the President of Nigeria who belongs to the People's Democratic Party. How have they worked? Nobody, but the two, can know. But press reports indicate that Dr. Ezeife remains himself and retains his principles and consistency. He praises Obasanjo for keeping him for so long in spite of basic differences on issues. He was only months in office when he made that statement.

Okwadike, an Igbo, was a founding member of Alliance for Democracy, a party dominated by the Yoruba of South-Western Nigeria. Why did he do that? As he explained, he believed that the Yoruba needed to be encouraged to remain in one Nigeria after the trauma of the annulment of the June 12, 1993 Presidential election, the annulment that he fought to the very end. It is his creed that one Nigeria where things work, is bigger and better than his ambitions for any office.

9

Yet he aspired for the presidency under AD. He expected to lose but was surprised that the Northern elements of the party gave him massive support. In the end, he lost to Chief Olu Falae in what he privately said was a totally compromised primary election. Yet he unleashed a resounding endorsement of Falae as soon as the "result" was announced and joined his campaign. He led the leaders of the campaign to Ohanaeze and to the country home of Dr. Alex Ekwueme. In the end, he said that the presidential election was clearly rigged, yet he did not support resort to the court. Okwadike, an Igbo, was a member of NADECO and did not stop fighting for the actualization of June 12, 1993, Abiola mandate until the man died. Indeed, Dr. Ezeife as the only SDP governor in the East, galvanized Eastern votes and dumped same for Abiola, enabling Abiola to escape narrowly the snares set for him by even some of his tribesmen. He was to campaign for Abiola in Lagos; nowhere did Abiola go to in Eastern Nigeria during the campaign that he did not go with Anambra siren. It was either Dr. Ezeife or his Deputy, Dr. Chudi Nwike, who accompanied the presidential candidate. Close to the election, Dr. Ezeife, the Garkuwan Fika, discovered and burst the rigging plans designed against Abiola.

A founding member of G-34, Dr. Ezeife joined in opposing Abacha's self-succession. His own consistent attack on the devices of Abacha was extremely risky. At one point he was hidden in a pastor's room for six weeks – not seeing the sky. That was when the dragnet of the dictator missed him by whiskers. It is a tale of some-thing good from foolishness. He knew that he was on the unofficial wanted list; he was so alerted by his friend, Admiral Ndubisi Kanu. Yet Dr. Ezeife joined Rev. Father Adasu, Ex-Governor of Benue and Chief John Oyegun, ex-Governor of Edo, to Kam Salem House, to visit those on the same wanted list who had already been arrested (Gov. Osoba, C.C. Onoh, David Jang etc.). This overtly foolish, audacious act actually tipped him off to avoid arrest even though the Policemen on duty were punished for letting him go. Chief John Oyegun was also on the wanted list and benefited from the same folly.

Dr. Ezeife, Akintolugboye of Egbaland, alarmed his supporters and sympathizers when he opened his mouth far too wide on the Diya & co coup allegation. Asked what he thought about the advertised confessions of the "coup plotters", he said he was not knowledgeable in pharmacology (suggesting that the persons might have been drugged). Asked further about the video evidence, he said something to the effect that he was not a photographer ("not an expert in cinematographer") suggesting that the video could have been doctored. He left no one in doubt that he did not believe the coup story. He had taken similar risks when Ken Saro Wiwa and Ogoni 8 were slaughtered. It looks strange that a progressive like Dr. Ezeife should enjoy traditional titles so much. Dr. Ezeife does. He celebrates his recent titles: his turbanning as Garkuwan Fika, his installation as Fiwajoye of Itori and, of course his Akin Tolugboye title. Since the Akin Tolugboye ceremony, traditional titles (of which he has already more than 16) have been pursuing Dr. Ezeife the way the vulture pursues carcasses. Offered are: Ibol Mkpeli of Ugep, Dan Amar of Jama'a, Okwadike Ndibo of Urum and more. According to Dr. Ezeife, he cares now for honours from non-majority groups. He does not want to have only Wazobia titles. Early in 2001, the Yoruba people resident in the North, awarded to him a certificate of merit at the Merit House Abuja. He was further declared a permanent Member of the Yoruba Community, worldwide- an award which Okwadike apparently enjoys so much. His official memo pad contains this declaration as if it were a chieftaincy title.

The Peoples Progressive Party (PPP) was born in the office of Dr. Ezeife with Balarabe Musa, Segun Osoba, and an empty seat meant for Chief John Oyegun, as the initiators. Dr. Ezeife was later to accept the post of National Secretary, leaving Rev. Adasu with the post of Chairman. Why did the

June 12 people want to participate in the Abacha transition? Dr. Ezeife had the answer. "We are politicians, not merely social critics or political activists. Politicians go for political power. Besides, those who understood and supported us would have been disappointed, if we did not give Abacha the chance to show that he did not mean well. It was not easy to persuade the core Yoruba elements to join. They had no faith in the Abacha move, neither did the rest of us – then non Yoruba. The UPGA boycott of the 1964 election was brought in as proof of the unreasonableness of boycotts. In the end, it was the argument that we should not be seen as too rigid, which won the case. By the way, that was the best party Nigeria never had – the PPP. There was total commitment and self-abnegation, men and women would zip open their purses, turn them upside down forgetting to take out even money for transport back. The espirit de corps was exemplary". Of course, neither the PPP nor the All Nigerians Congress nor even the Social Progressive Party, which contained the leading progressives who worked with Abacha, was registered. Instead, we got what the inimitable Bola Ige called "five fingers of a leprous hand!

Dr. Ezeife is a member of Murtala Mohammed foundation. How did he get on that? "I do not know. Long before I was appointed Political Adviser, I got one strange letter in which I found big names like Obasanjo, Babangida, Gowon, Danjuma etc". Till today he still does not know how he got named into the Board of trustees. Now, this is how he puts it: "my past has caught up with me. I did not know that people appreciated me. I was just doing what came naturally to me, playing the robot in the hands of God" that is how Akintolugboye explains his recognition at the National level.

Sometime, in the year 2000, the NTA network news showed Dr. Ezeife's in his traditional white, red cap and red beads, addressing a mammoth crowd in Kano stadium. It was the remembrance of Mallam Aminu Kano and his NEPU.

Garkuwan fika was the only southern person, of note, in the large gathering. Balarabe Musa, and Abubakar Rimi invited him. Dr. Ezeife has a connection with the Gamji Forum. He has featured in the activities of the forum a number of times. Some of his south-western associates wondered if he was jumping boat. Akintolugboye was just being himself.

Right there in Arewa house in early 2001, before he became the Special Adviser (Political), he responded to the northern irredentist speeches made by most speakers. He blasted Northern-interest-only advocates, especially, the military among them whom he accused of wrecking Nigerian and then singing a new and strange song of "Northern Interest Only".

Dr. Ezeife understands the basis of the agitation for resource control and agrees that the present situation of revenue allocation is grossly unfair, however he continues to advocate that national interest must count – that no part of Nigeria should be allowed to suffer while other parts are in plenty. "There must be something in Nigeria for every group."

A diehard advocate of One Nigeria, "if even as an economic union", Dr. Ezeife, at the height of Sharia controversy, called on Nigerians to do quickly what they have or want to do. Break up quickly if to break up you must. "But do so at a round table conference, not in the field of battle". Why the condition? "Because no part, or group of, Nigeria(ns) can walk away from the Nigerian System feeling triumphantly". And if the break up is accomplished at a round table conference, it will not be long before every group realizes its folly and a strong and better-ordered Nigeria, *where things begin to work,* will be the result". He feels it is in his bones, and asserts that "*One Nigeria* must survive." There will be no **Odua Republic, no Biafra, no Arewa Federation**. It was during the same Sharia controversy that Okwadike, a practicing Christian, showed his vast knowledge of Moslem literature, especially the Qur'an. He quoted copiously from the Qur'an to show that violence is not a necessary feature of Islam ('man killing God's children in defense of God.') that breaching the treaty (Constitution) is not Islamic. That there is distinction between the "way" (sharia) and the law of God and this enables the "way" to change in response to the changing times while the law of is God is permanent.

In his book: **Remarking Nigeria with Progressivism**, Akintolugboye showed essentially that Godly people are Christians and Moslems at the same time, irrespective of which religion the Godly persons prophess. He quoted the Bible where what counts is said to be fearing God as well as keeping his basic law, which is," Love thy neighbor as thyself" Anyone, who obeys this, is approved of God. And such, it is, who submits to Allah. When Jesus Said, "I am the way…" he means basically that love is the way. Okwadike Nd'Igbo believers that God, who has the power to make any one to be born anywhere, and the knowledge as to where the person is born, which often determines the person's religion, will not turn round and consign the majority of his creation to eternal burn fire, merely because of the accident of their birth. There is convincing Kernel of truth in this, it is even more convincing when ones reads Dr.Ezeife, Garkuwa Fika's direct arguments. Certainly God will not be merciful, loving, almighty, knowing everything, being everywhere and yet set just one path to Himself, which, as of now, a majority of his creation, due to no fault of theirs, do not traverse!

Dr. Ezeife's progressivism is seen in his universalism. But he has a special place for Black and African peoples whom he calls the original sons and daughters of God. His basic belief in One Nigeria is forced by the Original sons and daughter of God. His basic belief in One Nigeria is forced by the need for Nigeria to develop in to super power, so as to "restore the respect and dignity of Black and African Peoples the Original sons and daughters of God", who today, are like "the footman of the world". His progressivism also finds expression in his demonstrated support for youth, and women empowerment. On women empowerment, he makes the distinction between appointive and elective offices. As governor of Anambra State, he practiced the empowerment of women. He appointed two women Commissioners (one for works), six women Directors-General, three women Judges and a women Director of State Protocol. On elective office, he chides the women for not grabbing his suggestion of women exclusive constituencies, which he has made repeatedly in the last many years. He explains that each state has three senatorial zones. He proposes one additional Zone, the whole state, which becomes exclusive female senatorial constituency. In the same way, three counsellorship wards, three House of Assembly and three house of Representative constituencies, become one female exclusive counsellorship ward, one Assembly constituency, one of Representative female exclusive ward/constituencies, respectively. This guarantees 25% of legislative positions to women. And women are still free in the general orbit the non-exclusive constituencies. Some women may prefer to compete in the open or non-exclusive constituencies. They can! On the youths, represented by the students, a forum for regular dialogue must be created because there are legitimate bases for clash of interest among generations. A Government, which plays deaf and dumb to youths' demands, risks seeing them on the streets with attendant destructions!

Okwadike, the true progressive, accuses most Nigerian politicians of not having ideological addresses. He is in the mold of Zik, the Nationalist, and admires Awo; a republican and democrat, he respects Ahmadu Bello. Somewhat of a radical intellectual, he sees Shehu Shagari as a model of humanity, and quiet achievement. To IBB, he gave the title of Izu Atu (no conspiracy can get him and admires his elephantine memory, superb public relation, and superior knowledge of Nigeria and Nigerians. Who is Okwadike's

15

hero? "I like Zik's nationalism, I like Awo's solid planning; Ahmadu Bello's developmental zeal impressed me deeply. Murtala Mohammed led by example, although he ruined the civil service. "I wish I could satisfy you by naming just one person. I tried to imitate Aminu Kano but that has led me to unacceptable poverty". Dr. Ezeife does not look, at all, like a pauper but he does appear disdainful of any show of wealth.

Progressivism makes Dr. Ezeife a people's man. When he called himself "the People Governor of Anambra State", people who were distant from him must have scuffed. Okwadike is at ease with the high and mighty and the humble-the maigida and the maigadi. He makes absolutely no effort to relate the poorest and lowest, it comes natural to him. It is something to behold. This person whose dressing and carriage appear to be saying "touch me not ", this man whose acid ink on paper suggests that he must always be at war, this man whose talks and writing reflect transparency and superior intelligence, which should suggest that he did not suffer fools, is indeed a people's man. People! All manners of people, the poorest and lowliest get the same treatment as the high and mighty. Akintolugboye is the very incarnation of humility and simplicity and these come to him with effortlessly ease. You do not see in Dr. Ezeife's dealing with the lowliest, any sign of a condescending attitude. Everything is so natural. His office is congested at the presidency, his residence is equally congested, and what disparate classes of persons from every ethnic group in Nigeria.

From what we have described, the question should arise as to how Dr. Ezeife is seen by his Igbo people and Eastern Peoples. This is a most interesting dimension. Okwadike is very Eastern all the way. Read his chastisement of Easterners who did not raise a finger at the destruction of Odi. He thanked Northern Senators for taking the lead in condemning the Odi Massacre and wanton destruction "the blood of Odi

People is painting Nigeria red. Since then, it has been blood, blood and more blood and no part of Nigeria is spared". His Eastern View is fully expressed in his 1999 Zik Lecture delivered at the Nnamdi Azikiwe University (the University, he handed over to the Federal Government). In it, he chided the Easterners of being blinded by their ancient grudges of wrongs done each group by the other, especially, the Igbo. Some of the "wrongs" were real; some are matters of the imagination. Even now, "those who do not want Eastern unity play on the issue of abandoned property which is best forgotten in the interest of the East. Those who grabbed the so-called abandoned property are super-sensitive about it. They too should stop worrying and fearing that anybody will re-open the matter. It is closed –a dead issue. Nobody will divide the East again on grounds of issues that are dead and buried". The East is blinded by this emotional state from seeing the reality of their plunder –the so-called marginalization. According to that lecture, the East is like a group in a hunting expedition. The group killed the only, and very big, game. They came back, cooked the game and then sat on the floor fighting for the bones dropping from the table at which other groups are feasting on the meat of the same game, which the Eastern group killed and cooked.

He believe the East, on their own, can stabilize Nigeria by speaking "approximately with one voice". He has the concept of Edo and Delta being drawn into a larger East which should then work to bring together the Eastern flank of Nigeria from North to South: the Middle Belt, Adamawa, Taraba, Brono and Bauchi. This group can hold power fairly in Nigeria, giving every other group, principally, the Hausa/Fulani and Yoruba their adequate due, so that they do not rock the boat. When you listen to Okwadike talk of South-South Nigeria, he sounds like he is talking of the home base. This should not be strange to an inquisitive person who has spent time with him. He says it as if it really happened. He says that he is from Akwa Ibom State. Pressed further, he says Akai Ubiom Eket is his home. The Garkuwan Fika spent only two years schooling in the Salvation Army teachers' training college at Akai Ubiom Eket, Akwa Ibom state. He tells the story of one Etinan family, the Edduok family, who has a son, Donald, now in the USA. He spent holidays with that family and till today, he behaves as if it is his true home. Yet, apart from a few phrases, he speaks not, and understands not, Efik- Ibibio. Truly, Okwadike is very Eastern, but he is also very Nigerian. How does he see the Igbo, and how do the Igbo see him. This questions was not put to Okwadike. It is totally unnecessary. Apart, it requires no effort to define doctor Ezeife as the soul and conscience of the Igbo – the very definition of Igboness. He must have seen himself as such. There can be no doubt. He is not only an active member of Ohaneze, he is a founding member of Mkpuke the inner think tank; he lobbied for the founding of the lgbo political Committee the engine of Nd-Igbo, of which he chose to become the founding Secretary. He continues as an active member. It was the political committee, pushed by Igbo summit of January 2001.

What manner of man is Okwadike, A core Igbo, core Easterner, core One Nigerian? What made all these possible? Perhaps nature or nurture. His father was said to be tough, uncompromising and sworn to excellence. His mother is a model of equanimity and coolness under pressure.

Those who are close to his family testify to their openness and their acceptance of everybody. Perhaps, his education? He did not go to a secondary school, but read for GCE Ordinary and Advance Levels at home. This proves only his determination and acute intelligence. He took GCE qualifying test in January 1959, GCE Ordinary Level, January 1960 and GCE Advance Level in January 1961. The same year he went into the University College Ibadan where he came out as the best all round student in the Faculty of Economics and Societal Studies wining the Faculty Price in 1962-63. He read

18

for his M.A and PhD, as a Rockefeller Foundation Scholar, at the Harvard University January 1969- March 1972. He read all manners of books, from worked religions, to philosophy, to magic. Solid education appears to promote humility.

On work experience, he was a truck pusher, a petty trader, a pupil teacher, a head master, a teaching fellow at Harvard and lecturer (promoted to Senior Lecturer; Associate Professor if it were the USA) at Makarere University College, Kampala Uganda. He thereafter became a planning officer in the Federal Civil Service where he reached the peak as Permanent Secretary. He became an exporter, and he exported virtually every Nigerian commodity, except petroleum products. On politics, he became a member of the Constituent Assembly, the first Governor of New Anambra and a political Adviser to the President of Nigeria. Hear him on his governorship stint: "When Abacha kicked us out, many said I did nothing. Those outside Anambra, who do not go home often, are still saying the same thing. But those in Anambra now know better – as one Administrator after another commissioned projects, which I initiated, and half-completed. I blame nobody. I performed but did not inform. I make no apologies. If I am to go for a future political office, I submit to be judged by my performance in Anambra State. That I did not inform was a strategic choice whose effect would have amazed people if the rain did not soil the day. I was the only SDP governor in East. I wanted to win re-election with overwhelming percentage of the votes and I planned to attack all the fabrications against me at one go, close to the re-election. Nobody said that any Governor did better than I, however. Thank god that I handed Unizik, Oko Poly and Centre for Adaptive Technology, to the Federal Government. They would have been dead today.

Akintolugboye sees nothing unique in himself. He attributes much of his behavior to his religious organization, the Salvation Army, where the creed is "our hearts to God and our hands to man" and where "everybody is somebody"; men and women are treated virtually without distinction. Women hold any clergy office in the Salvation Army from the equivalent of Pope (General), to the equivalent of Catechist (envoy).

From where did Dr. Ezeife get the idea of being "a robot in the hands of God"? when Dr. Ezeife's family were concerned very much about him as a result of his attacks on Abacha, he would always yield to them and promise to stop making dangerous statements only to explode again at the next acts which he considered "dictatorial", iniquitous and unjust. In response to challenges of his not keeping his promise to stop attacking the Government, he declared himself "a robot in the hands of God" meaning that he could not resist the promptings to fight unfairness. At a stage, his death, in the hands of Government was taken to be a matter of time. That probably explains the rumour, which made rounds some years ago that he was dead.

Ask Okwadike Nd'Igbo what his political plans are? His usual answer: "everything is in the hands of God. I am a robot in the hands of God, "Indeed the Garkuwa calls politics, God's vineyard. Why? "Because politics deals with the affairs of men, the highest of God's creation, God cannot therefore be indifferent about what happens in politics. Nor can any man not pay for iniquities and atrocities committed in politics

"If the sea allows, we shall walk over it. Oshimilli kwe alia ya enu has become Akintolugboye's refrain in recent times. That is, indeed, the name of his last son. He named one of his sons (born after he had decided to run for Governorship), **Agbachukwu,** meaning, a covenant with God. And his last daughter conceived when he was in hiding from Abacha Government was named simply **Zobem,** short for **Chukwu Zobem** (meaning God hide me). Will the sea allow Okwadike to walk over it?

DR. Ezeife did not want the Igbo to start from early 2001 to challenge Obasanjo's second term in 2003. "There was no point in antagonizing the Yoruba until it becomes clear that Obasanjo is not re-electable." He had said that Obansanjo re-election was inevitable. That was prior to the Electoral Act controversy, the death of Bola Ige and the Sacking of the Savannah Bank.

Obasanjo was waiting for the voice of God. Dr. Ezeife is waiting for the prompting of God. One God for all Men. What will His decision be! Perhaps Okwadike may repeat his gubernatorial pledge in which he said: "if my being governor of Anambra State (President of Nigeria) is for selfish, egoistic interest, may god make it impossible, but if it is for the betterment of the people, may God make it easy". It is said that he lived up to the pledge as Governor.

(Special Interview Committee Nigerian Youths, August 2002.)

3

SUN NEWSPAPER INTERVIEW
IN COMMEMORATION OF THE 80ᵀᴴ BIRTHDAY ANNIVASSERY, 28ᵀᴴ OCTOBER 2018.

The military ruled and ruined Nigeria with 36 states, 774 local governments, most of them in the North and nothing was done with fairness."

Iheanacho Nwosu, *Abuja*

Former governor of Anambra State, Dr Chukwuemeka Ezeife who will turn 80 in the next couple of days has said that the parlous state of affairs in the country is making him to be angry on daily basis. He regretted that no Nigerian of his age could be proud of the country.

In this interview, where he x-rayed happenings in the country, the former presidential adviser on Political Affairs accused the incumbent administration of deliberately sidelining the South-East zone, saying that the panacea to the country's poor shape remains returning to the regions.

Excerpts:

What does turning 80 mean to you?

I don't know what it means to me. I thought it would mean great things – success, mission accomplished, etc. But today, I feel useless. I feel like a failure. I feel lack of accomplishment. I look at the younger ones and feel I disappointed. I look at Nigeria and I say to myself, why shouldn't I be the change, with the kind of things I could write or I should write? Couldn't I have done better? I was well prepared. I didn't go to any secondary school, but I told myself I would be properly prepared for leadership. So, nobody approaching 80 in Nigeria today should be proud or happy. This is a disappointment in the extreme. I did well at home and abroad. I beat every human being born by a woman in Ibadan. In the Faculty of Economic and Social Studies, I was number one. I came to the Civil Service; the first two years, I was a flyer. Then the problem of Nigeria, the civil war came and I went to America.

What is that you feel you should have done for Nigeria that you didn't do that evokes a feeling of failure in you?

I don't know, but I think maybe I would have been less haughty and more humble. There are things I proposed for 10 years and they were not done because corruption is serious. I proposed how to use petroleum industry to make Nigerian economy massively successful. I proposed to Obasanjo, I proposed to Jonathan, I proposed to Yar'Adua on his sick bed. They understood the issue. They appreciated the thought. But they could not implement. I decided that the best way for Nigeria is to use our petroleum gift by God to make our economy explosive. What I meant was we produce our own crude and sell it cheaply because every sector of the economy needs oil, whether it is your car, you are driving or your industry. You need petroleum product. So, I said we produce petroleum product, estimate how many litres of crude we need to satisfy our local demand. Once we establish it, even if we don't have the facilities, we go overseas and produce it, bring it back, sell it, use it to promote other economic activities. What killed it was corruption because to do that, you need to cut off importation of petroleum. There are some people who are so big, who are in charge of importing petroleum and they are gaining massively by so doing.

But this corruption has been with Nigeria for a long time. At what point would you say the descent really started?
We have always been in corruption practice. You remember during the coup, Nzeogwu said 10 percenters. That was infant level of corruption and you could survive. But eventually, the military ruled Nigeria and ruined Nigeria; it became monumental corruption and they pervaded every aspect of society. If you were a lecturer in the university, for a girl to score well, she would have to be under you. For a man to score well, he would have to be loyal. If you go to church, you will find corruption. Go to mosque, you will find corruption. Go to police, you will find corruption. Go to army, you will find corruption. Everywhere is pervaded by corruption. But it couldn't have been so massive and effective in destroying Nigeria if it were not for the destruction of the structure of Nigeria.

Who actually started the destruction?
Some time ago, maybe you were born; maybe you were not born; the World Bank said parts of Nigeria were growing faster than the rest of the world. Awo brought free education to the West; Ahmadu Bello tried to push the North up. It was not just the groundnut pyramid, Azikiwe, in the East. Every part of Nigeria was growing at its own pace and any man and woman, those who are intelligent, who are in public service had vested interest in what is done with the property of Eastern Region, Western Region. You are interested in how government spends money because it's your money. In those days, it is your tax. Whatever contribution you make to the

treasury, that's what the state is using. We didn't have oil. Therefore, we were interested in how those who are spending it use it. When the oil came, the size of corruption changed. If it were not for military, we would have been far better than where we are today because God planned it that way. Nigerians are great people, but the military messed up God's plan.

How did the military actually help in stunting the growth of Nigeria?

I have made the first point that the World Bank said that parts of Nigeria were growing faster than the rest of the world. There was a recent statement from a foreign leader. The Prime Minister of Britain came here and said Nigeria is one the poorest countries, that it is leading the world in poverty. The change from growing fastest to becoming poorest was effected by the military who ruled and ruined Nigeria. By 1954, our political leaders and founding fathers had decided on the structure of Nigeria. They decided Nigeria will run a federal system with regions as federating units and there were only three regions, then four. Federal system means that the regions have their own constitution and how you govern your own is your own making. But then there was a coup in January 1966. There was Nigerian/Biafran altercation about planning war, etc and the Nigerian military wanted to win the war and they wanted to win it fast. How would they beat Ojukwu who was fighting from the other side? They thought about it and they got the right answer. They decided that it is best to isolate the Igbo from the rest of Eastern Nigeria so that Ojukwu's command is just Igbo; the other people would not obey as much as they would have obeyed if nothing happened. That was achieved by creating 12 states in Nigeria. Southeast became Igbo state. That knocked out federal system based on regions. That's how Nigeria died. If after the war, the northern military leaders had ended this isolation, we would have been far ahead and the Igbo man would have been leading the world.

The argument is that yes, the military distorted the structure and the steps they took hurt the system. But we've also had politicians who took over, who have never shown interest in reverting to the old system, why?

You are wrong. The whole idea now is reversing to the old system. Restructuring is what we are talking about and that's why Atiku has won the PDP ticket. Restructuring is going back to our agreed structure.

Is restructuring all about going back to regions?
Yes, that is the correct thing to do. It's to go back to the regions as federating units. If we are going back to what we knew, what worked and what made Nigeria grow faster than other parts of the world, we are going back to true federalism with regions as federating units. I want to tell you something which many Nigerians don't know. Many northerners say they are opposed to restructuring. If the North insists on no restructuring and the South wants to grow, that's the end of it. But Nigeria is better bigger. It's the largest concentration of blacks in the world and what did God do with that? Maybe you saw recently the Hurricane Michael and it is around the world, except most of Africa. We don't have hurricane, we don't have tornado, we don't have those natural disasters. God made it that way. You can go naked outside and not die. Every vegetable can grow here. Anything you plant can grow here. God gave us every plant and animal. God designed for Nigeria unmatched greatness. God gave us all; but today, ignorant man in Nigeria has messed up God's design. Maybe this PDP something in Port Harcourt is a change. It was open, free, fair and everything was positive. The man who won talked like a human being with intelligence. Maybe we can still go back to what God designed for Nigeria. However, the military ruled and ruined Nigeria with 36 states, 774 local governments, most of them in the North and nothing was done with fairness.

The impression people have of you is that you are against this government. Is your stand on account of government's refusal to restructure Nigeria?
I am not against the government. I am against the government's policies. I'm not against Buhari. Buhari and I have been friends. I visited Buhari in his Kaduna home many years ago and he served me. He didn't call anybody to serve me. He respected me. But the government is ruining Nigeria's future. Nobody forced Buhari to say that he belongs to everybody. But do you know that Buhari has ruined Nigeria more than all the military people who ruled this country?

In what way?
There is something in the constitution of Nigeria called federal character. If you listen to those who know, you will know that Buhari did not come to use Nigerians to work. He has Nigerians who have superior intellects, superior ability, yet he does not use them because of where they come from. Instead he prefers to go to only Katsina and get people who have blood relations with him and dump them in government. They are sitting in the country and the country is going down. There is nobody who wants Nigeria to make progress that will like Buhari's government. I am Igbo, God made me so and God made Igbo people a people of destiny. No man can change it. The man as president has turned against the Igbo people. Any list of people who are being driven from office is dominated by the Igbo. On the list of new appointments, the Igbo are non-existent. The agenda is to pull Igbo down. Look at the case of Innoson, Emzor. Their containers are seized. As we are here today, if there is a meeting called National Security Council, nobody from South-East is there. This is not imagination. It's reality. Out of the 17 security bodies in Nigeria, 16 are headed by Muslim Fulanis. What can you say about that? The Senate and the House of Reps are there and this kind of policy is going against the constitution. Federal character is a matter of constitution. It's not a matter of individuals. I have good

prayers for Buhari, but I don't think he has enough preparation for what he got himself involved in. It was even clear from the first time he came as a military leader with Idiagbon doing virtually everything.

But he assured recently that if re-elected, no part of the country will be ignored. Do you not agree with him?
You are telling me what you will do when you will come back. You are already there and you have been there three years plus. So, does it make sense? Should he make that statement even when he has ignored most parts of the country? He has preference for people who he can use to work for Nigeria. If it is the will of God that Buhari will come back, no man born of woman can stop it and no force available to us in Nigeria can stop him from coming back and we don't know the will of God. God works in mysterious ways. It is possible that even what he has done is God's will for him.

But we've seen many people from your part of the zone also joining forces with him and defending him. Are you saying that there are things you know that they do not know?
Igbo people know themselves. They know their children. They know their leaders. They know what is prompting them to act in one way or the other. Some people see money and they move. The true Igbo behaviour is coming out. We believed in Jonathan and we voted for him. We may be losing, but everybody we are dealing with knows where we stand. We have some people who represent Igboness and we have some people that represent cash. Where money comes, they go there.

Some have continued to argue that the Igbo stood with Jonathan, but they got little for that support. Their roads are in bad shape, the Second Niger Bridge was not built, key infrastructure in the zone are neglected. Why did

you not also criticize the former administration for that?
I went to Uyo area where the first governor of Akwa Ibom
was buried. During the funeral, they gave me microphone to
talk. I said ladies and gentlemen, my brothers and sisters, I
did not bring any tribute. What I brought was a bomb. For as
long as the South-South, the South-East continue on parallel
lines and not meeting, for so long will they suffer in the
Nigerian system. But the moment they team up, what they
ask of Nigeria is what they get of Nigeria. I came back after
making that statement and we started meeting – South-South,
South-East at the home of Edwin Clark. It was like magic and
it turned things around. After that, we got the Yoruba. We
formed Southern Nigeria's People Assembly. Now, we have
gone to South/Middle Belt. God gave us Nigeria and made it
with unmatched greatness. We messed up God's design. But
man cannot dominate over God's will. Therefore, I have
hope that things will change. We have an election coming.
God knows me inside out. I will prefer that Buhari does not
run. It will be helpful to Nigeria if Buhari does not run. It will
be helpful to Fulani if Buhari does not run. If he does run, we
are just tearing further apart the Nigerian system. The Miyetti
Allah, my friends who supported me when I was going for
president, I understood their point of view and they
understood mine. They said they will support me, although I
didn't go far. Let us Nigerians lift our hands from the back of
Igbo. Let Nigerians stop pressing Igbo down because if you
leave the Igbo and he jumps up, Nigeria jumps up. Whatever
you call all those people who are backward, they are the
people to gain most from the revival of this country and it is
the will of God that it will work. There is one man from the
North who God used to keep me alive. That man is called
Justice Mamman Vatsa. He is from Katsina. I cannot hate a
person because of where he comes from.

4

AN ODE TO DIKE N'AGHA NDIGBO

(For Chukwuemeka Ezeife on his 80ᵗʰ birthday anniversary)

By Patrick Oguejiofor

To the rebellious hero
Who will not bow to deities
Forlorn gods of the desert
False celestial powers
Directors of Hell's Kingdom

Raging thunder in the forest fire!
Impregnable fortress of a sick black house
Mighty *Orji* in the forest
Belligerent giant among men
This day we honour your life
With thanks to the Great Man
To sent you to us 80 seasons ago!

Today the gods have done their deeds

Okwadike is eighty seasons
On this sacred soil rocks our hope of salvation
The secret of his ageless voice
Will continue to guide our steps

Through the sense forest
Through the storms in the desert
For today even the poet is
Possessed by your ageless prowess
For the barren bowels of the oppressor
Shall not stop our walk to our dreamland
Through several rivers
Through ageless deserts
Strength clung to your voice
Through the several seasons
Of the theft of our sweat

You have meandered endlessly
Through years of darkening labyrinths,
begging for our freedom
But once your dream got captured
In our hearts of hearts
We begin to court time
Our time to the Promised Land

And now it's only a matter of time
And the enemy will be vanquished
And we shall grieve no more.

*Patrick Tagbo Oguejiofor is an award-winning poet and a former
Chairman of the Association of Nigerian Authors, Abuja Chapter.*

5

CELEBRATING OKWADIKE @ 80

DEMOCRACY AND DEVELOPMENT: A PROLOGOMENA FOR GROWTH

Obiora Okonkwo PhD

Obiora Okonkwo is the Chairman of The Dome Entertainment and Hospitality Center, Abuja. He holds a Doctorate in Political Science from the Russian Academy of Science, Institute of World Economy and International Relations, Moscow.

The Okwadike at 80 celebration presents us with another opportunity to dialogue on the journey we consciously embarked upon, called democracy, for our own good.

Political philosophers of both ancient, medieval and contemporary times agree that man opts for government in order to create societal order and control through laws and regulations. Governments exist therefore, so as to establish organization, and provide parameters for societal behaviour and control while also defending people from aggression, which could be internal or external. Like Karl Marx espoused, property ownership is a huge source of social conflict which makes government a necessity. Outside these, what we probably would have is a state of nature where we live like savages with brutish, nasty and short lives as argued by

32

Hobbes. By agreeing to form a government, man surrenders his will to a group of persons whom he entrusts with the capacity to make policies and decisions that will work for his own good. This way, man is free to pursue other interests that will make him happy and ensure his well-being. Classically, government evolved as people discovered the need for protection which is easier when people stay together.

Overtime however, government responsibilities have evolved. They have also expanded to include economic planning and development. They have also come to include provision of social services that enables man enhance living. It is out of this expanding responsibility that we begin to have ideologies of differentiation of forms of government. That explains reasons behind what we have today as capitalism, welfarism, liberalism and all the ideologies that were developed to expand knowledge of what exactly government should be.

In our expression of our preferences, we have settled for democracy as a form of government that allows for mass participation. However, our form of democracy is federalist. This is different from other forms in which democracy is expressed. Other nation states adopt the form of democracy that best suits them. In our expression, we agreed to a presidential federalist democracy which supposes that we have a central government structure with semi-autonomous states. In other climes, parliamentary democracy is practiced. Some also elect to go with and infusion of monarchy and parliamentary democracy. However, what is most important is that whatever form of democracy that is in practice observes the basic tenets which include holding period elections, guaranteeing freedom of the people to hold plural opinions, associate freely, settle where they desire, pursue their business interests freely and also to express their faith without molestation. This is what makes the difference between a democracy and autocracy or dictatorship. I guess the fact that democracy offers the people the freedom to periodically chose their leaders and also, be free to pursue their interests and associate freely, is why many nation states prefer it.

However, there have been opinions also to the effect that democracy is the worst form of government to the effect that it allows for mob rule through majority vote. Some scholars have argued that the dictum of majority vote makes mob rule possible as the majority could be a bunch of irredeemable mongrels. Though views in this regard are not popular, I still recall the famous Winstonian thought that "democracy is the worse form of government expect for all those other forms that have been tried".

In appreciating the beauty that democracy offers, one may have to look back at Nigeria and see the differences. For 16 years, beginning in December 1983, this country was managed by the military. Many have argued that military government has never been the best. I agree. During these 16 years, there was suppression of rights, indiscriminate imprisonment of opposing voices, violation of human rights and other infractions against the people. This happened because the military did not see itself as accountable to the people. It was accountable only to itself but most especially, to the ruling group. This accounted for one of several reasons military officers contested to outdo themselves in planning coups.

Usurpation of government by military rule comes with one significant thing: suspension of the constitution. Implication of this is that rules, law and order were at the discretion of the military ruler. What he said was law became law as he had no parliament to work with. In such circumstance, the people live at the whims of the military ruler who is often the most senior military officer and as such, cannot be questioned by his juniors.

Despite these, there have been a long-standing debate as to

which pushes the frontiers of development better. There is no doubt that military regimes created states, a development which has remained almost impossible in a federal democracy like ours. This, I think, was made possible because of the command and control style of the military where actions are sometimes taken without minding the outcomes. Be that as it may, our national experience is one which says the military created states and "with immediate effect" decreed certain developments into being. However, I believe that democracy expands the frontiers of development such that both individuals and societies can develop using available resources in a more impactful and peaceful manner.

Taking Abuja, our federal capital, in context, one observes that though the military created it, and with military fiat relocated the seat of government, it also took military failures to derail it with abuse of the master plan which a civil democracy corrected using laws that passed the scrutiny of the people. It is debatable if the relocation of the Federal Capital to Abuja from Lagos would have been better handled by a civil administration. Similarly, is it possible that some of the infractions that occurred, like the forceful ejection of the original inhabitants of the territory, would have occurred in a democracy in the same way and manner the military managed it. Whatever our views on these are, preponderance of opinion suggests that development thrives better under a democracy because of the creation of the legal basis, through the parliament, for such developments.

This paper is however, not a comparison between military and democratic rule. I have drawn from the above to show why democracy, which entails periodic elections and thus change of administrators, plurality of opinions, freedom to develop at one's own pace etc., is preferable. Weiner, A. (2008), in *The Invisible Constitution of Politics: Contested Norms and International Encounters*, writes that the "literature on democratic ethics primarily focuses upon key components such as universal suffrage, free speech, legal equality, constitutional checks, political equality in practice, freedom of representation and enhanced participation". This essentially summarizes democracy.

That essential ingredient called participation is what really makes the difference. It further says that the absence of such democratic tenets like universal suffrage, free speech, legal equality, constitutional checks, political equality in practice, freedom of representation and enhanced participation removes from democracy what it should be. For if democracy is "government of the people, by the people, for the people" (Abraham Lincoln, 1809-1865), then, the people must participate to drive their own development using legal guarantees established by the parliament and protected by the government.

I believe this was what Okwadike attempted to do in Anambra state between January 1992 and November 1993 when he was elected by the people of Anambra and empowered to lead the charge and use governmental tools to put in place infrastructures that they need to drive their own development. I have no doubt that Anambra state would have been better had Okwadike executed the mandate without interruption. I say this because with hindsight, we see the trajectory of development discourse that Okwadike has pursued. He has remained a vocal advocate of restructuring aimed at putting power back in the hands of the people to enable them pursue societal development. At the 2014 National Conference, Okwadike stood firmly on his belief that for Nigeria to make progress, government must remain true to its social contract with the people and provide the enablers that drive industry. Okwadike has remained an unrepentant Igboist with a pan-Nigerian outlook. In his intellectual discourses, from his days in government, he never shied away from insisting that government must use its powers to remake Nigeria by creating a leadership culture that

36

NIGERIA - DEMOCRACY & STATE OF THE ECONOMY

is altruistic.

If we review Okwadike's propositions for the development of Anambra state for instance, we will be able to draw inspiration for the future of our state. Anambra is the leading light of the Southeast. It achieved that because of the enterprising zeal of its people. When I say this, I do not mean to humiliate or denigrate other states of the southeast. I rather want to instigate debate for the development of the region using government as a tool. For our people, government exist to facilitate development. As a people who have surrendered their will to a set of people who administer their commonwealth on their behalf, we expect, that in line with Okwadike's visions, that infrastructural development will be at the top of government contract with the people. The people believe that there should actually be no reason for them to suffer lack in social amenities given the huge human resource pool, and internally generated revenue, the state is blessed with.

Therefore, in designing a prolegomena for the future of Anambra state, we, the people of the state, must begin to look at government as a tool towards driving societal development. This view, which I believe is shared by many, aims to make us responsible for our development. It suggests that we must sit back and ask ourselves some hard questions and from the answers we generate, push for the constitution of credible alternatives to managing our commonwealth. Fact is, we cannot constantly bemoan our state of development but refuse to get involved in the process of using available tools to change our narrative. When we elect our leaders and representatives, it must occur to us that we are entrusting a set of competent, credible and honest people with our lives, our security, our resources etc. If we are deeply conscious of this, then, we would make the right move by ensuring that we design a system which will make us empower a set of people who will deliver the goods and show us outcomes of the

37

errand we sent them. Like I had argued elsewhere, government is not for self-enrichment. Government does not aim to produce the richest man. It aims, rather, to serve the people in a most honourable manner. It therefore beats my imagination, how, as entrepreneurs and employers of labour, we focus on recruiting the best of the best to grow our business visions, expand our investments, ensure profitability and return on investment but fall back to select, through election, the most incompetent, the worst, to manage our states, resources and infrastructure. At times I wonder if we really understand that elections are simply a job recruitment drive while campaigns are like job interviews? Do we honestly expect to plant mangoes and harvest apples? If we recruit the incompetent, how do we expect our societies to develop? How do we expect democracy to be of utilitarian value to majority of the people? Therefore, I believe we must begin to review at our leadership recruitment process with the aim of selecting, through elections, the best of our best to lead us. This should be the competent, the credible, the honest with proven success in private enterprise leadership and management.

I guess this is what China has done. China is a democracy. Its people sat back and fashioned out a democratic system that works for them. Several years back, we heard of China only in negatives. The West was at the forefront of attempting to export its own brand of democracy to China. But China closed its gates and while the West bamboozled it with negative media, it worked behind the curtain to push its development. When eventually China opened its doors to the world, the West started a new kind of diplomacy -to ask China to slow its growth. Today, China is the largest economy in the world. It did not achieve that depending on models exported to it by others. It designed its own.

Zhang Weiwei, Director of China Institute at Fudan University said: "China's rise has attracted global attention and many have focused on the economic model behind its rise, which is, of course, important. But China's evolving political change has somehow been ignored by many. In fact, without much fanfare, China has established a system of meritocracy or what can be described as "selection plus election", where competent leaders are selected on the basis of performance and broad support through a vigorous process of screening, opinion surveys, internal evaluations and various types of election. This is much in line with the Confucian tradition of meritocracy. After all, China is the first country that invented civil service examination system, or the 'KeJu' system."

Import of this is that China has been able to develop a leadership recruitment system that promotes merit across the entire political stratum. This leadership by merit is what now drives China's super-fast economic growth. For instance, as Weiwei said the "six of the seven top leaders of the members of the standing committee of the Politburo, elected at the 19th party congress, have run provinces or province-level municipalities, many of which, in terms of population and GDP are equivalent to many nations combined."

According to Weiwei "China's political and institutional arrangements and innovations have so far produced a system which has in many ways combined the best options of selecting well-tested competent leaders and the least bad option of ensuring the exit of the leaders who should exit for all kinds of reasons, through for instance, a collective leadership or age limits. The China model of 'selection plus election' is by no means perfect. It is still being improved upon. But, it is well-positioned to compete with the western model of popular democracy."

What China has done, in essence, is to educate us to the fact that we could strive to design a democratic leadership recruitment process that is based on merit and competence, which alters the incumbent system. We must design and develop a leadership system that promotes meritocracy through a selection process that identifies, and elects, the best of the best and entrust them with the management of the commonwealth. I believe that Anambra state needs such a process. It is clearly antithetical to common sense that, as a people, we succeed in private enterprise but fail in the management of our commonwealth. We must return to the drawing board, redraw the map and bequeath to the next generation a system that promotes competence, rewards excellence and drives development through selfless service to community. Meritocracy remains the solution.

PART II

**SELECTED WORKS OF DR. EZEIFE
NIGERIA – DEMOCRACY**

6

NIGERIA: HER MANIFEST DESTINY, AND BASIS OF UNITY

(Okwadike, Dr. Chukwuemeka Ezeife)

What basis of unity is there for Nigeria? Rather, are there bases for Nigerian unity? When General Gowon took over power by the coup of 1966, he made the oft-quoted statement that, "the basis of unity is not there"! What led him to do the somersault of later declaring that "to keep Nigeria one" is a task that must be done? Was he educated to, or did he learn, or, better still, did he come by the right vision of an abiding basis for Nigeria unity? Or was he quickly tutored on the Northern Nigerian interest in Nigerian unity? What is Nigeria's Manifest Destiny – God's purpose for her? Can it be related to the abiding basis of unity in Nigeria?

The purpose of this note is to propose an abiding and overriding basis for Nigerian unity which is forced by her manifest destiny. Of course, no basis of unity can sustain unity at all costs. Unity at all costs may even derogate from, be inimical to, the very abiding reason for unity. The abiding reason for Nigerian unity does call for every possible effort, or transformation, to create the conducive conditions for sustainable peace and unity in a dynamic, resilient, robust and fast growing Nigeria.

Where can we find, locate and identify this overriding and abiding basis for Nigeria unity? Where do we locate that impetus which should help us to suppress and diffuse conflicts and schisms? Thank God, we know where; we must go right back to the beginning – to the very beginning when God created the heavens and the earth.

Black Origin of Civilization

In the beginning, the *Elohim* created man in their own image and likeness. Today, ancient history, anthropology, archeology and natural science have combined to testify and confirm that the man created by the *Elohim* was black – a black African. Black humans were thus the original sons and daughters of God. It is important to state that the authority for these statements is not just the Torah (the five books of Moses), the story is the same for a Darwinian, an atheist, everybody! Natural science has confirmed that every human on the face of the earth has a great, great, great, great... grandmother who was black! Black humans were the first created and they were, therefore, mothers and fathers of the rest of humanity. The truth of these statements derives from the present state of knowledge. There is a more relevant truth which is backed by the certainty of historical knowledge which cannot therefore be doubted. It is the fact that the Black Humans, taught and gave to the world, the foundations of science and technology, astronomy and the 365 1/4 days in the year, 12 months a year, 30 days a month, 24 hours a day etc; geometry, trigonometry, writing, paper, iron, the knowledge of one God, and all the contents of the ancient Egyptian Mystery System. Black Egyptians, Cush, Nubians and their kindred, dominated the ancient world from earlier than 5,000 years before Christ, spreading knowledge and civilization to the blue-eyed "barbarians" of the "North".

Apart from using the knowledge of trigonometry to locate farm boundaries after the flooding of the Nile, and for a few other agricultural purposes, these Blacks enjoyed knowledge for its own sake treating it as a system of mysteries open only to the initiated. And the reason is not far to seek. In most of black Africa, a man can stay naked and outside shelter, round the year, and not die. This is because the climate is very favorable. Add to this, very fertile soil, few human needs and the advantage of early agrarian settlement and you get a contented people who attained early social and economic stability – life could continue without disturbances.

The ancient Blackman was in harmony with his natural environment. The material needs of man were met in this man-nature balanced situation. The psychic and intellectual needs of the higher society found expression and satisfaction in the Ancient Mysteries enjoyed for their own sake.

Non-Black Infiltration

It was not so with the barbarians of the "North" who faced very hostile climate and environment. They were indeed in conflict with nature, not in harmony with her. The Egyptian/African knowledge eventually got to the Europeans, through, mainly, the exploits of Alexander the Great who collected, and carted to Alexandria, hundreds of thousands of books and manuscripts from Egypt and neighbouring civilizations of Africa – the arts, sciences and technologies, which the ancient Blackman treated as mysteries. Of course, Greek authors attached their names to these African books and manuscripts, which is why Dr G M James wrote, "the authors o8f Greek philosophy were not Greeks, but people of North Africa, commonly called Egyptians, and the praise and honour falsely given to the Greeks for centuries belong to....Africans". The Europeans applied the sciences to develop technologies to conquer and dominate nature. One of the early results of the White man's efforts was the acquisition of the gun-powder which they put to aggressive use, first against the beast, then against their fellow barbarians and later against black Africans. Their successes and great achievements were celebrated by

Champollion-Figeac. First, he regrets the backwardness of the European, "clad in a hairy ox-skin, a veritable savage tattooed on various parts of his body..." "I am ashamed... since our race is the last and most savage in the series". (The ranking of the major races of the world in ancient times was as follows: first: Egyptians, second: Other Africans, third: Asians, and fourth and last: the Blue eyed Barbarians [Europeans]). Then Champollion-Figeac celebrated their great advancement: "there is something flattering and consoling in seeing them, (the savages) since they make us appreciate the progress we (the whites) have subsequently achieved" (Champollion-Fgeac, Egypt Ancient, Paris: Collections l'Universe 1839, pp. 30-31). Indeed, from fighting to wrest tolerable existence from nature, the white man started a process of unending improvement, developing and advancing – achieving and surpassing the comfort the African did not struggle or fight for. And, of course, over time the white man overtook the black man so much, and the gap widened so much that the white turned on the black to use him as tool, implement, slave!

The resulting onslaught on the cradle of civilization, by Northern, Middle Eastern, and other Eastern peoples eventually succeeded after more than 2,500 years of persistent pressure. Centuries before the birth of Jesus Christ, Black domination of the world had basically ended. The later black empires of Songhai, Ghana, etc, did wax strong but by the end of the fourteenth century A.D these empires had waned. And the sunset on black Africa turned her into "the Dark Continent".

Slave Trade and the White-Washing of History

The Arabs and Eastern peoples attacked North and East Africa, often carrying away black people as slaves. Then Europe and their outposts, led by the Portuguese, in the fifteenth century, started the massive depopulation of Africa, through the slave trade.

The most devastating result of Arab involvement was the degradation of the position of Black women who were traditionally revered and who led many black countries as queens and warriors. Black women were never regarded as inferior to men. A certain gender-co-operative equilibrium reigned. Even the present generations of Africans are still told, by elders, about the great women of the past. Tomorrow the story will be of great men only, unless some drastic action is taken to re-empower women and reverse the trend in gender discrimination.

European intervention with their Christianity did also degrade black womanhood by making them more subservient to the men.

The principal effect of European intervention in slave trade was, however, the *introduction of color prejudice*, which was hitherto unknown. To rationalize the trade in human "cargo" was the reason and origin of colour prejudice. The statement in the Bible (Songs Solomon Chapter 1:Verse 5) "I am black but (and) beautiful", has no relevance to color prejudice, though it was assumed to have been made in the fourth century B.C when black domination of the world had suffered serious reverses. The Holy Books of Christians and Muslims provide no basis for color prejudice, especially, prejudice against the black color – the color of the first sons and daughters of God.

Our new Christian predators were in search of some justifications or rationalizations for buying and selling human beings. So it was, that the African became "the half born ape" and, therefore, "subhuman". It then became, also, not even in the interest of the blacks themselves, that they should be allowed free to walk the face of the earth. Blacks have "sawdust for brains" and should be protected more effectively in captivity. Even, quite lately, Prof R B Carrell could write thus: "The savage, including the whole Negro race, should, on account of their low mentality and unpleasant nature, be painlessly exterminated"

They white-washed Egyptians – the swarthy complexion "and kinky woolly hair" of the Egyptians of yore - notwithstanding. If they were black they could not have been "negro black" – some "reddish black" perhaps. Moses, who led out more than one million Israelites – the offspring of the original seventy immigrants to black Egypt – and who were therefore thoroughly mixed with black Egyptians, through four centuries of inter-marriage and integration, Jesus Christ, his mother Mary, and other important historical personalities, became so white that they are depicted in pictures, today, with streaks of blonde hairs, and sometimes blue eyes. That is how it came to pass that the wheel of history has so turned that black Africa, the cradle of human civilization, became, and has remained, the foot mat of the world. And all these have happened because of the legacy of the same black people to the world. Where ancient wisdom had it that, "out of Africa comes something always new", today it is, "out of Africa comes something always horrific". The first has become the last and the last, the first! As Fela sang, "It is upside down! Disorganized! Kpatakpata!!" Black Africans became the primitive people – the object of study by "civilised" sociologists and anthropologists; they were found to be all emotions and feelings – with no ability to conceptualize or philosophise – Egyptian Mysteries having become the philosophies of the Hellenes.

Acceptance of Inferiority by Some Black

The white-washing of history, the preaching of racial superiority, all the "Bell Curves", supported by truly observed superior modern technology by the former "barbarians", make unenlightened, blacks, really feel truly inferior! It was shocking, but understandable, when a-not-highly educated black person said, while watching a television programme, that, "after God, it is the white". The danger runs very deep. How many Africa scholars, philosophers and literary giants know that Saint Augustine of *"Civitas Dei" (City of God)* was a black man? Or that one of the greatest generals of all time,

Hannibal, was black? What impressions do current political affairs in Africa give? Certainly they do not help the image of the black man. By not showing irritability, sensibility and sublimity, which define humanity, some African leaders appear to fit the tag of "the half born ape" or "sub-humanity".

We seek not to propagate racism or reverse racism; ours is to state the facts and define a task. We pray not for the wheel of history to so turn that Africans make foot mat of any peoples; our desire is that the wheel of history snaps and flattens out into a horizontal platform of equality of peoples, as God intended it. We state, restate and emphasize the truth of black priority and black legacy, not to incite arrogance but to inspire and motivate self-rediscovery, self-confidence and self-reclamation. Racial harmony in global love must replace racial conflict in inter-ethnic hatred.

The days when our needs were few are long gone. Our climate remains very clement, very favourable. But even if we do not want to, we cannot avoid seeing what modern science and technology have done to the world. The list of new goods is extending like our universe is expanding. We do not hate these new goods, we want them, we need them, we crave for them.

To exhume or recreate the greatness of the black race; to demonstrate that the black is not merely beautiful but capable too, to reclaim the proper position of the black race in the world, is a task that must be performed, a challenge to which must be responded, a mission which must be accomplished – and urgently!

The Quest for World Power is the basis of Nigerian Unity

Economic power, and its accompanying military might, are the only two indices of capability known to the world. The task then is to create a black economic and military power at the world level.

49

The making of a world economic power requires some crucial ingredients. Very high level of technological and economic development are necessary conditions but they are not sufficient. Switzerland, Luxembourg, the small Balkan countries, etc, are world great economic successes – world "economic beauties", but certainly not world economic powers. They are too small.

To be world economic power, number (population) counts and to a smaller extent, the geopolitical size of the country too, especially, for the military might dimension. Even the physical (geological) and, of course, the political stability, of the country also count.

Which black African country has the potentials, the natural and other pre-requisites, to become a world economic power? Maybe a few countries qualify for consideration. South Africa may qualify, but the credit for its attainment of world power status may not, without controversy, be given to blacks. Ivory Coast, Zaire, Senegal, Ghana, Kenya and some other countries may be considered.

Is it not obvious, are there difficult arguments required to arrive at Nigeria as the one black African country which has all the potentials in population, size, resources and history, to develop into a black world super power? It is clear that history and circumstance have imposed on Nigeria the task to develop into such a world super power, and to accomplish the mission of black re-emergence in world leadership. **What a conclusion! Why the tedious journey to this obvious conclusion?** With Nigeria as the largest concentration of blacks on the face of the earth, the conclusion should be truly obvious.

The "obvious" conclusion on the task before Nigeria is not obviously present in the consciousness of Nigerians, or it does not appear to be. Does it manifest in the actions of Nigerians and Nigeria? How many "leaders of thought" and key political functionaries of the government, let alone ordinary Nigerians, show awareness of this task? No past leader of Nigeria, military or civilian, had shown a craving for the economic development and growth of Nigeria. Do we appreciate why the happenings in Nigeria, Nigeria's actions and the prospects of Nigeria, should concern other black peoples of the world? Why they should "intrude" in what we may naively consider our "internal affairs"? They do not intrude; they have the moral right and vested interest in the affairs of Nigeria. Black peoples everywhere cannot be neutral in the affairs of Nigeria.

That the dignity, respect and place of the black man, everywhere on earth, is tied to the circumstances of Nigeria, as at present constituted, is a fact not open to disputation. Should Nigeria become a world super power, the respect, dignity and position of blacks everywhere will rise. Prejudice against the black colour will die a natural death. Today, as Nigeria, on the contrary, takes giant steps backwards, loses values and conscience, becomes a pariah nation, even a failed state, an outcast among nations, dehumanizing and brutalising her citizens, squandering resources of time, material and human, black people everywhere are deep in shame, and the friends of the blacks too. The ghost of the tag of "the half-born ape" haunts the original sons and daughters of God as the odium and opprobrium exuded by Nigeria spreads insult and humiliation on every black man outside the borders of his own and other Black countries. For Black Americans, Nigeria is a source of shame even in their own country! Black people do not carry labels saying "I am a Ghanaian, a Malian, a Black American, NOT a Nigerian!" The present situation, has persisted for too long, it is totally unacceptable – intolerable and must be rejected.

Nigeria has two options over which to exercise her pride of sovereignty. Each option has its implications. What are these options?
One, Nigeria may accept the challenge, accept to face the task of developing fast into a world super power, bringing respect and dignity back to the black man. Accepting the task and focusing on the great challenge will make us begin to forget much of our differences, make us see indigenous peoples in

Nigeria as Nigerians, as companions and fellow workers for the accomplishment of a great and crucial mission. That is, instead of squandering time and resources with debilitating inter-ethnic squabbles between Hausa/Fulani and the rest of Nigerian peoples or hateful jealousies between Igbo and Yoruba, even when the bases of discord and disapprobation had long disappeared, or endangering one Nigeria by politicians hiding behind perversions of religions, perpetually causing disharmony and destabilization.

But, as things are, the "focusing" may not be enough for sub-nationalities to accept unacceptable injustices. If we accept the mission and focus "on its achievement" – and there are serious detraction, the challenge of the mission will motivate and energise us to remove the detractions, to restructure or re-organise our system to achieve that sustainable peace, unity and political stability which are conditions necessary for the *achievement of the mission.*

There is the second option – the converse of the first, but God forbid that we should take it! The negation of the abiding basis for unity leads to the basis for disintegration. If we do not accept the great and noble challenge and task before us, or we are incapable of organizing or restructuring our polity for the *accomplishment of the mission,* Nigeria, as we know it, should cease to exist, and should, and indeed, must dissolve into several republics. There is no point in remaining perpetually a failed hope, a good dream that is unrealizable. We should not remain phony big among nations, like the old Nigeria penny among slimmer, but higher valued, coins. We cannot, should not, and must not, continue to raise and shatter the hope of black peoples. If we cannot elevate the black man, we should not continually pull him down. If we cannot give dignity and respect to black peoples, we should cease being the source of shame and ridicule to them. With smaller republics, the eyesore may clear up, no hopes are raised, none are dashed. We should stop being the flagship of Africa which is perpetually sunk or wrecked by the weight of its excess luggage of unending tribalism, religiousity and

52

sectionalism, worsening monumental, monstrous and all-pervading corruption, which has killed and buried the conscience of the Nigerian.

Indeed, disintegration is infinitely better than Nigeria remaining a hopeless hope, out of which comes something always shameful. We may console ourselves with the thought that God created the sub-nationalities which we are incapable of organizing into a meaningful country. If to disintegrate we must, that should be accomplished peacefully on a negotiation table. This way we are sure to eventually zealously re-integrate.

The path of honour for Nigerians is to accept the manifest destiny – Gods purpose for our country - of restoring the respect, honour and dignity of blacks, becoming the rallying point and big brother for all blacks.

7

TOWARDS GOD'S OWN NIGERIA

The manifesto of Okwadike, Dr. Chukwuemeka Ezeife
towards his Presidential aspiration in 2003

INTRODUCTION

Toward God's Own Nigeria is the war cry by Okwadike, Dr. Ezeife, in his quest for the leadership of Nigeria. Okwadike, who is also Garkuwan Fika, Dan Amar din Jama'a, Fiwajoye of Itori, Akintolugboye of Egbaland, Ochendo Umu-Akwukwo, etc remains committed to the pursuit of God's own Nigeria, the condition for the realization of which is the installation of God-centred leadership in Nigeria.

Asked if the quest is realizable – whether the objective will ever be attained – the Garkuwan Fika replies sharply: "there is no choice, no alternative, if we want the actualization of God's design for Nigeria as a super power".

Adamant in his belief in principled behavior, even in Nigeria politics (for him "politics is God's Vineyard)", uncompromising in his universalism and the idea of the moral equality of man to man, unflinching in his conviction that it is Nigeria's manifest destiny to develop to a super power and thereby raise the respect, dignity and joy of Black and African

Peoples everywhere, Dr. Ezeife is unrepentant about his puritanical politics. His refrain is "may God take control and keep control of, may He impose his will on, the affairs of Nigeria".

The Akintolugboye defines the problem of Nigeria as deficiency in leadership. He says, "ineffective leaders see liabilities and curses in the so-called diversities in Nigeria". The Akintolugboye sees the diversities as assets and blessing- "many sterling talents form many tribes".

The Okwadike Nd'Igbo says that every Nigerian is black "including the lightest Shua Arab," that Nigeria is greatest concentration of Blacks on the face of the earth; that today, the blacks are the foot mat of the world; that Nigeria has the geographical size, the population, the climate, stable earth; and even her history, to provide leadership for Africa. The message from these empirical condition is clear: "as goes Nigeria, so goes the Black man! Shouldn't Nigerians wake up to their responsibilities?"

These and more ideas are presented below for your reading pleasure. Perhaps they will touch your mind and motivate you to join the crusade, the jihad, to reform the minds of Nigerians, remake and re-engineer Nigeria for the welfare of man in Nigeria beyond.

OKWADIKE, DR. EZEIFE, DECLARES

SEND ME, GOD BUT ONLY AS A ROBOT IN YOUR HANDS

I do not have the billions of naira for a presidential contest in Nigeria. I do not have the connections to fund my election as President of Nigeria. I do not have the powers to direct anybody to do anything to facilitate my election. Yet, I feel this pressure, this prompting, indeed, I feel a compulsion to make myself available to be used by God, as President of Federal Republic of Nigeria, to **remake Nigeria,** to re-engineer Nigeria, to reform and integrate the minds of the Nigerian Peoples, for the welfare of man in Nigeria and beyond.

I am constrained, like all humans, not by material inadequacies alone. I know that, as Chukwuemeka Ezeife, I am nothing, I can do nothing. But God using me as a robot in His Hands, nothing will be left undone to make Nigeria a Super Power; I will leave nothing undone to uplift the welfare of Nigerians in body and mind. Nothing will be left undone to restore the respect and dignity of Black and African people and to contribute to world peace, unity and progress. God using me, nothing will be left undone to achieve, fully, the manifest destiny of Nigeria!

I therefore, hereby, declare and offer myself to be used by God, in the capacity of **President of the Federal Republic of Nigeria,** to switch back God's design for Nigeria and implement the same, to actualize the greatness of Nigeria, the happiness of Nigerians, to the glory of God. Send me, God, **but only** as a robot in your Hands.

When God gives me Nigeria, I shall return the country back to God. It will become God's own Nigeria!

In God's own Nigeria, we shall hurry back to land, develop long-range agricultural policies, and use our "Agrigan Model" to aggressively develop agriculture and agro-industries and to sweep unemployment. We shall create the enabling conditions for processing our raw materials. We shall help our manufactures to leapfrog to high-tech, fast growth, foot-loose industries. We shall develop counter measures to deal with the environmental constraints to manufacturing in Nigeria, we shall justify the same to the World Trade Organization, and arrest the de-industrialization of Nigeria induced by globalization. It will be farewell to massive unemployment!

Privatization will continue, indeed, we shall privatize all privatisables but our new strategy will be consistent with the good society, in which it is anathema for Government to nurture excessive, socially disruptive inequalities.

Our educational system will turn out persons trained to use their limbs, their minds and their intellect, persons in whom the spirit of enterprise is well developed.

Our government, which must be broad based, will focus on the commanding heights of the economy, emphasizing:

(a) The creation of investor-friendly environment, so that Nigeria money will be invested in Nigeria, and foreign money too.

(b) The provision of adequate and appropriate social and economic infrastructure facilities, including facilities for relevant "frontiers" education. On roads, we shall create a "Road Gan" system to nip potholes in the bud, and gradually indigenize the technology for building major roads.

(c) The creation of conditions for sustainable, fuller employment.

(d) The guarantee of regularly adequate supply of petroleum products, at reasonable prices. In this connection, rather than worrying about the smuggling of products (indeed any Nigerian-made manufactures) into neighboring countries, we shall expand greatly, the refining capacity, meet Nigerian demands, meet the demands of our neighboring countries and let them be glued to buying made-in Nigeria products. Over time, we must have increasingly, large quantities of refined products for export to the rest of the world – in line with the policy to export mostly processed goods

We shall empower our women, economically and politically-the political empowerment will be based on the idea of "gender exclusive constituencies" which we have developed. The views of the youths will count in governance. Such views will be ascertained from a forum for regular dialogue to be instituted to enhance intergenerational harmony. We shall promote cultural public autonomy among our many peoples. With persistent public religious education, given by recognized experts in the religious, we shall blunt religious fanaticism.

The people of Niger Delta will get the confident assurance that Nigeria loves and needs them more than the resources in their land. We shall heal wounds in Nigeria: Odi, Zaki Biam, others.

Our security forces will appreciate that **we need them** and they will be motivated to give their best. Nigeria needs her Police; Nigerians will get to love their Police. The military forces are indispensable, especially where diplomacy fails. Only bastard throw away their inheritance. God's own Nigeria will be worth risking death for! A super power Nigeria must live within secure borders. We shall repay those foreign loans made prudently and honestly. We shall embrace our manifest destiny; actualize the potentialities of Nigeria's greatness, with stable polity and Godly social values. Nigeria shall be a country, under God, where everything works, a country from which no group will want to walk away and none can leave feeling triumphantly. It will be goodbye to hunger, anger, frustrations and hopelessness, and therefore goodbye to hatefulness and violence. The family will be safe and happy again, wives embrace their husbands as they swagger home from the days' business with pockets bulging with high value currencies; children celebrate their mothers' return from markets with singing and dancing, assured of goodies in the market basket.

The world shall hail God's own Nigeria; we shall restore the respect, dignity and joy of Black and African Peoples. The ancient maxim shall return that "out of African always comes something new" and good. Yes, we shall remake Nigeria; we shall reform and integrate the minds of Nigerians. The giant in the sun will bounce back; the flag ship of Africa will set sail anew, never again to be mired in the mud. The eagle shall fly, aloft, on the wings of God's winds. We shall worship our God, we shall shout Hallelujah!

Brothers and sisters, Nigerians, let that spark of God inside you speak to you; the voice of conscience can be very low; let not primordial emotions shut it off. Reject moneybags, for the government by moneybags is always for moneybags, never for you. Sacrifice the transient, the short lived. Think long range and vote for yourselves, for your families, vote for Nigeria. Voting for me, as a robot in the Hand of God, is voting for Nigeria. I do not ask only for your votes. I ask, also, that you defend the vote you cast. Let us make the moral and material efforts to get the Nigeria we want, the Nigeria we need. God's own Nigeria! I pledge to you to be me, to remain truthful, steadfast and selfless. I pledge to you to slave for Nigeria.

God bless President Olusegun Obasanjo whom I believe has done that for which he was divinely selected. God bless Ide Alex Ekwueme, God bless all aspirants to the office of the President of Federal Republic of Nigeria. May God take control and keep control. May his will be done in Nigeria at all times. God bless all of you.

WHY I SEEK POWER

Today, January 2nd, 2003, with prayers to God, I picked up the nomination form for UNPP President Aspirants. I expect to become the "Alliance Candidate." The alliance should include APGA, which is already in negotiations with the

UNPP. Realism demands that the alliance should involve many, many more political parties.

Basic to the problems of Nigeria is hunger, which defines leadership failure in a country so bountifully endowed by the Almighty God. I have watched the ongoing primary elections. It may be easier to get water from rock than for credible leadership of Nigeria to emerge form these gimmicks, these fraudulent manipulations. We have refused to learn anything; we are not prepared to give true democracy a chance. Conscience is dead and buried and the worst of us are marauding the entire political space!

Many Politicians are offering themselves, seeking the power to administer Nigeria. They say they want to do so in the interest of Nigerians. We know better: we have heard them before; we have seen them in office before. Nigerians may pretend to be deceived, as they collect from the investor-politicians, change taken from the interest, earned on the peoples' money, looted directly or indirectly from national treasury!

I seek power to re-engineer, to remake Nigeria, and return her to God's original design for her greatness. I seek power to banish hunger, anger, frustration, hopelessness and therefore banish hatefulness and violence. I seek power to restore love, justice, truth, and good social order. I seek the power to return Nigeria to God. I seek power to install God-centered leadership in Nigeria. And God knows I tell the truth!

I have bought the Presidential nomination form at a whopping cost of three million naira.

But I cannot buy power in Nigeria. If Nigerians are not tired of callousness and falsehood, if Nigerians are not tired of callousness and falsehood, if Nigerians are not tired of comprehensive failures in all directions economic, political, religious and ethnic. And, above all, if God has not decided to forgive our many sins and turn His face and Grace to Nigeria, there is no way I can be President of Nigeria. My success depends on, and will signal, the arrival of God's Own Nigeria. I shall not, indeed, will not engage in politics as usual, the present dog-eat-dog politics of callous bestiality, insensitivity and insincerity – politics of conspicuous deceit! Nigerians must be committed to basic change. I want to be agent of that change.

Subject to the will of God, I have the best theoretical training, the best practical experience in economics, the social sciences and the art of governance, to re-engineer and remake Nigeria for the welfare of man in Nigeria and beyond. By training and from experience, I know where the switches are, and motivated by love of all God's children in Nigeria and beyond, I crave to switch on the lights! When the economic lights are no, the other problems of Nigeria will be better illuminated and made amendable to solutions with ease. Indeed, as ugly and as threatening as the problems of fanatical religiosity, consuming tribalism and hateful sectionalism may appear, they are really mere symptoms of the more virulent basic problems of hunger, which derives from self-centred ineffective political leadership in Nigeria.

I am aware of 419 religiosity in Nigeria but I must be me and not fear being mis-categoriesed.

We need to shift from man-centred, selfish leadership - leadership for self, relations, in-laws, and friends to leadership anchored on God, God centred leadership. It is that leadership, which makes the economic lights come on, which makes for baking larger national cake that may be surplus to requirement, because it generates loving care for all concerned. We only need to submit to our Creator.

And God is merciful and forgiving. To his call:

"Turn to me and be saved

all ye ends of the earth
for I am God and there is no other." **(Isaiah 45:22)**

Let us, in total submission, affirm:

"Thee alone do we worship and
Thee alone do we implore for help.
Guide us on the right path-the path of
those on whom thou hast
Bestowed Thy blessings…. **(Qur'an 1:5-7)**

May these pieces of paper, this UNPP nomination form, signal the beginning of the end of Nigeria as a rich/poor country, and for good!

NIGERIA HER PROBLEMS …LEADERSHIP

In the beginning, God created Nigeria and dowered on her abundant natural resources: vegetable resources, animal resources, water resources, mineral resources. He gave her good climate, round the country, round the year. God gave her stable earth: no volcanoes, on earthquakes. On top of the surplus material resources, God peopled Nigeria with among the most ingenuous human beings. They include world-beaters at Harvard, MIT, Oxford, Cambridge etc universities; they include the man who developed the World's fastest computer process today; they include World No. 3 in robotics; they include the aerodynamic expert who is currently redesigning the airplane. Nigeria experts are making waves at the frontiers of technology in foreign lands! Ridding greedy persons of their money, and other 419 activities, are not games dullard play. God has the power to make all Nigerians one people, with one culture, one religion and one language. In His wisdom, graciousness and mercy, he chose to give Nigeria, many peoples, many cultures, may talents form many tribes. Integrating the Nigerian peoples and training them to effectively exploit the bountiful material resources, cannot but make Nigeria a Super Power among nations. Indeed, this is God's design for Nigeria: to develop into a Super Power and restore the respect, dignity and joy of Black and African Peoples. This, also, is the manifest destiny of Nigeria. Clearly, poverty is not and cannot be, in our stars! Those who advocate "continuity" in suffering are in manifest error.

What has the Nigerian man made of God's design?

Today's Satan-Man's Nigeria: The State of the Nation

Personal safety, security of life and property, the favorable environment for genuine economic pursuits, are not there. The physical environment is degrading fast. The economy has been ruined almost completely. The polity is now in the zone of extreme self-centeredness, the zone of callous insensitivity, of dog-eat-dog bestiality, merciless brutalization of neighbour's minds and body, and worse! On law and order, the police have long been reduced to status of highway beggars/extortionists, and the judiciary has been compromised. Corruption, in high and low places, has eaten away the heart and soul of the society Satan-man in Nigeria has done everything to ruin Nigeria completely and comprehensively, morally, socially, politically, economically, not even hope has been spared! But Nigeria's manifest destiny - God's design for Nigeria as a Super Power – abides and must ultimately prevail.

Elements of the Problem with Satan-Man's Nigeria.

Development planning started even in colonial Nigeria, yet economic growth with development has never Nigeria. No leader, military or civilian, has shown great zeal, a craving, or a consuming desire, for the economic growth and development of Nigeria. Many leaders do not know what to do with economy and would not listen to advice. One military government sent soldiers to the market to shoot down prices. They thought it was a success as rice, auctioned by soldiers from private were houses, became so cheap as to be used for feeding local dogs!

One the polity, the seeds of some abiding problems were sown by those colonial masters, who followed their, biases and preferences. But we have passed 40 years as a nation; we cannot, therefore, blame other people for problems we have not generated the will to solve, even though it is in the long-term interest of every group in Nigeria that these problems are solved. Military domination of the political scene, since independence, has added to the problems. No Nigerian leader has developed enough guts to take the bull by the horn and solve the problems of the polity with loving care, sympathy and understanding.

Problems of sectionalism are growing by the day, especially over the last three years: there are the tribal divides, religious divides, geographical divides and other bases of negative solidarities. Nigerians are retreating to their primordial enclaves – making progress backward to primitively, tribality and fanatical religiosity! These problems cannot be deceived with superficial cleverness. We deceive only ourselves. They must be confronted and rooted out by a leader who is enabled by his guts, mind and mental development, to escape from sectionalism and negative solidarities. Corruption cannot be eradicated by formal law alone. Bribery cannot be the order of the day in the Government and people are successfully exhorted against corruption. It does not happen that way. The leadership must be committed and must lead by example.

The bite in the problems of the political process, in tribalism, in religious intolerance, geographical divide etc. has been seriously on the rise because of the intensifying economic problems. The average or ordinary Nigerian, and, even the not so ordinary, are hungry, angry, frustrated, hopeless and therefore hateful and violent. A man who cannot provide for himself and his family feels so frustrated that he finds no use in continuing to live. He sees dying in a sectional (tribal, religious etc.) war as more "honorable" than committing suicide! Such a man is a ready material for killing God's children in defense of God.

THE ABIDING PROBLEM:

The Leadership Nigeria Needs!

We may see the economy as a major problem area; we may identify the structure of the polity as responsible for some problems, and, of course, we can blame it all on ethnicity, religious fanaticism etc. no doubt, all these are problems. They count. But the mother of all the problems is the lack of effective political leadership. Nigeria is rich by God's design; man makes her poor. This is the contradiction of the rich poor country. But man's mess up, man can clean up.

Infective political leadership, characterized by selfish man-centeredness, myopia, lack of knowledge, and above all, sectionalism, sees negatives where there are definite positives. The infective leader sees our diversities as curse and liabilities, not as God's given blessings and assets.

Who fits the Leadership Bill for Nigeria?

The leader who can implement God's design for Nigeria must be knowledgeable, courageous, God fearing, God-centered, he must be able to escape from sectionalism and see the diversities in Nigeria as blessings and assets. He must be an integrator who will fire the minds of the Nigerian people, focusing them on the great, deserving goal of working on the abundant material resources to make Nigeria a super power. The search for such effective political leadership will not end until Nigeria gets gusty God-centered, principled leaders. The political leader of Nigeria has work to do –he has a burden to carry. It is not a matter of seeking power merely to administer the country for selfish and sectional purposes. The leader Nigeria needs must possess those correct and sound principles of personal characters, namely, integrity, telling the truth, courage, humility, justices as fairness, steadfastness, industry etc. He must be sensitive to the feelings and needs of the people. He must care- genuinely! He must accept and embrace the following basic ideas of God-centred leadership.

1. Politics as God's Vineyard:

"The ignorant says there is no morality in politics, that politics is a zone of the filthy, where anything goes – the abode of demons! This just cannot be true. Politics is God's vineyard, because politics deals with the affairs of men, the highest of God's creation. None can escape the judgment of God on things done in Politics. Therefore, onward Godly Soldiers, matching as to war, against the filth of our politics. Join hands! Let us remake Nigeria, let us reform the minds of Nigerians. So that, this country, Nigeria, will never be the same again!"

2. Equality of Man to Man:

The moral equality of man to man derives from the existence of a piece (spark) of God in every human. The spark in me is equal in every respect, except in conscious development, to the spark in you and in everybody else.

3. The Neighbour We Are to Love:

In the injunction, love your neighbour as yourself; your neighbour is any human with whom you come in contact. This injunction is the greatest law. It is also the most difficult. Your political opponent is your neighbour. If you love him, would you need, in electoral contest, hatchets, guns, acids, cudgels, running away with electoral materials and many other election-rigging device? Your adversary in any field, in everything, is your neighbor. To love him is the law of God. This law operate in every field of human endeavor and contact!

I believe in this basic idea and try to live by them. They have guided my thoughts and actions. The declaration statement above, is based on these ideas. Sometimes, I find that I have no choice and no control over my actions. I broke solemn promises I made to my mother, to stop the life – endangering habit of attacking military dictators. It was then I realized that some Higher Power is prompting and using me. I had to accept that I am a robot in the hands of God!

NIGERIA NEEDS INTEGRATION

The God-centered leader who should be an integrator must imbibe this basic ideas, which should form the foundations of his thought and actions. With them, he will see every Nigerian as a brother, a sister, or a neighbor.

On my path, I should like to be confirmed as a mere robot in the hands of God. Playing a role like that should help the integration of Nigeria. For without doubt:

Nigeria needs integration
Integration calls for an integrator
The integrator will bring together
The minds of Nigerian's many peoples
Their many talents and many tribes
And move Nigeria towards Super-Powerdom

WHAT IS INTEGRATION?

Integration is bringing together, and uniting the minds of Nigeria's many different tribes, and putting to work, their many different talents, to make our country, a super power.

HOW DO WE ACHIEVE INTEGRATION?

We must touch the minds of Nigerian peoples, open their eyes to see God's gift of many talents from many tribes as blessings and assets, not as curses or liabilities. These blessings are just like our surplus natural resources, the good climate, stable earth (no earthquakes, no volcanoes) etc. we must make Nigerians know that, by working with one mind, we can produce so much larger national cake that every Nigerian can have as much as he needs and there will still be surpluses to give, as Zakat, to poor countries. We must make Nigerians see, and accept the challenges of our being the largest Black Country in the world. By fixing our minds on baking the much larger national cake and on the challenge of our blackness, we will learn to see each other as comrades working to lift up Nigeria, and to bring back the respect and dignity of black an African people, everywhere!

WHAT SHOULD WE DO?

Bad leadership can make our blessings of many tribes with many talents, and even our surplus natural resources, look like curses and liabilities. Such bad leaders are small-minded, sectional, selfish, shortsighted, and lack knowledge.

We must pray God to let his grace shine upon us and give us an Integrator for a leader; a Leader who fears God, sees every Nigerian as a brother or sister; and sees blessings and assets in what they call our diversity; a Leader who accepts the challenges of our being the largest Black Country in the world; a Leader who is determined to make Nigeria a Super

Power and, having the knowledge, is ready, willing and able to do so; a see-through Leader who can switch on the mind of Nigerians at home and abroad.

May God guide us on the path of those on whom He has bestowed His blessings and give us an Integrator.

SOME THOUGHTS OF OKWADIKE, DR. EZEIFE

THOUGHTS ON THE POLITY

1.1 Nigeria: The Basis of Unity.
Nigeria is the one Black African Country, which has all the potentials in

Population size, geographical extent, resources and history to develop into World Super Power. It is the manifest destiny of Nigeria to develop into Super Power and raise the dignity and respect of Black and African Peoples everywhere. If things can be made to work in Nigerian system feeling triumphantly. One Nigeria is in the interest of Nigerians, in the interest of Black and African Peoples, in the enlightened interest of the World.

1.2 Political Ideology.
Basic principles or ideologies make the difference between political parties and bands of armed robbers (who have agreed on how to share the loot).

Progressivism, as an ideology, is an attitude of the mind, and to life, anchored on justice as fairness, which requires that any product of historical process or any social situation, which is, significantly, not as good as it should be, should be changed, reformed, in pursuit of a progressivism derives from the injunction to "love your neighbor as (almost) yourself".

1.3 Political Leadership in Nigeria.

Nigeria needs an integrator. The integrator must begin by appreciating, as blessings and assets, not as curses and liabilities, the so-called diversities of Nigeria that He gave her, not only, abundant material resources, good climate and stable earth (no volcanoes, no earthquake), but also many peoples and cultures, many talents from many tribes. The integrator will fire the minds of Nigerians, focus them on the good great goal conceived by him, and tap the material resources to make Nigeria a Super Power. The search for such effective political Leadership will not end until Nigeria gets God-centred, principled leaders. A political leader of Nigeria has work to do, burden to carry. He will need Knowledge, wisdom, vision, and more. He must possess correct and sound principles of personal character, namely, integrity, telling the truth, courage, humility, justice, steadfastness, industry etc. He must be sensitive. He must care genuinely.

1.4 Political Empowerment of Women.

Women, especially, women as mothers, bear the brunt of bad government. They soak up, from all the members of the family, the shock and frustrations arising from failures of government. Women should therefore have the greatest vested interest in good governance. Besides, women respect, and play by, the rules, more and have superior integrity to men, in public offices. These two propositions, support greater empowerment of women, for both appointive and elective political offices. The solution with regard to elective (legislative) offices can be found in creating two sets of constituencies: "free constituencies" in which men and women qualify to contest, and "gender (women) exclusive constituencies". To make women occupy at least 25% of legislative offices, there should be one-woman exclusive constituency to every three free constituencies.

1.5 The Youth and Governance

Legitimate conflicts interest do exist among generations. The enlightened interests of the younger generations should be more in tandem with the permanent interest of the society, while the older generations, usually, control the government. To neutralize these intergenerational conflicts of interest and boost harmony, an institution must be created to routinize dialogue between the youth and the government. It will not pay to ask the youths to await their time. A government that chooses to play deaf and dumb to the youths, usually represented by the students, risks seeing them in the streets, with collateral damages.

THOUGHTS ON THE ECONOMY

2.0 The Economy and the Polity.

Political Stability is a condition necessary for economic growth and development – for economic greatness. Economic growth and development and the resulting improvement in material welfare reduces tension and insecurity, thereby enhancing political stability. The greater is the visible hand of economic performance on political stability and happening in polity. Nigeria has moved away from the dominance of the private sector, to the dominance of government. This results from the heavy weight, on the overall economy, of the petroleum sub-sector, which the government largely controls. The performance of the Nigerian economy today, is super-sensitive to the wisdom, competence, integrity in, and the stability, of government.

2.1 Economic Development and Democracy.

Economic development may, or should, lead to democracy but the relationship is not reflexive. There is no guarantee that democracy should necessarily lead to economic growth and development, especially, where democracy is not an accepted culture, but merely the electoral basis of choosing leaders and the electoral process is ruse, *banza* and devoid of fairness.

2.2 Economic System.

History has demonstrated, personal psychology has confirmed, that the propelling force of self-interest, which private enterprise exploits, leads to, incomparably, greater productive power than socialism/communism. But state intervention is inevitable in distribution. The spirit of capitalism should dominate production; the spirit of socialism should dominate in consumption or distribution. To keep both spirits alive, and in balance, is the responsibility of the government, as the agent of the society. That is why, preferring private enterprise, the progressive will, nevertheless, not hesitate to let government intervene in the economy, to achieve a good society. We predicted the collapse of socialism/communism as a system of economic management more than one decade before it happened. It was our submission that it is not natural to man to behave as socialism/communism requires.

2.3 Privatization

Privatise all privatisables in the public sector, routinize all routinisable, commercialize all commercialisables; deregulate all deregulatables, all, only subject to good society. It does not make for good society for privatization of public assets to be stood on its head. Offering public assets first to the so-called shady "core-investor" and offering only the remnants to the public, is standing privatization of public assets to be stood on its head. Offering public assets first to the so-called shady "core-investors" and offering only the remnants to the public, is standing privatization on its head. The privatization strategy is sowing the seed of such serious, class problem in Nigeria as to alarm men of vision. We get better result, socially and economically, by adopting reform privatization, which combines the privatization of management with a more ruthless exploitation of self-interest of the workers, through worker-empowerment strategies, which, we developed about a decade ago. Or, we should push controlled sale-privatization only at the rate which the capacity to buy under controlled individuals buying, and buying by the state, and local governments (to warehouse for future controlled sale to the people) can allow.

2.4 Education

The level of effective and relevant education of the populace sets the limit to, or removes the limits from country's growth and development possibilities. The output of the educational system, at all level, should, as much as possible, be wholesome, resulting in trained body, mind and intellect, and in the development of entrepreneurship abilities.

2.5 Agriculture.

The clarion call is "back to land" with consistent long range policies.

The "Agrigan-System" a system which does not allow any arable land to lie fallow while men die of hunger and decay, is the basis of a food self-sufficiency policy, agro-based industrialization policy, it is also the sweeper of unemployment. Agricultural policy must be clear, consistent and sustained; no stop-go policy will work. Sustainable policies should be developed for peasant, small scale and large scale farming. Land development, input price support and the rational defense of farm income against the vagaries of climate and output, must be part of long-term agricultural policy, carefully work out.

2.6 Manufacturing Industry.

Nigeria is being de-industrialized. The pace of de-industrialization is progressively accentuating by further globalization. Needed, are policies to re-start industrialization. Such policies must depend on a thorough understanding of the constraints of the environment of manufacturing in Nigeria Vis-ă-vis manufacturing in foreign lands. This should lead to defensible environment-compensating measures, which will be consistent with both Nigeria's self-interest and the requirements of World Trade Organization. Lack of knowledge, and incompetence, make people commit suicide believing they are complying with rules they can't change. The most pragmatic approach to industrialization of Nigeria should be two-prong; namely combining the aggressive mundane processing of agricultural and other available raw materials with creating conditions to enable leapfrogging to some foot-loose, growth industries.

2.7 On Smuggling

Smuggling products into Nigeria can be injurious to the Nigeria economy and should be combated. Combating the smuggling of products, especially manufactured products, from Nigeria to our neighboring countries, is not, clear-cut, a wise policy. We should like to get our neighboring countries glued to Nigerian manufacturers – including petroleum products. These neighboring countries are natural extensions of the Nigerian market. The challenge is to expand production (and employment) not to fight smuggling when our competitor countries are dumping manufactured goods in Nigeria and her neighboring countries.

2.8 The Commanding Heights of the Economy.

Government must concentrate on the effective management of the commanding heights of the economy. Today, these commanding heights are: the environment for economic activities by both foreign and national investors (for Nigerian money to be invested in Nigeria, and foreign money too); the assurance of: regularly adequate and relevant educational and manpower training facilities, conditions for fuller employment, adequate socio-economic infrastructure facilities, and the regular available and reasonable pricing of petroleum products. On roads, as part of the infrastructure, the policy will be anchored on nipping potholes in the bud using a "Road-Gan" system. The "Road-Gan" system makes road maintenance a continuous activity. We do not wait for the total collapse of roads and award big contracts to rebuild them.

2.9 The Global Economy: End of Economic Problem

Ultimately, democratic communalism will replace democratic capitalism as technology so enhance productive capacity that it comes in conflict with the profit motive. Slowing this trend is the primitively and blinding tribalism of the man; rigid antiquarian and anachronistic conceptions of territorial integrity, national sovereignty and the attendant non-interference in the "internal affairs" of nations. (Nations, which can neither feed their citizens, nor guarantee basic internal security and personal safety, should have no claims to these conceptions. Instead, the United Nations should develop into a World Government to manage countries which cannot effectively manage themselves-including small dependencies).

3.0 THOUGHTS ON ETHNICITY

Kins and cultural groups need to associate and to have a fair control of their own affairs. Political structures and organizations should allow, at least, cultural autonomy for various ethnic groups: from those, who occupy many states to those who are only part of a local government area. These structures must be in the context of One Nigeria if even as an economic Union.

4.0 THOUGHTS ON RELIGION

Only the slow process of pointed, religious, public, general, education, given by acknowledged experts of particular religions, to the generality of the people-adherents and non-adherents alike-can solve the problem of religious fanaticism. Acknowledged experts are necessary so that it does not look like propaganda but, rather, commands the respect of, especially, the adherent and also the non-adherents. What many fanatics do in name of their religions (like killing God's children defense God) find no support either in the scriptures or in the theology of particular religions. There is need for gradual, but persistent, exposure of the basic tenets of each belief system, to Nigerians something like comparative religion brought down to the level at which ordinary people can understand and appreciate. Such education will, over time, reveal the exploitative employment of religious favor for selfish, often political, interest of some leaders. It will expose the leaders who do not hesitate to urge their followers to heaven (to lay down their lives) in mad wars, only for the same leaders to readily run for dear life at the sign of the slightest dangers to themselves. It will give adherents the knowledge and confidence that non-adherents understand and even appreciate their religion. This may reduce the propensity to defend religions violently. This kind of education will show Nigerians that Judeo-Christianity, based on Abraham, Musa, Isa and Mohammed (may peace be on his name) are only branches of the same tree, sharing roots and stem!

5.0 THOUGHTS ON A FEW PRESSING PROBLEMS

5.1 The Environment

The environment is "common cause" to humanity, every

nation must bear its share of the burden. However, special considerations must be given to the less developed countries to help them cushion the impact of some self-denial environmental protection measures, like avoiding deforestation to improve the world environment.

5.2 National Debt

Lending goes with the risk of loss of the money lent, through default! The insurance against default and bad debt is the prudence in the lending activity. It is not the job of current National Governments to insure lenders against bad debts incurred from past reckless lending activities. While foreign debts properly and reasonably incurred must be paid, the lender to Governments (Local, State and National) must beware. When lenders aid public functionaries to plunder public treasuries, through their lending activities, the debt need not be paid. Foreign national debts must, therefore, be x-rayed to identify justifiable and unjustifiable claims. A case can, indeed, be made for the refund of some debts already paid. There is also the issue of interest payment. When the principal has been paid several fold and the debt keeps ballooning on account accumulation of interest, a basis exist for negotiating away the interest "debt". There remains the problem of the legitimacy of the borrowing government. Should a deal by a lender, operating from a stable democratic environment, with other than a government of the people, by the people is considered legitimate?

5.3 The Niger Delta Problem

For decades, the Nigerian Governments, especially, the military governments have behaved as they preferred the material resources of the Niger Delta area to its people – as if government would have wished the region were a desert. It is the accumulated feeling of unwantedness and neglect over the decades which fuel the confrontation, conflict, bloodshed, the breakdown of law, and the tearing asunder of order, in the

Niger Delta. Compensating affirmative actions are required. And they must be comprehensive and adequate. Bonny cannot remain without a road link to Nigeria! The present Government has started well in this regard except for the totally unnecessary and provocative onshore/offshore litigation. Men write constitutions; men people Supreme Courts; God puts peoples and resources where He pleases!

NIGERIA: AS A SUPER POWER.

WHERE EVERYTHING WORKS!

Nigeria, a Super Power? Where everything works? How can? Is that Nigeria possible? What is the truth? Which is the truth? The answer, my dear, is clear like clean water in a clean glass and the evidence for it is strong like iron. That Nigeria is possible. It is not only possible. It must come to pass! Nigerian must become a super power, where everything works.

For God so loves Nigeria, that he gave our country everything good in plenty! Our climate is so good that a man can walk around naked, sleeping outside, all the year round, and not die! He cannot do that in many parts of the world during some months of the year, and last for one night. Our soil is fertile. Because of good climate and fertile soil we can grow all kind of plants. Today we eat apples and wheat grown in Nigeria. Jos and Mambilla Plateau make it correct to say that we can grow most crops known to man! Our shores are full of the best prawns and fishes of all kinds, which is, in spite of the pollutions caused by oil mining. Animals, wild, domestic, large and small, are surplus, even without any serious effort by us to rear or conserve them. Under the soil, the earth is pregnant with minerals, known and unknown, and these minerals are available, not just in traces, but in large commercial quantities. In energy resources, we have crude oil and gas, the princes of today, we have uranium, the hope of tomorrow and, can anybody say which day the sun does not come out and shine brightly on us for long hours? Our earth is stable no earthquakes, no volcanoes? Our various peoples? Great peoples-the original sons and daughters of God, very gifted, very talented. Our peoples are as skilled in soccer and other activities requiring the working together of mind and body, as they are in intellectual (or brain) pursuits. Our scientists, Doctors, Engineers and other professionals are making waves at the frontiers of science and technology in foreign lands. Our peoples are great peoples, before some of whom, the white man confesses feeling inferiority complex! We salute the God of Nigeria.

Nigeria, a super power, where everything works? Yes! Of course! It is not only possible; it is indeed, God's design, God's plan, for Nigeria. Man may mess up God's plan, but only for a time. In the end, God's plan must prevail must come to pass. Nigeria is destined to be, and must become, a world super power, the leader among nations! We owe this to no man.

We must forget the present hopelessness and nail-biting suffering in poverty, which nobody ever thought, was possible in Nigeria. Were you an adult in 1960, you would have had no doubt, then about the prospect of Nigeria, where everything works. It was more natural and more easily believed than the present nose-diving Nigeria where nothing works. We must forget the collapse of everything in every way. We must forget that inside Nigeria we are treated like people with sawdust for brains, manipulated, frustrated, pauperized and humiliated. Not having any guns and being played one group against the other, we pretend to believe, accept and even applaud our own sons who enslave us in our own land. Outside our country, still an outcast among the community of respected nations, we are treated like lappers, even worse, we are treated like pieces of cheap shit!

This is not the Nigeria of God's design: it is the result of uncaring, unfeeling, soulless and prolonged military dictatorship. Perhaps we have sinned very much and must bear this temporary, but very harsh, punishment. We must pray to the Merciful Almighty God, who loves us, to forgive the sins of His children, actualize his designs for our country, and bring a new dawn to Nigeria. That Dawn will lay the foundations of, and let us see with our own eyes, that Nigeria, where everything works!

Yes, where everything works! In super power Nigeria, we'll play God with electricity. Turn on the switch, and there must be light: bright full-current light! It is not a matter of trying luck. Turn on the tap, and water pours, gushing or rushing out of the tap: a large container is filled in seconds. You lift the telephone receiver with the blessed assurance that the pior-or-or-orh dialing tone must be there. To cook is a matter of turning on the gas cooker, letting natural gas liquids turn to clean flames which burn so hot that the toughest stock fish, cow hide or beans, becomes soft in seconds. The gas comes as if from nowhere because, like the water, electricity and telephone, it flows through a network of under-ground pipes which enter every home, office, and factory in townships and in many villages too! You wash and (tumble) dry your cloths in machines, no looking at the face of the sun.

The streets are clean, well lit; they have beautiful flowers on the sides. Large urban roads have flowers on the right, the left and the Centre. All road users are well provides for; the cars and clean buses do not threaten the pedestrians, the cyclists and the Okada users. The high ways are wide, have many lanes and they are clean, neat and beautified. The driver must look out, but only for other road users, not at all, for potholes which do not exist. No lights from vehicles on the other side of the dual carriage way disturb the drivers at night. Corners and bend are carefully provided mainly to keep the driver awake. It is so good that every highway bye-passes the townships and never enters them. You want to go to another town, visit the village or just want to enjoy movement? You can choose from among clean cars and buses, urban rails, and inter-town, over-ground, under-ground and on the-ground rails, the inland waterways or long distance pleasure boats and ferries. Of course, the air mode is quite safe, fast and clean as the Salvation Army white uniforms.

The urban areas have green parks and play grounds, almost like the serene villages. The villages are not just quiet and beautiful; they also have the light, the water, the gas and the telephone like the urban areas. Cottage, small and medium-scale, industries operate in industrial zones and created for them in the villages. In both the urban and the rural Nigeria, well-fed, robust and healthy Nigerians move freely without fear for personal safety. Some sneak to the parks at night and sleep there all night, no fear. Health-care delivery is ever quick, ever ready, with a combination of traditional and modern medicine, no fakes. Ovie, Musa, Etim, Okolo, Ayo happy nationals, all move and mix freely like brothers just like in the Colonial days but without the Colonial masters! Unity, Peace, Love and togetherness replace the hatred and suspicion smuggled in and rules forever. Nobody (now) talks about "born to rule". Everyone has accepted to be Nigerian and to share with other Nigerians what is Nigerian including political power. And nobody regrets! No Nigeria can now be likened to that local dog, which happily follows the overfed man in the hope that sooner or later, if he does not vomit, he will defecate! Indeed, it is the foreigners in our midst who provide us the opportunity to fulfill our religious duty of giving the Zakat. For no Nigerian, except the very seriously handicapped, needs Zakat anymore! The national cake has been baked so large that everybody has enough to eat and enjoy, with greater peace of mind. Nobody waits to be fed anybody, nobody slaves for anybody.

The psychologically balanced and emotionally stable, cheerful children, all of whom sucked their mother's breast for at least one year, celebrate heartily the mothers' return from the market, because they are sure of many goodies. Mothers and their children jump for joy at the approach of the husband/fathers. While children sing and dance the mothers rush to embrace their husbands who swagger home with confidence. The children mark this climax of the parents' welcome ceremony by looking away and smiling at each other with eyes that says, "Marriage must be sweet". The wives/mothers caress the bulging pockets of Daddies-front and back pockets bulging with high value currencies. One leaf of the wad of notes can buy a crate of soft drink and leave enough change for the biscuits money and school transport fare to school, for six children, the coming school day. It is not like today where there can be reasonable doubt as to which weighs more, the vegetables bought or the money used to buy them.

On education, Nigeria is at the frontiers of knowledge at all levels of education.

The churches and mosques are overflowing with happy worshippers who praise Allah, the God, for His Boundless mercies and great deeds. Not like today's worshippers whose faces are grim, twisted and disfigured as they "bulldoze" and shout in pains, begging God for daily bread, employment, promotions, marriage partners, personal safety and more.

Outside Nigeria, we are admired, even feared, we are given the respect which befits the original sons and daughters of God! And because of Nigeria, all blacks regain their joy, respect and dignity. At summits of Heads of States, every head of state wants to shake hands with, and embrace the Nigerian Head of State, who is reputed for making peace among nations and whose emissaries even stop wars and conflicts between countries.

The Nigerian Police? Happy professionals doing their

thing: well equipped, well-paid and true friends of the people. Ring 777 and, in no time, they are with you, worried as if their lives depended on helping you.

The Military? Well supplied with State of the art equipment, integrated, mobile & well oriented people's Armed Forces. They monitor the designs of the outsiders and are loved at home. Bakasi? No way? Who dares touch the tiger's tail, even if the tiger looks dead? The risk remains that a soldier may die at war, but then, that Nigeria is worth risking death?

Did I hear you say, wake up? You make a mistake. This is no dream, only a realistic picture of what must come to pass, based on God's great love for, and surplus gifts to Nigeria!

Ok, how does it come to pass? We have all learnt the word "actualize". How is this actualized? Who can do it? Who can pull us out of the present rot, move us forward and take us there? Who knows the way?

Good questions, but first things first. First, no military dictator can do the job. None can lead us to the Promised Land. They do not know the way. Secondly, no proxy of, from, or for, the military, can take us there. His liabilities will not let him. What qualifies him to be the proxy of the military totally disqualifies him from being able to move us forward. Finally, no person who just wants to be president, because he can fund the campaign, can lead us to that Nigeria where everything works!

Then we are stuck! Why? No, we are not! We have people but most of all, there is God! He works through persons and in mysterious ways. When God wants something to be, He says: let it be! And the thing becomes! When God takes charge and moves, man gives way- including those who think they are high and mighty.

Then God will show us somebody whom he will use to clean things up. He will give us the Moses, the Joshua, the Deliverer. God will provide the opportunity to clean up our national iniquities, allow us to affirm our unity, cause all hands to be on deck, pushing the ship of state in the same direction. The potentials and talent of all Nigerians will then be released and pulled together for the good of all. The "Giant of the sum" will tear away in great speed to catch up with, and overtake, the growing nations of this world. God will give us the person who will lead us to that Nigeria where everything works.

And now, go out, let it be known, that hope is on the way back. The hope of greater tomorrow, a greater Nigeria! A super power Nigeria! Let it be known in homes, tell it in public places, break the news in towns and villages. Everyone, Nigerians and Non-Nigerians must know and accept that the bones shall rise again, the Eagle must fly again, and this time very high. Yes, let it be known that when we "remake Nigeria with progressivism" the result will be a super power country, under God, where everything works!

Sai Nigeria! Beni! Enyimba! Insha Allah, Deo volente! The Eagle must fly again, aloft on the wings of God's wind.

LEADERSHP, DEMOCRACY AND GOOD GOVERNANCE

In the affairs of men, leadership, above all else, should be the source and driving spirit of any society, the rallying point for the people's aspirations, the catalyst and dynamo for positive change in the political, economic and social performances.

Laws for ordering all social processes issue from the leadership and these laws, when they are fair and reasonable, must be obeyed. They regulate social life, economic life, political life, religious life and general living. Whatever the leaders do, in discharge of their responsibilities as leaders, have impact on the society. Thus, the relevance of leadership to democracy and good governance should be axiomatic. Is it not rare for a people to rise above their leaders? Without first rising against them, and removing them?

In terms of relevance of leadership to democracy, we may need to refer only to Lincoln's plebian definition of democracy as the government of the people, for the people and by the people. The elementary assumption of this definition is that the leadership holds governmental powers in trust for the people. Every action of the government must therefore be guided by the interest of the people.

When the government, created by the constitution, is a democracy, the leader must clearly appreciate the challenges of democracy. He must understand the principles of democracy and their practical significance. He ought to know the reciprocal nature of democratic power, which seeks to balance the power of government against the power of the people. He ought to know the context in which he is the trustee of power for the society and the purpose of that trusteeship. He must lead by persuasion not by dictation. If the people do not understand, it is the role of the leader to educate not to bulldoze. A leader who fails to understand these is bound to twist and distort the practice of democracy. This will lead to a situation where the benefit of democracy will come only in half measures or not at all.

In our opinion, the mere observance of democratic principles does not amount to good governance. Indeed democracy in itself alone, does not guarantee good governance. It is only an approach to, or, rather, an instrument for attaining good governance. However, it occupies a cornerstone position in the modern-day conception of good governance. Good governance is the careful and guided application of governmental resources to the upliftment of standard of living of man in the society. The indices of living standard include availability of the basic need of life (i.e., food, shelter and clothing), the presence of social amenities (such as drinking water, roads, power supply, communication facilities, etc.) it also includes intangible elements such as state of health, level of education of the people, security of life and property, and a feeling of social and political relevance (man likes to feel that he counts in the scheme of things in the society).

Good Leadership & Democracy

Good leadership is a friend of democracy. A good leader emphasizes the welfare of the people. By so doing, he will create a conducive atmosphere for growth and development. He will create conditions for the material and physic welfare of the people. Physic welfare refers to the rest of mind, the feeling of personal safety, and the feeling of relevance, which are inherent in an atmosphere of fairness and justice. Therefore, good leadership, whether it is provided by a dictator, an oligarchy or any other form of rulership, is a friend of democracy, because growth and development inevitably leads to democracy. A leader who is consumed by a craving for the greatness of his country and for the physic and physical well-being of his people may get the people to do what is good for them and what he wants. That is the hallmark of God-centered leadership.

It is often said that political leadership has been the weak link in Nigeria's development effort. It is necessary to be clear on what we are talking about before assessing the truth or falsehood, or, at least, the extent of the truth or falsehood, or, at least, the extent of the truth or falsehood, of this assertion. We cannot have problems with what does not exist unless, of course, its non-existence is itself the problem.

Before independence in 1960, Nigerians participated

in electing the leaders of their self-governing regions. Thus, we can talk of some political leadership and following in pre-independence Nigeria. The experience was not disastrous. On the contrary, the leaders responded reasonably well to the yearnings of their followers. They, even educated their followers on what to yearn for. That must be why, at independence, the sun of great expectation shone so brightly in Nigeria. Nigerians were full of hope, some foreigners were full of envy and some of admiration.

Since independence, we had political leadership from October 1960 to January 1966, from October 1979 to December 1983 and from May 1999 till date. The period of our political leadership has been shorter than the period we have been under military rulership. The biggest problem of democracy has been that of orderly succession, peaceful change of political baton.

LEADERSHIP AND FOLLOWERSHIP

Leadership is not everything; follower-ship counts! But he gets better following who leads better. Leading better by examples, consistent behavior and gutsy decisions, all anchored on blind fairness and justice, a good leader who is such, seen through like a transparency, by his people, gets followed and his examples are copied by his lieutenant and the entire populace.

But followership counts! Indeed Nigerians can choose between poverty and wealth, between independence of families, in terms of economic self-sufficiency and begging; between freedom and bondage, between Nigeria as a super power and Nigeria as a contradiction of a rich/poor country. Nigerians can choose between switching on the light and remaining in darkness. Nigerians can choose between heavy moneybags and principled visionary leaders who will be fair to all concerned, and get committed to actualize the abiding reason for one sustainable Nigeria: namely, the need to raise the respect and dignity of Nigerian and African people in world affairs.

THE NEEDED LEADERSHIP:

We need a leadership that makes people do the will of the visionary leader as if they were following their own will. This is the leadership, which makes very intelligent and independent minded followers follow like robots, like zombie while the leader surrenders himself like a robot in the hands of God, anchoring his thoughts and actions on God. The followership which copy from the leader, the fear of God and respect for man, as the "abc" of wisdom, that is the followership which is generated by the right leadership; such followership can also generate good Leadership. Leadership and followership are thus the two sides of the buttocks rubbing on each other and equilibrating the social body giving it the poise!

The immediate task of political leadership in Nigeria is to restore hope. To pull our people out of the pit in which they have found themselves. To rescue the people from the ravage of military dictatorship and from the ruling clique. The strategic goals, objectives or task must be to actualize the reasonable expectations, hope or potentialities, which the situation of Nigeria clearly justifies. The challenges before political leadership in Nigeria are enormous, serious, urgent and important. A political leader of Nigeria has work to do. He will need vision, organizing ability, wisdom, administrative skills and more. But everybody cannot possess all these in abundance. Some of these attributes can be acquired by a leader through wise recruitment and effective use of the talent in other persons. What cannot be loaned or hired are those correct and sound principles of personal character, which generate good thoughts and right actions.

What are these principles? What is their source? No correct and sound principle is inconsistent with loving our neighbor as yourself. Caring, integrity, telling the truth, courage, humility, fidelity, justice, steadfastness, industry, etc. these are correct and sound principles.

These correct and sound principles have their sources in Godliness. Possessing the correct sound principles, a leader can make up for other leadership deficiencies, but nothing atones for lacking them. Godliness! In politics? Yes! Our Godliness must find expression in our politics as in our other activities of life.

It is common Nigerian fallacy that politics is the domain of the filthy. The fact is that we cannot be dirt in politics and be acceptable in the sight of God. There is no domain in human life from which God can be excluded. If there were to be any, certainly politics, which deals with the affairs of man, God's highest creation, cannot qualify.

To serve the interest of the people, to meet their aspirations, to improve the quality of their lives, must therefore, constitute the general purpose of government policies and actions. If this is achieved in the contest of democracy, the credit will go to good leadership. Good leadership will then have made democracy as good in idea, as in practice. It needs to be added that, for Nigerians today, it is good leadership, not the form, or the philosophical basis, of governance that matters. As has been indicated already, good leadership will ultimately lay the foundations for the demand for democracy. Nigerians do not find bases to hope. Civilians must beware! But, no military government in Nigeria had come close to the quality of good leadership.

ELECTORAL EMPOWERMENT OF WOMEN

Any promise by party leaders to help women wins nominations in our present political system, will either be empty or lead to unfairness – be undemocratic. Beyond helping women with campaign support, party leaders cannot effectively and meaningfully help women to gain nomination without taking undemocratic actions. In which constituencies will they choose to impose women and disenfranchise men? In a multi-party system, even if a party succeeds in imposing a woman, the woman may still not win unless the constituency is a captive one for the party.

Effective and meaningful empowerment of women is a constitutional matter. It calls for the creation of two sets of constituencies. One set of constituency will be free for all, for men and women. The other set of constituencies should be gender exclusive – exclusive to women – women exclusive constituencies (WEC). If we want to retain the existing constituencies in the country, they may be designated "free for all constituencies". In addition to these, we should create additional constituencies, which should be exclusive to women. To guarantee that women occupy 25 percent of legislative positions, one women–exclusive constituency (WEC) must be created for every three constituencies. The senatorial constituencies (zones) are the easiest to use to illustrate. Each state has three senatorial constituencies. To add a women-exclusive constituency (or zone), the whole state is made to constitute one exclusive constituency for women. The same method can be applied to councillorship wards, House of Assembly constituencies and House of Representative constituencies. That is, three existing councillorship wards, three House of Assembly constituencies and three House of Representative constituencies will constitute one women-exclusive councillorship, House of Assembly and House of Representatives ward/constituencies respectively.

90

We may think that having so many more constituencies is unacceptable. Then we have to re-organize the existing constituencies. For example, we can create two free senatorial constituencies and one women exclusive senatorial constituency in each state. That leaves each state with three senatorial districts. How? The whole state is divided into two for the free senatorial constituencies; the state as a whole then constitutes the women-exclusive constituency. The same method will be applied to all other constituencies/wards: councillorship, House of Assembly and House of Representatives. In this case, women will be guaranteed at least $33^1/_3$ percent representation in legislative houses.

Women who feel strong enough not to want the concessions made to women by the device of women-exclusive constituencies, are of course, free to contest in the free constituencies.

The concession to women to increase their participation in governance is in the interest of the society. As I have argued, elsewhere, women, especially women as mothers, suffer most from bad governance. And, on the average, women have greater integrity than men. These two propositions justify deliberate effort to increase the participation of women in appointive and elective positions in government. I have not found a way to empower women fairly for elective chief executive offices; Local Government Chairman, State Governors and President. Only campaign-support, to women who are going for such offices is possible. Even this is seriously problematic. How do we decide on those deserving of our support?

Unless women enjoy merely chanting their electoral disabilities, they should pick up this proposal, which has been lying for more than half a decade! Recent experiences have shown that even in this era, when party bosses picked and imposed candidates of their choice, seemingly, in their absolute discretion, women aspirants fared even worse than in the past. What women aspirants could offer, were inadequate to meet the demands of the party bosses. Women would, perhaps, have done better in a system of direct primary elections. Since the direct primary system is also better for the country, in terms of reduced "conspicuous deceit" and greater fairness, women should join in propagating the merits of this 'grassroots democratic system" and its adoption by all the political parties and for all general elections.

AKINTOLUGBOYE ON PRESIDENT OF IGBO ORIGIN

I should comment on the issue of Nigerian President of Igbo Origin. Igbo or non-Igbo, I am eminently qualified to be president of Nigeria. I am Igbo. Should this fact disqualify me?

Whether or not there is any agreement on "one term for the incumbent President, the source of North-South rotation idea is the 1994/95 Constitutional Conference. There appears to be also an understanding that the rotation is for the two terms of successful presidency. When it became clear that the incumbent president did not deserve a second term, reasonable persons, who understand the dynamics of Nigerian politics and also think long range, started considering the prospects of killing two birds with one stone. To ensure the stability and permanence of one Nigeria, they reasoned that the presidency should remain in the South for four more years but moved to the East, in particular, to the Southeast. The Southeast has clearly demonstrated its full willingness and readiness for the presidency even if some detractors and shallow thinkers invent imaginary problems for the Igbo people. They do not remember that more aspirants came out from the North, when the NPN zoned the presidency to that region, than have now come out from the Southeast. Ultimately, the North pruned the aspirants and brought out one person for the one party – NPN. The Ohaneze has organized to do better, even in the environment of 30 political parties. And, Of course, the southeast has a super abundance of presidential materials – if the truth is to be told. Had only a few aspirants come out, the same detractors would have pointed to that as evidence of lack of interest. Of course, the competitive disabilities of the Igbo, a truly republican, highly individualistic people, operating a personal – merit- driven system, in a larger society, dominated by privilege and the ascription of positions and statuses, must be given due recognition. Thus, it will take time for the Igbo, used to a freely competitive, open system, to adapt to the system of manipulative compromises prevalent in the larger Nigerian society.

I should have preferred it, if my self-interest had dominated my adherence to truth, principle and nationalism, so that I do not make the next points. But, God is in charge and He created me the way I am. He does not make mistakes. I yield to God and tell the following truth as I see it:

Those who care for one Nigeria, her stability and greatness, should act with caution and wisdom in this delicate period. The presidency should remain in the South for another four years; it should be moved to the South-East or South-South: where this is not feasible for whatever reasons, it should be left where it is. This is the course for the permanence of One Nigeria, her stability and her greatness.

We must discount the defeatist decision by a timorous leadership who do not, at all, appreciate the depth of the feelings of the people they lead.

THANK YOU PRESS CONFERENCE

I thank all my supporter across Nigeria, both those, from many states, who joined Okwadike Campaign Organization and those who defied instructions and voted for me at the Eagle Square. The office bearers among them, whose positions are threatened for defying instructions, should rejoice in the Lord that they followed their consciences – the sparks of God inside them.

I regret nothing, I feel no bitterness, I remain undaunted and committed to a goal of installing a God centered leadership in Nigeria. I will remain so committed all the days of my life. I will have no part in politics as usual in Nigeria – *politics Nigeriana.*

In or out of office, my song will be the same: politics is God's vineyard. May God confirm me as a robot in his hands? Nigerians must continue to pray for the advent of God's own Nigeria. We must persist in prayers, no wavering, or as apolitical supporter says, "No Shaking". God knows the best. He will guide us all right.

Nigeria must go back to the grassroot democratic system and allow the people to select candidates in direct primary elections. This is the first step to positive change.

The dominance, in the political scene, of generals, the military Heads of State and Retired Military Officers, who held political offices while they were in service, is a threat to our civilian rule (we have civilian rule, not democracy). First, as the Igbos say, we must cure a mad man of madness but not of his mad gaits, his style of working. We have seen the effect of this in the current civilian government of General Obasanjo. Secondly, it is difficult to convince currently serving military officers against adventures into political arena when they see the dominance in the country's politics, of their retired colleagues who held political offices as serving

94

military personnel. It is also a submission to the god of cash and an extolment of corruption. The ex-military succeed, not because of their superior political acumen, but possibly because of superior cash fire power, the result of their impact on the coffers of the State.

But no power on earth is beyond the power of God. Therefore, we must pray, in the belief, that in the fullness of God's time, He will take control. Keep control and impose his wills on the affairs of Nigeria. So to implement, His design for Nigeria as a super power.

8

THE IMPERATIVE,
AND A,B,C,
OF RESTRUCTURING NIGERIA

(Okwadike, Dr. Chukwuemeka Ezeife)

Fellow Nigerians, all true friends of Nigeria, and all those who wish Africa and all blacks well, ladies, gentlemen, and Nigerian youths - male and female - there is one truth, a truth which cannot be honestly doubted, controverted or wished away: every serious thinking Nigerian, even with minimum sincerity, knows this bothersome truth: that our dear country, Nigeria, the largest concentration of blacks on the face of the earth, will, without urgent serious political re-engineering or restructuring, go into extinction - cease to exist!!! This is the only truth! Don't mind some people who talk idly about Nigeria remaining united and being "indissoluble" without restructuring!! This truth defines the **IMPERATIVE** of restructuring Nigeria. The recent fate of *devolution of powers* in the National Assembly, defines the need to lay bare, the **A,B,C** of restructuring Nigeria.

Nigeria's Manifest Destiny and Efforts To Abort It
God designed for Nigeria, unmatched greatness, to enable

NIGERIA - DEMOCRACY & STATE OF THE ECONOMY

her achieve His purpose for creating her. That purpose is Nigeria's Manifest Destiny. To restructure Nigeria, and make her able to achieve her Manifest Destiny is the task every Nigerian should pray for and help to bring about!!! This task must be performed, and urgently too. Surely, Nigeria was not an accident of British imperialism. No! God created Nigeria using British imperialism merely as a tool. And God created Nigeria for a purpose! What purpose? It is reasonable to say that God created Nigeria to be a rallying point and big brother for Africa, and, indeed, for all the blacks on earth. Population and geographical size are important in the ranking and power play among nations. Nigeria cannot achieve God's purpose for her unless she develops into a Super Power among the nations of the world. And she needs her present large size to achieve that. Nigeria developing into a Super Power among world nations will raise the respect, dignity and prestige of all the blacks of this world. Income per head, population and geographical size contribute to the ranking of world powers. Nigeria is the greatest concentration of blacks on earth and has massive geographical size. To ensure very high income per head, God endowed Nigeria with a stupendous abundance of resources. Nigeria's ultimate purpose for being, clearly appears to be: to wipe away the shame of slavery from the faces of all blacks!!! Nigeria achieves this by attaining the status of a Super Power among nations. We should elaborate on the endowments that make this possible.

Think of the climate in Nigeria and you are forced to easily see that the climate is meant for human beings. One can be naked and stay in the open for much of the year and not die, come rain, come sun shine and all. Thunder storms are minimal, there are no hurricanes as happens in the Americas, nor typhoons as in Asia. The winds are not too fierce nor are the rains too heavy - tsunamis are not really known. We have occasional flooding, but not, at all, comparable to what is observed in other parts of the world. The geo-physical structure of Nigeria is solid, rugged and favourable, there are no volcanoes, no earthquakes, landslides and erosions are manageable. Nigeria and Africa appear to have been originally designed for human habitation. Material resources are simply surplus. Every plant can grow in Nigeria. Those that cannot grow in Igbo Ukwu, can grow in Mambila Plateau and similar places in the country. We have gold, silver, gem stones, oil and gas, limestone, iron, tantalite etc - all in large quantities. And, it does not appear that we know, yet, all the mineral resources the country is endowed with. Of animals, Nigeria is home to anything that moves or breaths. What of human resources? Not only does Nigeria boast of large population, we can also boast of many talents from many tribes.

Nigeria's endowment with equable climate and huge material and human resources disposes her to unmatched greatness. This was not, and is not, hidden. The British saw clearly, this potential in, or of, Nigeria and, fearing that her former colony would fast develop into a Super Power and challenge her in world affair, she contrived strategies to keep Nigeria down, underdeveloped, and for them, hopefully, undevelopable. The colonial masters assessed the potentialities and made choices to stifle the growth of Nigeria. Some of the colonial officials who were used to implement the strategies have confessed about their manipulations. But the time seems to have come, and it seems to be now, that, as ordained, God's Will must dominate, prevail over, and neutralise, all the negative efforts of man, foreign man and the chosen local man, to mess up His design of unmatched greatness for Nigeria!!!

Fellow Nigerians, our God is great. He answers prayers. Let no groups of Nigerians blame themselves or other groups. For some of us were merely used - it was not the making of those who have been used!! Our God works in mysterious ways. As It appears, this is His time. He will open the minds of every group to see the group's greater long term benefits, in a politically re-engineered or restructured Nigeria. He will also give the dialoguing or negotiating groups, the mind to accommodate necessary interests, where they are merited. Let us not yield to the devil and help tear down, and demolish, the gem of a country, given to us by God. No group of Nigerians, large or small, can happily walk away from Nigeria, properly restructured, and with justice, as fairness, prevailing. God will forgive those who know this truth, but who, for whatever reasons, including clearly myopic delusion supporting the sustainability of unsustainable unfair advantages, or cheating, or those who will like to delude themselves and their people, that the status quo can continue and Nigeria survives - does not go into extinction. Those who may have been at the receiving end must find ways to love their neighbours as themselves. And "neighbours" mean any other Nigerians. The saying "God's time is the best", is the truth!!!

The National Assembly Experience
Recently, the National Assembly dealt with the issue of *devolution of powers,* which is a key element in the restructuring of Nigeria. Devolution of powers deals with the sharing of powers between the centre or federal government and the federating units. It is what makes a federation a federation. When powers (the power over electric power, the power over external relations, the power over all internal affairs, the power over weights, measures and currencies, the power over primary and secondary schools, the power over the exploitation of minerals, the power over external security, the power over all internal security or police affairs, markets, courts, religion, the power over revenue etc) are concentrated in the central government, it defines extreme unitary government. As it were, by their rejection of devolution of powers, the National Assembly is saying no to the appellation: "Federal Republic of Nigeria". Although we expect patriotism, and service to the people, justice as fairness, to prevail, we must be aware of myopia. This is a clear case of short-sightedness, a clear case of baseless hope that clearly unsustainable and unfair advantages can be

sustained. The National Assembly is part of the problem and needs to be restructured to work in the overall interest of the country. It is clearly unrealistic to leave the issue of restructuring Nigeria to the National Assembly as it is, at present, composed. Ask the National Assembly whether Nigeria should have bicameral or unicameral legislature, or whether legislation should be part time or full time job, it will give the same answer as it has given to the question on devolution of powers. In this case the conflict of interest is naked. The answer to the devolution question defines a clear case of living in the past, and of closing eyes to stark naked current realities. It may look like arrogance in the extreme. But we must accept that man is man and has limitations, which include, conflict of interest. Who did the voting? How did they vote? The result is a clear dramatisation of the unfairness of the actions of the post-civil war military leaders from the North. The only surprise is what appears as extreme short-sightedness and total lack of patriotism. As shown below, the post-civil war Northern military rulers of Nigeria gave the North more states (therefore more senators), more federal constituencies (hence more representatives in the House of Representatives), and, by far, more local government areas. All these mean more money in a system without fiscal federalism.

A,B,C OF RESTRUCTURING NIGERIA

Nigeria has failed man and God, she has failed comprehensively and woefully. Instead of providing a template for good governance to Africa and wiping shames off the faces of blacks, we are leading Africa in corruption and bad governance, and, generating more shame for all blacks! For Nigeria not to go into extinction i.e., not to cease to exist, we must restructure her and make justice, as fairness, prevail in the restructured country. Now, what is restructuring Nigeria? What does it call for? In substance, restructuring

Nigeria simply calls for our *going back to the "agreed Nigeria", that is, going back to the structure or political arrangements of Nigeria, as agreed by our founding fathers - our heroes past!* **To that** "agreed Nigeria", we add all, or some of, the results of the 2014 National Conference. This is the A,B,C of restructuring in Nigeria!!! Elements of the agreed Nigeria are in the independence constitutions of the federal and regional governments. And the Report of the 2014 Conference is readily available, if even in the archives. As is well known that "agreed Nigeria" was a federal structure, with regions as federating units. Initially there were three regions: Eastern, Western and Northern regions. Midwestern region was created later, making four regions: three in the South, one in the North. Each region had its own constitution and operated fairly autonomously. The Federal Government handled issues universally agreed to be federal responsibilities - issues like: external relations, currency, weights and measures etc.

There was fiscal federalism, as the resources for running the Federal Government came, basically, from the federating units. Each region controlled its resources and grew at its own pace. The people owned their regional governments, in the sense that people in the regions were, particularly, concerned about how their regions were run and their finances spent. That was mainly because the money spent in the regions was basically internally generated - contributed by the people of the regions, through taxation, other payments etc. That is different from the present situation, wherein revenues "come" from the Federation Account to the federal, state and local governments. With that agreed structure there was peace and satisfactory progress. The *agreed structure* was rubbished by the Nigerian military in 1967, at the beginning of the Nigeria/Biafra conflict and was not resurrected after the civil war.

The Rubbishing of the Agreed Nigeria

To win, the Nigeria/Biafra war, easily and fast, the military government, under General Gowon, adopted the strategy of isolating the Igbo from the rest of eastern Nigeria. Twelve states were thus created: six in the North, six in the South, with the Igbo bottled up in the Southeast state. The running of Nigeria was also made more fully adapted to military central command system. This central command has given Nigeria a unitary, as opposed to, the agreed federal, structure of government.

After the war, the military rulers continued to run the government in Nigeria - making it progressively more unitary and more dictatorial. It was thus easy for the military to, basically dictatorially, create not only new states, but also new local government areas (LGAs), without considering the fairness of their distribution. Today, we have 36 states plus Abuja, sometimes treated as if it were a state, 19 states plus Abuja in the North, 17 in the South. The imbalance in the distribution of local government areas (LGAs) is, by far, more pronounced. For example, Kano and Jigawa (which was created out of Kano) have between them almost as many local government areas as the whole of the Southeast geo-political zone; Kano has 44 LGAs, Lagos 20, Bayelsa 8, etc. The North has 419 local government areas, and the south has 357. Both the federal, states and the LGAs, get allocations of revenue (funding) from the Federation Account. The unfairness of these military creations should be obvious and problematic, and should be a major reason for the clamour for restructuring. However it, indeed, is its consequence that is the main problem. As the country is currently structured and run, the country is growing backwards - indeed, taking giant steps backward. The Nigerian people, at federal, state and LGA levels, do not police the expenditure of revenues allocated from the Federation Account, and this and other factors, have led to the monumental corruption which has eaten deep into, and permeated, every fabric of the society, leading to the comprehensive and woeful failure of Nigeria.

Restructuring Nigeria and
Completing the Unfinished Business of 2014
Conference.

We note that the very well composed 2014 National Conference approved the creation of additional 18 states. Those who doubted the wisdom of so many new states, should think of the new suggestion of twelve regions and 52 states for only the Middle Belt. The problem is that the extent of dehumanisation and suffering to which some Nigerians are subjected cannot be imagined by many Nigerians. Without taking account of the new information from the Middle Belt, we have 54 states plus Abuja to deal with. We should adopt the least controversial and most efficient approach to restructure Nigeria, instead of rediscovering the wheels with attendant new controversies. The line of least resistance, which can also yield fairly efficient solution, appears to be: to adopt the present six geopolitical zones, which have been used, even if informally, for decades now, as the Federating Units, and allow the states, in each zone, to work out their constitutions, with the recommendations of the 2014 Conference and Independence Constitutions of the former regions as guides. Of course, they may introduce new elements, forced by current realities. One such, is to make the zones responsible for their internal security - with external security left with central government. In this case, the coexistence of Zonal and State Police Commands, should be seriously considered, for greater effectiveness and efficiency. There is, of course, the option of treating the 54 states as federating units, leaving it open to interested states to somehow cooperate. Beyond, perhaps, satisfying theoretical completeness, no knowledgeable analyst will take this option seriously in the empirical context of Nigerian. Whether we want to adopt the above line of least resistance or choose any other approaches, we must be aware that we are running out of time. We should note the following:

(1) The materials/templates for the work of restructuring Nigeria, including the 2014 Conference Report and the Independence Federal and Regional Constitutions are available.

(2) The existing states have their interests which need to be fully accommodated. Members from the states should work to ensure that, there is not, for any state, a reasonable bases for the feeling of
"going back to Egypt".

(3) A restructured Nigeria, with justice prevailing, is in the best interest of every group in Nigeria, large or small.

(4) There is time constraint.

THE PROGAMME FOR RESTRUCTURING NIGERIA

A. By mid, or end, of September 2017: the Federal Government should set up a body (perhaps Sovereign National Conference/Constituent Assembly/ Some Other) to work out details of a New Nigeria based on improvements to our old durable foundations of the agreed Nigeria, aided by the Report of the 2014 Conference. Perhaps, the first month of the body's work should be devoted to the participants from each zone working out their zonal constitutions, which will then go to the State/Zonal Assembly for any further action.
B. The structure of New Nigeria is adopted by mid-2018. A chunk of the Conference/Assembly time should be devoted to developing anti-corruption measures with a view to achieving, as much as possible, a zero-tolerance of corruption in the New Nigeria. The Body should also work out ways to

empower women for electoral offices, in view of their special good qualities. This can be done by creating women exclusive constituencies.

C. The new structure is fully implemented before the end of the first quarter of 2019.

CONCLUSION

We pray to the Almighty God, our Father in heaven, to give us, Nigerians, the mind, the understanding, the passion and the determination, to save Nigeria, by restructuring Nigeria, by letting justice prevail in Nigeria, thereby empowering Nigeria to develop into a Super Power, and achieve her Manifest Destiny!!! Amen!!!

9

THE IMPERATIVE OF A NEW NIGERIA
EZEIFE LEADERSHIP FOUNDATION

(Okwadike, Dr. Chukwuemeka Ezeife)

Reasonable persons believe that God has a special purpose for creating Nigeria - even though He used the instrumentality of British Imperialism to bring her about. What could be God's purpose for creating Nigeria? In other words, what can be called Nigeria's Manifest Destiny? To attempt an answer does not seem to require advanced spirituality or great political insight! The fact that Nigeria is the greatest concentration of black persons on the face of the earth, is clearly suggestive. Add to this the events of world history involving the blacks. It seems clear that God intended Nigeria to be the big brother and rallying point for all blacks. And God's bounteous resource endowments on Nigeria must be to enable her achieve that Manifest Destiny, which has to involve Nigeria developing into a Super Power among nations, thereby raising the dignity and respect of Blacks on earth. To wipe away the shame of slavery from the faces all of Blacks, has to be the ultimate Manifest Destiny of Nigeria. And God endowed Nigeria with every ingredient she needs to it.

The climate in Nigeria is equable - no extremes. It is even possible for a man to stay naked outside, in the open, round the year, and not die. There are no hurricanes, no tornadoes or typhoons. We have never been affected by any tsunamis! Our geo-physical structures are stable - no volcanoes, no earthquakes, landslides are not known. Our endowment of material resources is super-abundant. Any plant found anywhere, is, or can be grown, somewhere, in Nigeria. Our animal resources, including anything that breaths and moves, are surplus. All valuable minerals, known to man, are surplus in Nigeria: oil and gas, gold, silver and diamond, gemstones of every type, limestone, iron ore, aluminium etc. Everything!! And more are yet to be discovered. As for human beings, Nigeria is superbly gifted - many talents from many tribes! It is clear that the Almighty God designed Nigeria for unmatched greatness!!!

What has been the result? So far, it has been colossal failure, unmitigated! The Nigerian humans, especially the men, are working tirelessly to mess up God's design for our country. The main cause of the total failure of Nigeria is monumental corruption which has saturated every element of the social structure. Far from raising the respect and dignity of Blacks, Nigeria has become the generator and accumulator of shame to all Blacks. And it has now come to the stage that all Blacks are being suffocated with shame emanating from Nigeria. Not even those who are not affected by the odium of our failure are, any longer, keeping quiet. Not long ago, a white man, Donald Trump, the Republican aspirant for the Presidency of the United States of America, said something to the effect that:

Africa, especially Nigeria and Kenya, should be re-colonized for another one hundred years. His reason is that, we, Africans, learnt nothing from our ex-colonial masters, that our pre-occupation in political office is to cart away the wealth of our countries and dump same in foreign banks.

Nigerians emigrate, in large numbers, as a result of the mismanagement of her economy, and in the USA, they take away jobs meant for the citizens. He, indeed, threatens to deport Nigerians if he wins the presidential election.

He accused our political leaders of never considering the interest of the people they lead. He clearly implies that **politics in Nigeria is exclusively for self, not for service to the people or society.** Donald Trump may have been blunt, unprotocolic, unfriendly, even totally unsophisticated. But he said the truth - the crude truth. He called a spade, a spade.

Condemnations are now pouring in from many quarters and individuals. **A respected international organization announced that all about 50 countries of the world, which are governed by blacks are the most backward and very poor.** An Afro-American pastor, declared, with bitterness, that blacks are good only at feasting tables. Blacks, according to him, have contributed nothing to societal growth, have invented nothing and developed nothing. And a blunt Jewish Leader has this to say:

> **"The only thing blacks understand is consumption. Blacks don't understand the importance of creating and building wealth.... Their leaders steal from their people and send the money back to their colonial masters .... Every successful black wants to spend his money in the country of their colonial masters, they go on holiday abroad, buy houses abroad, school abroad, go for medical treatment abroad etc. instead of spending this money in their own country to benefit their people."** In comparison with the Jews, he said **"this is why Jews are at the top and blacks are at the bottom of every**

ladder in society".

All Backs should be sorry for the colossal failure of black political leadership. But the greatest failure and therefore, the greatest shame should be my country's - Nigeria's - the supposed big brother and rallying point for Blacks, whose Manifest Destiny is to raise the dignity and respect of black and African peoples!!

But it is important to remind the reader of this note, that contrary to some statements which seen to demean Blacks, the black man was, indeed, the creator and developer of the basics of all knowledge: science and technology, mathematics, religion, including the idea of one God. In the ancient of days, the wise saying was that, out of Africa, always comes something new and good. It is true that when the white men (who used to be the foot mat of the world and we called, the "blue eyed barbarians") took hold of black knowledge from, especially, Alexandria, where most of the books and manuscripts were dumped after the conquest of Africa, they put it to use to fight their hostile environment, and, over time, they arrived at a process of continuous improvement. After much improvement, the whites looked back at the blacks in Africa, who remained, mostly, in their state of nature, enjoying God-given favourable ecological balance. Noting the wide gap, in living standards, between themselves and us, they started to wonder whether we, the Blacks, were humans like themselves, or were, somehow sub-human, like, half-born apes. They debated our suitability to be bought and sold as chattels. That was the foundation for the slave trade. The truth is that the black man has not always been the foot mat of all the world. They were once the topmost.

Yes, we Nigerians have failed in our Manifest Destiny, and have no basis for continued existence, except as a totally changed country!!!. We must become the opposite of what we are now. Extra-ordinarily system-saturating monumental corruption brought us to this colossal failure. That corruption must be exterminated, totally, from our land. There must now be zero tolerance of corruption in Nigeria. No half measures can do it!! Zero tolerance must be zero tolerance. And it is achievable in Nigeria. We must achieve success in re-making Nigeria!! Because the Almighty God, who gave us this mission and gave us the where withal to achieve it, does not change. Man can try and appear to succeed for a time. But man cannot permanently mess up God's design. It is the will of God, not that of man, that will dominate. Now is the time, to deal finally with all who try to mess up God's design for Nigeria as a nation of unsurpassed greatness. It must be Operation Total Clean Up. **Away** with all corrupt institutions! **Away** with all existing political organisations and parties. **Away** with all agents of corruption. Away with untruths, deceit and lies. No more sacred cows! No more untouchables! To keep Nigeria clean to achieve her Manifest Destiny, is a task we must commit to. Members of the, yet to be formed, new political parties (preferable two to begin with) both the new members who were not in politics before, and the truly reformed old politicians, must swear to new political principles or oath, including the oath of service to the people, as the reason for participation in politics. Every adult Nigerian must swear to the oath not to sabotage Nigeria (and corruption shall be defined clearly as act of sabotage). Working with the will of God, man can clean up man's mess. In the new Nigeria, women must play a major, if not the dominant, role, so that their superior qualities can raise both the quality of governance and the welfare of the governed. The superior qualities include the following: 1) The milk of human kindness flows more in women than in men. ii)

Women are, usually, more concerned with the welfare of their children (offspring) than men. iii) As I stated in my book, "Remaking Nigeria with Progressivism," in 1987: a).

"Women bear the brunt of bad governance," and "should have greater vested interest in good governance." b). As a rule, and on the average, women

110

are less corrupt than men in public and private offices."
c) Women obey the rules and keep to the principles
more than men. d) "Even where materialism rules both
men and women, men plunder the public treasury more
devastatingly than women, because women have,
generally lower material expectations".

The path to New Nigeria must be very tough and rugged: it includes remaking the polity, remaking the private sector and social groups, remaking the church, the mosque, the school and education system, the clubs and associations, remaking the judiciary, the police the army, the town unions and traditional organisation, trade unions, the market associations, the age group system, the old boys associations, old girls etc. Sure, to Remake Nigeria must be a daunting task. But there is no way to run away from it. It is time to confront what confronts us. For knowledge, experience, competence and intellect, we shall draw from the bounties in every part of Nigeria. For funds, we may approach able Nigerians, including the repentant erstwhile looters of the country. To Remake Nigeria, we must!! God helping us, as we work on His purpose for Nigeria!!!

10

RIGID ZONING AND ROTATION OF OFFICE OF GOVERNOR IN STATES

(Okwadike, Dr. Chukwuemeka Ezeife)

A political entity performs best in the atmosphere of peace and unity, which are generated by equity, justice and fairness. Equity, justice and fairness are most evident where every member of the society, from every section of the political entity, sees himself/herself as equal to, and has the same rights as, every other member of the political entity. All fair-minded persons will accept the above as not only truly desirable, but, indeed, optimal.

The Problem

The problem is that this optimal situation which looks so natural does not, at all, come automatically, even where no bases exist for segregation among the peoples in the political entity. That is, even where equality of persons, in every aspect, is widely accepted, it may not lead to fair distribution of political offices among the various sections of the political entity. Differential availability of resources usually accounts most for this. Thus on a "laissez faire" basis, the Governor of a state may keep coming from one section of the state, and, overtime, people from that section may develop "a born to rule psychosis". The result will be the destruction of bases for peace and unity and therefore, the stifling of progress in the political entity. In the extreme, the other sections may conspire to keep the "dominating" section permanently out of power in the state - leaving the political entity permanently without peace and unity, and therefore underproductive and underdeveloped.

Efforts At 2005 National Conference

To avoid these negative outcomes is the reason for zoning and rotation of leadership in a political entity. In the 2005 National Political Conference, at Abuja, I served as the Chairman of Power Sharing Committee. In spite of the hot heads packed in that Committee, we were still able to come up with fairly unanimous recommendations on zoning and rotation of offices, from the Local Government Level, to the National Level. But we were not quite able to rigidly define the sequence of rotation at the national level. Also our recommendation for zoning and rotation at the Local Government Level was, expectedly, left hazy and did not really go beyond the statement of the principle. However, the recommendation for zoning and rotation of the office of Governor was very clear and definitive: - the office of Governor will rotate among the three Senatorial Zones of the State.

Producing People's Gubernatorial Candidate with Minimum Hassle

Although the recommendation for gubernatorial zoning and rotation have been seen, widely, as eminently reasonable, it has not succeeded in every state. One of the reasons is ethnicity and the choices by political parties, where the sequence of rotation is not made legally binding. The lesson is that for zoning and rotation to work perfectly, it must be sold to, and accepted by the people of the state as a whole: the voters, the political leaders, the town unions, individually as well as at the level of the Anambra State Association of Town Unions (ASATU)), the churches, the market unions, trade unions, the traditional leaders, the religious leaders, and all the major publics in the society. This is because we want the people to own the system and defend it with their votes. The necessary legal backing then becomes an expression of the will of the people. The system has to be made robust and rigid so that there is no doubt or confusion as to from which senatorial zone the Governor should emerge. This is not just optimal, it can easily be achieved and can comprehensively elevate unity, peace and progress. There are many more benefits: the costs and impact of money on governorship election will be drastically reduced and these costs include costs to the society in terms of electoral disruptions and violence, human casualties, damages to property, mutual suspicion and antagonisms. Also the candidates are better and more seriously screened, imposition of candidates is reduced or even eliminated, and the emerging candidate becomes more of a peoples' candidate than a godfather's candidate.

Necessary Ingredients

1) Each Senatorial Zone holds Governorship Power continuously for two terms of 8 years.
2) Each Political Party selects its candidate from the Zone whose turn it is to supply Governorship candidate, at both the first term and second term stages. Thus the Party whose member is in power has the right to select or drop the incumbent Governor for the second term. The electoral umpire ensures rigid compliance by not accepting candidate from other than the zone whose turn it is.

Enhancing Governance

3) A serving Governor must hold at least two town hall meetings in each Senatorial Zone during each of his/her term of office.

4) Government Accounts shall be for the scrutiny of the people, not only for the House of Assembly. Provision 5 below helps in this regard.

5) An unpaid **People's Council** consisting of Elders, Women, Youths and representatives of key stakeholders in the society may be constituted to help make non-binding inputs in the budgetary process. Such a body may also help with (4) above and with other needs to consult the people.

6) Suggestion Box System (which may also be used as whistle blowing opportunity) shall be maintained securely by the government, and made effective use of, as a serious anti-corruption/anti-abuse device.

Moving Forward

So far, the Zones in Anambra state have held Gubernatorial Power as follows:

	Zone	Years in Office
1.	Anambra South	5 Years and 10 months.
2.	Anambra Central	11 Years.
3.	Anambra North	3 Years.

Thus, the rigid sequence of zoning and rotation calls for Anambra North, after completing 8 years in office, to hand over to Anambra South, which will after its turn, must hand over to Anambra Central and this rolling stone gathers moss.

Exporting to All Southeast, And Improving Governance

Such a rigid rotation will be good for Anambra State and should, as early as possible, be exported to the whole Southeast zone. And there can be no serious problems in so doing. Why?

1). Virtually every LGA in Anambra state, not to talk of a senatorial zone, can boast of several worthy candidates for Governor. So, there can be no true shortage of suitable or capable candidate from each senatorial zone.

2). The Senatorial Zones in Anambra are fairly evenly endowed with competent men and women.

3). As goes Anambra, so virtually, goes the rest of Southeast. We should provide this vital leadership.

4). We want Anambra politicians from now on, to see politics as rendering service to the people, not service to self. Competition among politicians is now to be seen in efforts to improve the welfare of the people. Every candidate for political office must swear to a special oath of service to the people.

5) The voters of Anambra state, must now take clear ownership of their state and avoid any special, especially material, inducement, to vote for any candidate. Indeed, any candidate who offers such inducement, shall have, by so doing, declared himself unfit for the position. It is the duty of the people to ensure that the money received on their behalf - from internal or external sources is judiciously expended.

The above propositions, even if they may sound like pontifications, can be added to or, subtracted from, to arrive at Ohazulume Charter for Anambra Politics.

Yours for Nigeria As a Super Power!

11

ENGR. CHARLES MBANEFO
DISTINGUISHED LECTURE, 2017.

(Okwadike, Dr. Chukwuemeka Ezeife)

Distinguished high class members of the highly esteemed Nigerian society of Engineers, Ladies and Gentlemen, other distinguished people present, you are welcome. To what am I welcoming you? Indeed, why are we here? What brought us all here? We are here to do the needful. We are here to celebrate a living legend: the 21st President of the Nigeria Society of Engineers, who has lived "his life in pursuit of a better life for all", "a paragon of virtue", a "Monument of virtue", a Registered Professional Engineer of Ontario, Canada, a COREN Registered Engineer, a member of Canadian Geotechnical Society, and a Fellow of Nigerian Society of Engineers, Engr Charles Mbanefo. He is the Founding Chairman of the Nigerian Society of Engineers, Abuja Branch. This is the man "for whom mentoring of the young has always been his passion and he has a long list of young engineers he has mentored and is still mentoring" . This is the man who "where others would speak a hasty word or act in anger, he is the patient one, seeking to heal and bring together". This is the man whose compelling achievement-dominated life, we are here to honour; this is the living legend who accumulated valuable knowledge, expertise and competence in diverse fields, including engineering and life in general, and who applied such capabilities, seemingly effortlessly, with a commitment to improve the life of man on earth. Chief Charles Mbanefo is chief in engineering, chief in tradition, chief on merit. Chief Mbanefo, Nnwa-amulunanma of Onitsha, commands automatic respect and is automatically respected in his engineering field and in all life. As already indicated, he is a mentor per excellence, who has mentored and is mentoring, so many persons, in and outside his profession, and do not know he is mentoring them. Surely, the time we have here in not enough to adequately celebrate this great Nigerian. A brief summary of his profile has been prepared for the purpose. It is believed that the thoughts generated in the reader of this short summary profile will resonate, vibrate and be of the frequency to induce, and attract the best of mentorship and benefits to the reader.

But it will be, simply, inexcusable, to have the opportunity of meeting with this assemblage of highly educated and concerned high stake holders of the nation and not deal with the urgent or immediate matter of *Nigeria: to be or not to be?*

Fellow Nigerians, all true friends of Nigeria, and all those who wish Africa well, Ladies, Gentlemen and members of the Press, there is one truth, a truth which cannot be honestly doubted or controverted: our great engineering czar, Engr. Chief Charles Mbanefo, who we celebrate today, and every serious thinking Nigerian, even with minimum sincerity, knows the bothersome truth: that our dear country, Nigeria, the largest concentration of blacks on the face of the earth, will, without urgent serious political re-engineering, cease to exist!!! This is the only truth! Don't mind some jokers who talk idly about Nigeria remaining united and being "indissoluble" without restructuring!!. But God forbid that Nigeria will collapse, disintegrate, and cease to exist!!! Nigeria must be re-engineered, not only to survive, but to achieve her Manifest Destiny!!!

To re-engineer Nigeria is the task we must perform, and urgently too. Surely, Nigeria was not an accident of British imperialism. God created Nigeria. He used British imperialism only as a tool. And God created Nigeria for a purpose, that purpose is for Nigeria to be a rallying point and big brother for Africa. God further endowed Nigeria with stupendously rich resources, to enable her to develop into a world Super Power and, in the process, raise the dignity, prestige and respect of all blacks. God's ultimate purpose for Nigeria, otherwise, *Nigeria's Manifest Destiny,* is for Nigeria to eventually, wipe away the shame of slavery from the faces of all blacks!!!

The British saw, clearly, this potential in, or of, Nigeria and, fearing that her former colony would fast develop into a Super Power and challenge her in world affairs, she contrived a strategy to keep Nigeria down, underdeveloped and, hopefully, undevelopable. But God's will must prevail over, and neutralise all the negative efforts of man, local man and foreign man, to mess up His design of unmatched greatness for Nigeria!!!

Fellow Nigerians, our God is great. He answers prayers. Let no groups of Nigerians blame themselves or other groups. Our God works in mysterious way. It appears, this is His time. He will open the minds of every group to see the group's greater long term benefits, in a politically re-engineered Nigeria. He will also give the negotiating groups the mind to accommodate necessary interests, where they are merited. Let us not yield to the devil and help tear down, and demolish, the gem of a country given to us by God. No group of Nigerians, large or small, can happily walk away from Nigeria, properly re-engineered, and with justice as fairness prevailing. God will forgive those who know this truth, but who, for whatever reasons, including clearly myopic delusion about the sustainability of their unsustainable advantages, or cheating, will like to delude themselves and their people, that the status quo can continue and Nigeria survives.

WE must re-engineer Nigeria. In substance, such re-engineering really, simply, calls for our going back to the "agreed Nigeria", that is, going back to the structure or political arrangements of Nigeria, as agreed by our founding fathers - our heroes past! That "agreed Nigeria" was a federal structure, with regions as federating units. Initially there were three regions: Eastern, Western and Northern regions. Midwestern region was created later, making four regions: three in the South, one in the North. Each region had its own constitution and operated fairly autonomously. The Federal Government handled issues universally agreed to be federal responsibilities - issues like: external relations, currency, weights and measures etc.

There was fiscal federalism as the resources for running the Federal Government came, basically, from the federating units. Each region controlled its resources and grew at its own pace. The people owned their regions in the sense that people in the regions were, particularly, concerned about how their regions were run. That was mainly because the money spent in the regions was basically internally generated - contributed by the people of the regions, through taxation, other payments etc. That is different from the present situation, wherein revenues "come" from the Federation Account. With that former structure there was peace and satisfactory progress. The *agreed structure* was rubbished by the Nigerian military in 1967, at the beginning of the Nigeria/Biafra conflict.

To win, easily, the Nigeria/Biafra war (then predicted to be only a "police action"), the strategy was adopted to isolate the

Igbo from the rest of eastern Nigeria. Twelve states were thus created: six in the North, six in the South. The running of Nigeria was also made more fully adapted to military central command system. This central command has given Nigeria a unitary, as opposed to, federal, structure of government. After the war, the military continued to run the government in Nigeria - making it progressively more unitary and more dictatorial. It was thus easy for the military to, basically dictatorially, create not only new states, but also new local government areas (LGAs), without considering the fairness of their creation or distribution. Today, we have are 36 states plus Abuja, sometimes treated as if it were a state, 19 states in the North, 17 in the South. The imbalance in the distribution of local government areas (LGAs) is, by far, more pronounced. For example, Kano and Jigawa (which was created out of Kano) have between them almost as many local government areas as the whole of the Southeast geo-political zone; Kano has 44 LGAs, Lagos 20, Bayelsa 8, etc. Both the states and the LGAs get allocations of revenue from the Federation Account. The unfairness of these military creations should be problematic, but that is not the main reason for the clamour for restructuring. The main problem is that as the country is currently structured and run, the country is growing backwards - indeed, taking giant steps backward. The Nigerian people at federal, state and LGA levels do not police the expenditure of revenues allocated from the Federation Account, and this and other factors, have led to monumental corruption which has eaten deep into, and permeated, every fabric of the society, leading to the comprehensive and woeful failure of Nigeria. We note that the very well composed 2014 National Conference approved the creation of additional 18 states. Those who doubted the wisdom of so many new states, should think of the new suggestion of twelve regions and 52 states for the Middle Belt. The problem is that the extent of dehumanisation and suffering to which some Nigerians are subjected cannot be imagined by many Nigerians.

Without taking account of the new information from the Middle Belt, we have 54 states plus Abuja to deal with. We should adopt the least controversial and most efficient approach to restructure Nigeria, instead of rediscovering the wheels with attendant new controversies. The line of least resistance appears to be to adopt the present six geopolitical zones as the Federating Units and allowing the states in each zone to work out their constitutions, with the recommendations of the 2012 Conference and Independence Constitutions of the former regions as templates. Of course, they may introduce new elements forced by current realities. One such, is to make the zones responsible for their internal security - with external security left with central government. In this case, the coexistence of Zonal and State Police Commands should be seriously considered, for greater effectiveness and efficiency.

Whether we want to adopt the above line of least resistance or choose any other approaches, we must be aware that we are running out of time. The following suggestion is based on these considerations:

(1) The materials/templates for work, including the 2014 Conference Report and the Independence Federal and Regional Constitutions are available.

(2) The existing states have their interests which need to be fully accommodated. Members from the states should work to ensure that, there is not, for any state, the feeling of "going back to Egypt".

(3) A restructured Nigeria, with justice prevailing is in the best interest of every group of Nigerians, large or small.

(4) There is time constraint.

THE PROGRAMME PROPOSAL

A. By mid, or end, of September 2017, the Federal Government should set up a body (perhaps Sovereign

National Conference/Constituent Assembly/ Some Other) to work out details of a New Nigeria based on improvements to our old durable foundations. Perhaps, the first month should be devoted to the participants from each zone working out their zonal constitutions, which will then go to the Conference/Assembly for further actions as necessary.

B. The structure of New Nigeria is adopted by mid-2018. A chunk of the Conference/Assembly time should be devoted to developing anti-corruption measures with a view to achieving, as much as possible, a zero-tolerance of corruption in the society. The Body should also work out ways to empower women for electoral offices, in view of their special qualities. This can be done by creating women exclusive constituencies.

Let Us Choose One Nigeria Properly Structured With Justice Prevailing!!!

The above structure may have defects. Combining this structure with justice prevailing, will maximise the welfare of all Nigerians. I need only emphasise what I said during the Save Democracy even some weeks ago: Time is running out on Nigeria!!
The above deals with necessary structural changes. There is also need to re-engineer the core values which serve as the foundation and pillars of the edifice.

As said already and as is generally well known, God endowed Nigeria with every ingredient she needs to it. The climate in Nigeria is equable - no extremes. It is even possible for a man to stay naked outside, in the open, round the year, and not die. There are no hurricanes, no tornadoes or typhoons. We have never been affected by any tsunamis! Our geo-physical structures are stable - no volcanoes, no earthquakes, landslides are not known. Our endowment of material resources is super-abundant. Any plant found anywhere, is, or can be grown, somewhere, in Nigeria. Our animal resources, including anything that breaths and moves, are surplus. All valuable minerals, known to man, are surplus in Nigeria: oil and gas, gold, silver and diamond, gemstones of every type, limestone, iron ore, aluminium etc. Everything!! And more are yet to be discovered. As for human beings, Nigeria is superbly gifted - many talents from many tribes! It is clear that the Almighty God designed Nigeria for unmatched greatness!!!

What has been the result? So far, it has been colossal failure, unmitigated! The Nigerian humans, especially the men, are working tirelessly to mess up God's design for our country. The main cause of the total failure of Nigeria is monumental corruption which has saturated every element of the social structure. Far from raising the respect and dignity of Blacks, Nigeria has become the generator and accumulator of shame to all Blacks. And it has now come to the stage that all Blacks are being suffocated with shame emanating from Nigeria.

All Blacks should be sorry for the colossal failure of black political leadership. But the greatest failure and therefore, the greatest shame, should be my country's - Nigeria's - the supposed big brother and rallying point for Blacks, whose Manifest Destiny is to raise the dignity and respect of black and African peoples!!

But it is important to remind the reader that contrary to some statements which seen to demean Blacks, the black man was, indeed, the creator and developer of the basics of all knowledge: science and technology, mathematics, religion, including the idea of one God. In the ancient of days, the wise saying was that, out of Africa, always comes something new and good. It is true that when the white men (who used to be the foot mat of the world and we called, the "blue eyed barbarians") took hold of black knowledge from, especially,

Alexandria, where most of the books and manuscripts were dumped after the conquest of Africa, they put it to use to fight their hostile environment, and, over time, they arrived at a process of continuous improvement. After much improvement, the whites looked back at the blacks in Africa, who remained, mostly, in their state of nature, enjoying God-given favourable ecological balance. Noting the wide gap, in living standards, between themselves and us, they started to wonder whether we, the Blacks, were humans like themselves, or were, somehow sub-human, like, half-born apes. They debated our suitability to be bought and sold as chattels. That was the foundation for the slave trade. The truth is that the black man has not always been the foot mat of all the world. They were once the topmost.

Yes, we Nigerians have failed in our Manifest Destiny, and have no basis for continued existence, except as a totally changed country!!!. We must become the opposite of what we are now. Extra-ordinarily system-saturating monumental corruption brought us to this colossal failure. That corruption must be exterminated, totally, from our land. There must now be zero tolerance of corruption in Nigeria. No half measures can do it!! Zero tolerance must be zero tolerance. And it is achievable in Nigeria. We must achieve success in re-making Nigeria!! Because the Almighty God, who gave us this mission and gave us the where withal to achieve it, does not change. Man can try and appear to succeed for a time. But man cannot permanently mess up God's design. It is the will of God, not that of man, that will dominate. Now is the time, to deal finally with all who try to mess up God's design for Nigeria as a nation of unsurpassed greatness. It must be Operation Total Clean Up. **Away** with all corrupt institutions! **Away** with all existing political organisations and parties. **Away** with all agents of corruption. Away with untruths, deceit and lies. No more sacred cows! No more untouchables! To keep Nigeria clean to achieve her Manifest Destiny, is a task we must commit to. Members of the yet to be formed, new political parties (preferable two to begin with) both the new members who were not in politics before, and the truly reformed old politicians, must swear to new political principles or oath, including the oath of service to the people, as the reason for participation in politics. Every adult Nigerian must swear to the oath not to sabotage Nigeria (and corruption shall be defined clearly as act of sabotage). Working with the will of God, man can clean up man's mess. In the new Nigeria, women must play a major, if not the dominant, role, so that their superior qualities can raise both the quality of governance and the welfare of the governed. Those superior qualities include the following: 1) The milk of human kindness flows more in women than in men. ii)Women are, usually, more concerned with the welfare of their children (offspring) than men. iii) As I stated in my book, "Remaking Nigeria with Progressivism," in 1987: a). *"Women bear the brunt of bad governance," and "should have greater vested interest in good governance." b). As a rule, and on the average, women are less corrupt than men in public and private offices." c) Women obey the rules and keep to the principles more than men. d) "Even where materialism rules both men and women, men plunder the public treasury more devastatingly than women, because women have, generally lower material expectations.*

I call upon all Nigerians to adopt Engr. Charles Mbanefo's seriousness and commitment to the remaking our country, Nigeria. The core values of truthfulness, respect for life, genuine service to the people, integrity and patriotism, which are the foundation and pillars of a good society, must be re-engineered and re-activated in Nigeria!!! Nigeria must survive!

12

WHAT FEDERATING UNITS? STATES OR ZONES/REGIONS? OBJECTIVE BASED FOR CHOICE?

(Okwadike, Dr. Chukwuemeka Ezeife)

States or Zones, which should be our Federating Units? How do we rationally make the decision? The difference between states and zones is size - geographic size and population size. The smallest zone in Nigeria - the Southeast - has five states. The largest zone, Northwest, has seven states. The rest of the zones have six states each. Therefore zones are, by far, larger than states. The question is what difference, if any, does size make. Size difference refers to population size and geographical size. Both are relevant to the size of the market. Does large size confer any advantage? This requires a consideration of what the economists call "economies of scale". Basically this concept states that, up to a point, the larger the unit of production, the lower is the unit cost of production. Of course, the lower the unit cost of production, generally, the lower the market price per unit, and thus, the more units a consumer can buy with a given amount of money. What this says is that the consumer/people can derive greater welfare in a lager unit than in a smaller unit.

Thus if the welfare of the people is the dominant consideration, the preference should be for zones, over states, as federating units. Of course, states can be chosen for other strategic considerations. Post-coup Nigeria provides a clear example of states being chosen for other considerations, this time, clearly, out of military strategic consideration.

Nigeria had, in 1954, agreed on, and chose, a federal system of government with regions as federating units. This agreed system was perfected in 1963 and it worked very well. The regions were growing at their own paces. That the World Bank declared that parts of Nigeria were growing faster than the rest of the world, confirmed the suitability and excellence of the system. Not only was welfare higher, there was greater peace, there was effective security, and progress was assured. Problem started with the coup of 1966 and the civil war that followed in 1967. The military government wanted a strategy to win the war more easily and faster. It decided to isolate the Igbo from the rest of the Eastern Nigeria and thereby reduce the influence of the Biafran leader. Because of this, the government abandoned the regional structure and created 12 states (six in the north and six in the south) out of the four regions, with Igbo basically contained in the Southeast state. If, after the war, Nigeria had returned to the agreed structure that worked, we wouldn't now be talking about restructuring. What actually happened was that successive military rulers from the North created increasingly more states until we got to the present number, 36, plus Abuja, sometimes treated as if it were a state. The various military leaders also created local government areas, by far, more lopsidedly in favour of the North.

Thus, it is not for all purposes that zones/regions have advantage over states as federating units. It was purely military strategic considerations that led to the abandonment of the agreed structure that worked. It can be shown that the greater material welfare of the people is not the only advantage zones have over states as federating units.

Take the increasing calls for state police, and the fears

people have about possible abuse of state police by the governors. It can be shown that a combination of state and zonal police will be better - safer - than purely state police, controlled totally by the state governor. Some years ago, at the heat of the agitation for state police, the following illustration of possible blatant abuse was given. Officers from the state police, even on their own initiative, invaded the home of an aspirant who was challenging the incumbent governor's second term bid. The police officers ordered the aspirant's wife from the family dinner table. While marching her to detention, they castigated her saying, "look him 'nyash', she wants to be first lady". The chance of this is drastically reduced in a system of zonal/state police where the state police is supervised by zonal police which is controlled by all the states in the zone.

We can also see a clash here between the welfare of the people, and the desire of the politicians to be in full power. Politicians who hope to become governors may have a preference for an arrangement which guarantees them unfettered use (or abuse) of political power. Such politicians will prefer states to zones as federating units. There is an interesting case from the Southeast. Experts in the Southeast zone, with the agreement of the Governors, carefully worked out and designed "Southeast Economic Development Commission" many years ago. The objective was to, through joint development actions by the states, raise the welfare of the people. Up till today, the Commission is not yet functional and has not, therefore, impacted on the welfare of the people. Governors have been picking and choosing and disagreeing. As it turned out the governors never agreed, so the Commission has not operated. With zones/regions as federating units, the zonal/regional constitution will define zonal and state responsibilities and the whims and caprices of individual governors do not intrude. The problem implied here defines the weakness of providing for states to voluntarily integrate. All those who want greater welfare of the people will prefer outright zonal arrangement over states as federating units. The provision for voluntary integration, will rarely work. It is best to agree on outright adoption of zones as federating unit leaving it to each zone to work out the details of its constitution.

There is an ancient anachronism which makes some people see going back to the agreed structure of federation, based on regions/zones, as federating units, as "going back to Egypt". This is best illustrated with the position of Ebonyi state in the Southeast zone. In the ancient of days, the people of Abakaliki (the dominant city in Ebonyi state, Afikpo, the other city did not share in some of the disadvantages) had a disadvantage in education. Abakaliki city was dominated by people from other Igbo areas, especially people from the present Anambra state. These outsiders controlled and dominated commerce in Abakaliki. Also, with the disadvantage in education, Abakaliki people were not well represented in the civil service of the southeast - in Enugu - the regional capital. The result was a feeling of inferiority complex by people from Abakaliki, and it was real. What is it like today? Today, Abakiliki town is more beautiful than some eastern capitals. Ebonyi people now dominate activities in Abakaliki city. What is more, the people from Ebonyi state now dominate many villages and towns in other states of the Southeast. They marry the indigenes of those states and the population of Ebonyi people is fast increasing in many towns and villages in the Southeast. They control and regulate the supply of various social and economic services and they are indeed at the frontiers of politics, especially the politics of secession - they dominate youth membership of IPOB and MASSOB. Indeed some indigenes of their host communities are beginning to worry about the dominance of Ebonyi people in the local activities of their areas. Of course, some older people of Ebonyi state, may still remember what it was like, in Enugu, in those ancient of days. And some fear that the capital of Southeast zone must be Enugu. But nothing stops Abakaliki from becoming the new capital of Southeast Zone. And since zones must be given the opportunity to agree on their internal constitutional and governance arrangement, Ebonyi state can make demands of conditions for their agreement. They may insist on their preferred form of government for the Southeast, they may insist on supplying the first political leader of the Southeast in a rotational arrangement etc. And the next reluctant state, Enugu, may supply the next leader in a possible 8year rotation arrangement. What applies to Ebonyi State should apply to the most reluctant states in other zones. And the other states in the zones must bear with the reluctant states, knowing that the welfare of the people should come first, and that zones dominate states in guaranteeing the highest welfare of the people.

One point made by politicians who favour states as federating units is that, using zones disposes the country to easy disintegration. It is argued that since the zones are already quite large, they are more likely, than small states, to easily opt out of the federation - to be on their own. This may have some merits but the easier it is to opt out of a federation, the more important it must be for the operators of the system to ensure that justice, as fairness, prevails. Indeed, large market is the towering abiding basis of unity in Nigeria. In Nigeria, the large market derives from large population with divers peoples, and many talents from many tribes; our large market means large geographical size which accommodates divers ecological and climatic zones with varied flora and fauna. It also means diversity of mineral resources: iron ore, crude oil, gold, silver, gem stones, lime stones etc. Britain had to educate a Nigerian military Head of state, who had wanted to pull his part of the country out of Nigeria saying that the "basis of unity is not there". He learnt very fast and retreated from *araba*! Large market is the reason why every group in Nigeria, large or small, must gain from One Nigeria organised or restructured to work and for justice to prevail. Because of her large market, no group in Nigeria will happily walk away from the country well organised for equity and fairness. This is why many groups in

Nigeria are still hanging on, in hope, even when they believe they are grossly unfairly treated and that the country appears to have crossed the red line to extinction.

We should appeal to Nigerian politicians to put the interest of the people uppermost. This means considering the welfare of the people beyond any other consideration. This gives the states no chance as federating units. Therefore, the need to honour the agreements of our heroes past, the lessons of history, respect for what works and very importantly, caring most for the welfare of the people, make the choice of zones as federating units of our federal system compelling!!!

Some politicians have argued that with zones as federating units, the cost of governance will be higher and will thus reduce the welfare of the governed. In the case of Nigeria the cost of, say, six zonal governments has to be added to the cost of 36 or 54 state governments. Of course this assumes that even with zonal governments the cost of running state governments will be the same as with zonal governments. While this is possible, conscious efforts can be made to reduce the cost of running state governments. After all, the job is now shared between the two levels of government - the zone and the state. States and state governments must remain but the state governments must be run at much lower cost than as of today. After all, the job of the state governments are now shared between it and the zonal government. This issue can be easily resolved by reference to pre-military coup experiences in Nigeria. But it, is indeed, a policy matter - what weight should the state government carry. The tiers of government are federal and zonal/regional!! We remember the days of Okpala, Akintola, Ahmadu Bello, and Denis Osadebe!!!

13

AN APPEAL TO FELLOW NIGERIANS

(Okwadike, Dr. Chukwuemeka Ezeife)

I pray that it pleases the Almighty God, our Father in heaven, the only true God worthy to be worshiped, to open our eyes, our hearts and our sixth senses, to see, perceive and appreciate the real truth about the state of our country, Nigeria! We can, on the positive side, see the unmatched greatness, designed by God, for One Nigeria, as the Super Power giant of Africa. And on the negative side, because of man's mess up, there exists the imminent danger of Nigeria's collapse, disintegration and going into extinction! May God uphold His Will and positive designs for Nigeria, and forbid the consequences of the mess up by man, colonial masters, and local.

There are stones, there are also gem stones: tourmaline, aquamarine, sapphire etc. Among countries, Nigeria is, by creation, a gem. We watch television, local and international, we have access to newspapers and other print media and we listen to radios, foreign and local. We read, see and hear constantly of natural disasters caused by hurricanes, tornadoes, typhoons, tsunamis, volcanoes, and earthquakes. As I am writing this, the CNN is describing what it calls Monster Hurricane Harvey - said to be the worst such hurricane in the USA, in 12 years (it turned out to be the worst on record). We do not experience such disasters in Nigeria - in Africa. Take away the few cases of flooding, and erosion caused by man's abuse of our eco-system, and we find nothing near the magnitudes of natural disasters experienced in mostly non-African countries. Even among African countries, Nigeria is specially blessed, spared of, even, some minor disasters that occasionally happen in Africa, like the recent one in Serra Leone.

Which country on earth can compare favourably against Nigeria, in term of God's endowment of abundant natural resources. Virtually every plant can grow in Nigeria, if it cannot grow in Igbo-Ukwu, it can in Gembu. I have heard, only recently, that there are miracle elements in our bamboo, which can enhance the development of solar power. Virtually everything that breaths and moves - man and other animals, are plentiful in Nigeria. In terms of minerals, we have stones, gem stones, lime stones, all manners of sands, stones and clay, oil and gas, gold and silver, iron ore, tin, columbite etc. All these are in large deposits. And we do not yet know all the valuable mineral deposits we have in Nigeria. For human beings, we have many talents from many tribes - large population, also, large geographical size. Our men and women are participating in making waves at the frontier of technology in near and distant lands. Indeed our humans have demonstrated no inferiority, in brain power, compared with any colour of man, as they beat most of those with whom they compete in the best universities in the world!

God would not have endowed us with all these without a purpose, especially with large population and geographical size - the largest concentration of blacks on the face of the earth. I believe that God's purpose for Nigeria is to be the rallying point, big brother and template/model for black Africa. By effectively utilizing the resources endowed on us, and developing into a Super Power among nations, we raise the respect, dignity and prestige of the black man and ultimately wipe off the shame of slavery from the faces of all blacks!!

Yes! Our former colonial masters intervened, manipulated, manoeuvred and made choices to keep Nigeria down, for fear of having to complete with her former colony, in world affairs, not long after independence. But, clearly, we should, from now on, own up our failures. That Nigeria has failed is due to Nigerians - we are, today, the cause of our problems. We sit on, and keep down, our great potential as a country, bickering among ourselves, and dispensing excruciating poverty, among the people, while our leaders cart away and dump our financial wealth in foreign banks, or in deep wells, after becoming tired of acquiring foreign assets. We must now honestly , look at ourselves, group by group, to purge ourselves of the negatives that keep Nigeria a failure - generating shame to all blacks on earth, instead of wiping shame off their faces!!! We need total change!!! We need a New Nigeria. We must remake Nigeria! But first, we accept that our nation is at crossroads and that a national discuss or conversation is imperative. That imperative national discuss or conversation must be on restructuring Nigeria.

The statement: "change begins with me", is becoming a cliche in Nigeria. I should apply this to me and the Igbo people of Nigeria. We, the Igbo, like to feel proud that we have taken modern development, in term of modern houses, education and businesses, to every part of Nigeria, from the former capital city, Lagos, to the present capital city, Abuja; from every township in Nigeria, to most villages in Nigeria. It is the Hausa, not the Igbo, to whom is credited, the statement: that "if a person gets to a place and does not find the Igbo there, the person should pack and go, far the place is not fit for human habitation".

Now, are we the Igbo, in consequence, celebrated and praised around Nigeria? Should we be celebrating? Not at all! On the contrary, we have just been given a "quit notice" by some Northernern youths. It does not matter that those who gave the quit notice may be a tiny minority, or that good reason might not have guided their deliberations and decision. The saying that wealth generates envy may be part of the explanation, but something deeper appears to be at work. The Igbo must introspect! Are we in the best of terms with our host communities? If the answer had been yes for decades, has it remained yes? Where could the problems have originated? Is it that some people think that we are now no longer needed?

Decades ago, Igbo people would go, virtually empty handed, to a town or village outside Igbo land, and start, virtually at the very bottom, to search for economic survival. They would do all manners of menial jobs. They would graduate, usually, to trading, opening shops. And, over time, they make a success of whatever they were doing and get rich enough to building palatial houses - houses that are often better than what their hosts could afford. What happens? Igbo audaciousness comes to play, or, is then recognised. The Igbo would sit cosily in front of their palatial houses: ***oozing out more confidence than the original owners of the land.*** In some cases, mostly involving people from my state, Anambra, bad month, in form of boasting aloud, may follow. These generate the envy of the host communities, the envy grows to jealousy, jealousy to hatred, and it can get worse. The audacity of the Igbo is fed by their feelings of innocence, justice as fairness, openness, and accommodation. There is also the strong Igbo maxim that "ebe onye bi ka ona awachi", meaning that where one lives, one mends (builds). This gives the Igbo such a serious commitment to where he settles down that he so feels for the place, no less than the indigenes. The Igbo does not set out to make his host jealous or unhappy. He does, in the open, whatever he gains from, leaving it open to anybody to emulate. However, no self-justification can do.

The Igbo must now actively pursue friendship with their host communities; plant a variety of enduring seeds in the host communities; respect the customs and traditions of the host communities; use the town union system, which they have everywhere, to educate new comers to know and respect the dos and don'ts of the host communities. We must blunt our forwardness or audacity, with some diplomacy and studied silence. Of course, no individual Igbo chooses to behave the way he does, by himself; it is a matter of up-bringing, not much of personal choice. I became Igbo, *on arrival,* not by choice. So did everybody from every ethnic group of any size. This should make for greater understanding and accommodation among groups. Indeed, much the same thing applies to religious affiliations among people. I was purely monotheistic, worshiping Chineke through mediums, *on arrival* and later I became Christian, and even this, is not by my choice, but simply as a result of the family into which I was born, and where they reside. I had no choice! Did you, Femi? Did you, Hassan? Etc. We did not choose what tribe to belong to, nor did we freely choose to what religion to belong. The choices were made, for us, by God, Who decided where to plant each of us!!!.

Like the Igbo, many other Nigerian groups must introspect. The Fulani needs introspection most, as their superiority psychosis, is really getting out of hand. How fair and reasonable is their "quit notice" to an autochthonous group, like the Igbo.

The Igbo, like other successful groups in Nigeria, do whatever they do for economic success in the open, not in secret. The Yoruba, the Kano Hausa, the Kanuri, the Ibibio and many other successful groups in Nigeria are all using, or applying, learnt behaviour, or knowledge, which other groups can also learn or emulate. The greater the number of groups which assimilate achievement motivation, the greater the welfare and happiness in Nigeria.

Fellow Nigerians, it is time to break with our past of recriminations, jealousy, hatred and blind selfishness. Time to resurrect Nigeria. We must become our neighbours' keepers. Time to be concerned about fairness to all concerned. No longer should we turn blind eyes to the discriminations against, or the marginalization of, other groups in Nigeria. The octogenarian, Chief Edwin Clark, is leading the way to the New Nigeria of neighbours' keepers. He loudly condemned the marginalisation of the Southeast zone. Let us, all Nigerians, join him and try to love our neighbours as ourselves and shout against injustices to any groups. I am happy to see many condemnatory statements from many parts of Nigeria, against the injustice done, and disdain shown, to the Southeast in the recent appointments to the NNPC in which the North (which produces no oil) got 10 appointees and the whole South (where all oil is for now mined) got half of that, with none to the Southeast. This change of mind will kick-start the New Nigeria. It would not have been acceptable behaviour to watch as President Muhammed Buhari, at the beginning of his tenure, make more than 40 appointments, without a single one of them appointed from the Southeast, nor should other groups have kept mute where, in a six-geographical-zone and six-major-protocol-offices situation, the Southeast was not given even the least of those offices - the Secretary to Government. There are very many more cases of the marginalisation of the Southeast. Most people kept mute at the sacking of mostly southern, and particularly, Southeast officers, from military and other security offices; none complained at the virtual exclusion of the Southeast from capital development, including the development of the railway. National silence greeted the complete absence of the Southeast, from the National Security Council, the scarcity of the Southeast and southern persons from any list of new Federal appointments, and the dominance of the Southeast persons in the list of those being removed from federal offices. I spoke out against some of these actions and the killings, and some people had the callousness to accuse me of tribalism. I was shrieking that President Muhammed Buhari was forcing the Southeast out of Nigeria, and fuelling the fires of IPOB and MASSOB. Today, Igbo land is in turmoil; Igbo youths, in reaction to the negative happenings, and the long detention of Nnamdi Kanu, became disdainful of their elders, roundly and insultingly castigating them, especially, those who live in Abuja and those in leadership positions in Ohanaeze. What is worse, after months of staying out of the country, the President came back, not repentant, but with even what looks like re-enforced zeal to push the Southeast out of Nigeria, this time, with everything, especially, military might.

Let me repeat what I have been saying and writing for many decades. Every group in Nigeria, large or small; Igbo, Yoruba, Hausa and especially, Fulani; Urhobo, Ijaw, Kanuri, Ibibio, etc will gain stupendously, from One Nigeria that is made to work. The crisis-urgent, make-or-break, issue of today is the restructuring of the country. Restructuring may sound like big grammar, but it is not. It simply requires our going back to "agreed Nigeria" that worked very well, with some adjustments to reflect current realities. That is, going back to the political structure/system of Nigeria as agreed by our heroes past - those heroes who so cared only for the progress of Nigeria and the welfare of her people, that for some of them, their people had to contribute money to build homes for them, after they left offices. Today, to the 36 states plus Abuja, we should add the 18 new states carefully assessed and approved by the 2014 National Conference. That gives a total of 54 states, plus Abuja. What to do? Have them as 54-plus federating units? We may adopt the six geo-political zones we have known for decades, as the federating units, or make some adjustments to them. That is the line of least resistance. We should then request the states from each zone to develop a constitution they can live with. A federal body, with sovereign powers, may be set up to resolve any problems and complete the restructuring of Nigeria by mid-2018. The raw materials for the job are readily available: the federal and regional independent constitutions, and the reports of various Conferences, especially the 2014 National Conference.

The structure we have today resulted from the impositions from the military rulers, who ruled and ruined Nigeria. First, to isolate the Igbo from Eastern Nigeria and make it easier to win the civil war, the military created 12 states out of the four regions of Nigeria, and contained the Igbo in the Southeast state. After the war, the military rulers created more states and local government areas to fit their biases, with no consideration for justice as fairness. Any Nigerian politician, of age, knows all these. Those who are behaving and talking as if they are confused, are just being grossly dishonest and deceitful.

With meaningful and effective restructuring, and with justice, as fairness, allowed to prevail, Nigeria will escape from the colonial cage and experience explosive growth, to the pride, to the increase in welfare and happiness, of every Nigerian, irrespective of ethnic group or religious affiliation. Only the antiquarian feudalist, who may miss the sight of downtrodden masses, swept away by massive development, may regret!

God and good men, know that One Nigeria, effectively restructured, for justice to prevail and things, to work, cannot be to the detriment of any group in Nigeria. No! By God, not at all!!! On the contrary, it will usher in explosive growth in peace and tranquilly, enabling Nigeria to become a Super Power among nations, thereby raising the respect, dignity and prestige of all blacks and eventually wiping off the shame of slavery, from the faces of all blacks on earth; thus making Nigeria achieve her Manifest Destiny!!!

The hearts of kings are in the hands of God. May the Lord God of Abraham, Chineke, Olorun, Ubangiji, the Monotheistic God of most of Nigerian misunderstood religions; the One who created the heavens and earth and everything in-between; the only One true, living God; may He touch the mind of our President, Buhari, and the minds of others in power, to urgently do the needful, to keep Nigeria One, and let justice prevail in her system!

14

WHY I PREFER RESTRUCTURING NIGERIA TO BIAFRA

EZEIFE, FORMER ANAMBRA STATE GOV

SUNDAY SUN 21st May 2017

By Chidi Obineche

Former Anambra Governor, Dr Chukwuemeka Ezeife CON. has accused ailing Nigeria's president Muhammadu Buhari of coming into the office with the mission of "pushing the Igbo ethnic group" out of Nigeria. He insisted that if the onslaughts continue, "Igbo must go". He speaks on the basis for one Nigeria, which he says must be based on going back to the agree true federal system with region as federating units frame work of restructuring. The former federal permanent secretary reviews the 2015 presidential elections saying that ex-President Goodluck Jonathan, knew about the plot to rig him out months before the election. Jonathan would have returned as President, if he wanted. He speaks on his ordeal in the hands of Buhari alleging, but paid tribute to Buhari for rejecting a plot to frame him(Ezeife) up and silence him. He speaks more on other national issues in this interview with Sunday Sun at his Abuja home.

You just released a small pamphlet entitled 'Nigeria: The Basis of Unity', do you specifically see any basis for one Nigeria?

There is a basis for the one Nigeria. If Nigeria is restructured and justice is made to prevail, no group in Nigeria can, as things stand, consider moving out of Nigeria. There are many reasons for that, but the basic reason is economic, something the economists call "economies of scale". And what does that mean? With larger output you should be getting lower, unit prices up to a point. And then, you have one market. One very large market you produce in Sokoto and sell in Calabar, Kano, Lagos etc. So I started by defining the welfare of the people as the decision criterion. The welfare of the people Should be the guiding principle for what is good and what is important for the Country. So, the production of goods and services are the basis for the welfare of the people. And this is cheaper in the larger population and geographical area than in a smaller one. Nigeria should be properly structured for the people regions to take care of their affairs including their internal security, or there will be no Nigeria.

In other words, the agitations and secession threats by IPOB (Indigenous people of Biafra) is misplaced?

No. Ok, let me go to the beginning IPOB(Indigenous People of Biafra) is Igbo. MASSOB (Movement for the Actualization of the Sovereign State of Biafra) is Igbo. Igbo captivity committed most suicides during the slave trade. Why? Because the Igbo say Eji ndu eme gini? (Life without honour is not worth living). The way we are in Nigeria today, especially under Buhari is useless - without honour. At the start of his government, he employed more than 40 people without a single South easterner. He denied Southeast, the post of Secretary to the Government of the Federation, which is the lowest of the six positions that are critically important. He sacked Igbo people and other Southerners from the military, Customs and other offices. He killed our people for no just cause in Aba, Onitsha, Port- Harcourt and Asaba. The Port- Harcourt bloodletting is the one that drives me crazy. I don't know what to make of that one. Because some boys were rejoicing that Trump won in America they were massacred. How does it concern Nigeria security and they came and slaughter them in their numbers. What that says is that our position in Nigeria is reaching the point eji ndu eme gini? Therefore we may consider quitting. My own submission is that Biafra becomes inevitable if this injustices, marginalization, dehumanization, inequity, all forms of bad things being done to the South-east, continue beyond Buhari, then we must not keep on hanging in for any reason. Remember IPOB was not there during Obasanjo's regime, it was not there during Yar'Adua's time, it was not there during Jonathan's tenure as President. But because Buhari came with his Islamization agenda and a decision to push the South-east out of Nigeria we are going, and we must go if things continue the way they are. But not all of us believe that things will continue like this. Why do we believe that thing must change when every day we are confronted with more reasons why our stay here is injurious? Even people who never thought of it are now getting conscious of the humanity of our continued stay and are changing their opinions. They are now taking about giving the Igbo the Presidency. Today, Igbo are a great majority group in Nigeria. We are pushing for restructuring, so are the Yoruba, South-south. Middle belt. So, four zones are talking about restructuring. Even among people of the North-east, many are asking for restructuring. So, it is a matter of understanding where you are going. Those who say Biafra outright is better than restructuring, I doubt they are right. If you are waiting for something better and you don't get it, then Biafra becomes an option - a fall back.

What would you think is responsible for the reluctance of some segments of the society that are opposed to restructuring?

What is restructuring? Ultimately, restructuring is going back to what we know; what our heroes past agreed - a federal system of government with regions as federating units. And what has happened? We had four regions - the North, the East the West and Midwest. Three regions in the South, one in the North. As the civil war started, the military worked out a strategy for winning the war fast. They decided to isolate the Igbo from the rest of the East so that Ojukwu should not have power beyond the Igbo east, and as a result, created 12 states out of the four regions. After the war the Northern military leaders also created even more states. Now, we have 36 states. And how did they create them? Today, we have 19 states in the North, 17 in the South. And sometimes Abuja is treated as if it were a state making it 20 states in the north. Even the number of the states, is also important. South-east has five states, North-west has seven. Then, you come down to the number of local governments. Where are the 774 local governments? They are mostly in the north. Look at Lagos with a very massive population with only 20 Local governments while Kano has 44 Local governments. That is the issue. Bayelsa has only eight local government areas and that is where oil is. Funding from the centre goes to the local governments. Since they have dominance of states, dominance of local government areas, if they agreed to restructure and say Ndigbo stay in your place, Yoruba stay in your place and we adopt fiscal federalism, they think they will lose Income - revenue. Most Northerners who are against restructuring think that because of resources control component of restructuring, morning after the night of restructuring, revenue from oil will dry up for the northern states. I know that a project to generate internal revenues will be launched in all states. And it must go on for some years before the stoppage of revenue sharing that is the myopic reason why some northern people are talking against restructuring. It is known to most people including Sanusi the Emir of Kano, that the north lose most with the breakup of Nigeria. What is the literacy level in the north? And when did education become second to anything in development? So, even right now, what can they boost of? Tomato is alright. Yes. We are not seeing the groundnut pyramids again. But it is not what they are using to build the North.

So they are not contributing anything to the nation pool?

That is not even the Issue, there is nothing they are contributing to the national revenue today, but they are taking more than those who are contributing. They have food, but they are not contributing to revenue in Nigeria. Food is not enough. That is why I prefer One Nigeria because I can see the potentials of things being much better with organization, better structuring and justice being allowed to prevail.

Those who want Biafra now-now are right. But the best thing that has happened is IPOB and the way it is going about Biafra which calls for referendum. It is most reasonable. We will just vote like the people in Canada, Yugoslavia, Britain, and Scotland even northern Cameroun. Even Southern Cameroun people are now saying they are Biafran now. So far me, I do not quarrel with anybody who is saying Biafra now-now-now. For after delaying waiting for restructuring and we do not get it we will regret the delay. But I know that if we get restructuring it will be superior to Biafra now-now. I am not complaining because of the war experience. During the Biafra - Nigeria war we committed all kinds of 'Ibenne' taboos and at the end of the war people just pick up their briefcases and walked away and would not come back unless they make enough money to come and bamboozle the people at home - to show them that they have arrived with money. With IPOB, there is no need for cleavages, no need for divisions. Since there will be an opportunity of stating your own views. But people must remember that some of us have roots outside. I don't have any. This is my compound. Finished!

You like the vision of IPOB. What about the leadership as represented by Nnamdi Kanu?

That is the effective leadership they have. I don't know Nnamdi Kanu very well. But if a person can say, "my life means nothing to me" and puts everything into whatever thing he is championing, that person should be respected and honoured. I would like them to take cognizance of other views. A person saying no to structuring does not seem to have full understanding of history or the society of Nigeria.

And what is that understanding of the society of Nigeria?

The history behind it. We were alone - on our own in Biafra. We committed all manner of 'Ibenne' atrocities. **(taboo).**

What is the recurring 'Ibenne' taboo?

Yeah! Our culture does not allow us to do certain things to blood relations for example, we must give a sleeping ground to a relation. What happened at the outbreak of the war? Our people would come back and be welcomed home happily by relations. In two weeks, disharmony will set in. That is why we have today, excessive individualism. We used to be individualistic. That is our system. But after the war we became excessive individualistic because some people went out in anger because of what their brothers did to them. No land is given to you to cultivate cassava and they will ask you where you have been all this while. You dare not inquire into certain family assets but when you came back you were celebrated. We are better with restructuring. With restructuring we control our affairs. We are able to generate power for ourselves; we are deep with ecological problems. We need to take advantage of the land mass of Nigeria and the advantage of being in our space which is the largest concentration of population in Africa. I am emphasizing the economic aspect because that is where the action is. And then the psychic satisfaction of being in one Nigeria. I believe it is not the British Imperialism that created Nigeria. I believe that God used the invention of Britain to create a country which should become big brother and rallying point for all blacks on earth. A country which will eventually develop into a Super Power and raise the dignity and respect of all blacks and the African people and ultimately wipe away the shame of slavery from the faces of all blacks. That is Nigeria manifest destiny, or God's purpose in creating Nigeria. And we cannot achieve it without being big. Look at Sweden, Norway and all the small countries where the income per head is very high but they are not populous. With Nigeria, for our population we will easily become a Super Power .

You earlier accused Buhari of accentuating anti Igbo policies. What is in the Igbo person that is reprehensible and provocative?

Go and read Buhari speeches years ago. About 15 of them are talking about Islamization of Nigeria. He may not even hate the Igbo. I was in his compound. I sat in his parlour and he gave me food. That was about 16 years ago or more when we were trying to make friends politically. Today, Nigeria's Security Council will met and no South easterner is there. There are so many actions of Buhari that are irritating and provocative. Right now, they are sending herdsmen to the East to cause commotion and fight on Islamic front. If you think they are planning Islamization you are very dull person. They are making great progress with implementing Islamization. Benue State governor said that 12 local government of theirs have been taken. And the strategy is that they talk to a farmer and ask him to change to Islam. If the person agrees, no problem. If the person doesn't agree, after some time they will bring cattle to the person's farm and then gradually they will take over the farm. They will fight you, kill you and what house is left they will move in and build more. Incremental Islamization is already on in Nigeria. Anybody who does not understand it is not thinking fast. Of course you know that the South-east is predominantly Christian.

Why blame Buhari? Why not Ex-President Goodluck Jonathan who had a rare opportunity to change the situation with the 2014 National Conference report but failed to implement it until he was removed ?

He had no time within which to implement it. But he did everything including adopting it and taking it to the National Assembly for legislative action. Where you can blame him is that he did not see early enough the need for national confab. And some of us who kept telling him to do it were disappointed that he did not do it early enough. However, a man is not perfect in every direction. **Jonathan did a good job.** When he came for a meeting in Enugu, I told him that his ministers are sabotaging him on Eastern Federal road. Enugu to Port Harcourt, Enugu to Onitsha, the two big Eastern roads, nothing was done on them. I don't know whether we have the right to blame Jonathan for that. In terms of personnel Jonathan brought our people into government and gave them reasonable positions, Why didn't they use those position to improve on the lot of the zone?

He also dispensed with them conveniently, people like Stella Oduah, Barth Nnaji

I don't fully understand that one and I don't believe it either. What I know is that in terms of personnel, he gave us positions we never had before. He gave us positions. With which we should have used to help our own people. We did not and turn round to blame him. Let me tell you, we had a meeting of South-south, South-east, before the creation of one including South-west, we had to go to Jonathan. I was the spokesman and you know I say things as I see them. We were not very happy with the appeasement strategy, which Jonathan adopted towards the North. He was trying to appease people he cannot appease. The Northern people cannot be appeased. You gave them one, they want two, you gave them two they want ten etc. That is in the nature of man. especially, the northern man. If you are bringing they will be demanding.

That was one of his undoing? That was why he lost easily?

No, Jonathan is a very good man naturally, an easy going Christian from all indications. He said it with his mouth that his political interest was not worth a drop of anybody's blood. He knew there were problems but he felt that stopping the problems may create more problems. If he had insisted on winning he would have won. There was no way he didn't know what was going on. We got the minutes of meeting of northern leaders on how they planned to rig the elections. Eight days to the election. I was with Jonathan. I told him that Jega will not use his mouth to announce him as a winner. I discovered later that there were people who had told him the same thing three months earlier - that Jega cannot use his mouth to pronounce him as the winner. Everyone thought he would act. People saw children who were voting in the North. The distribution of voters cards was in favour of North. The cards were not available for our people in Lagos and the south and the minutes of the Northern elders called for registering everyone in the North whether they are of age or not. When you go to the East be extremely niggardly, that is, allow only a few to register. This was written in black and white. Initially we saw it and reviewed it. Eventually we saw it in the field, under-aged kids had a field day voting in the north. Even Card Reader rejected President Jonathan. These things were planned in detail. The rigging was carefully planned.

But some people accused Jonathan of naivety.

It is not naivety. The Man didn't want to cause loss of blood. He knew what was going on. Eventually I got intelligence report from our people in the North that the thing was no longer voting; that it was a matter of infidels versus believers. Adamu Muazu, the PDP national chairman, and other people who worked at the top level of Jonathan's campaign, were said to have voted against President Jonathan. He saw these things coming and monitored them carefully. That was why it was easy to persuade him to congratulate Buhari even before the final result was counted. It was un-African and wonderful to have done that. I know I don't know enough of anybody but I must say with what I saw and the close discussions I had with him, the man wanted to prevent massacre. Do you know that even in Abuja the equipment for killing were distributed? Killing who? Christian and Southerners. I don't know, maybe he dreamt about them also and tried to save people's lives. This is a Christian man, a gentleman and realistic in the extreme.

Ifeanyi Uba has been arrested by the DSS over some oil deals with NNPC. Are you okay with the reasons advanced for the arrest?

Unless it is just happenstance it seems to be a co-ordinated effort to ruin the economy of South-easterners. Many of the containers owned by South-easterners are seized and taken to IDPs in the North. Most manufacturers and industrialists from the East are in trouble. Ibeto for long has been put aside. Emeka Offor, I don't know if everything is moving well. Look at Innoson, the vehicle manufacturer, I don't know he is getting all the cooperation he needs from government. And he is the only manufacturer of cars in Nigeria. There seems to be a strangulation policy for South-eastern economic people. DSS invited Ifeanyi Ubah for interview and he honoured the invitation. He was not detained. Then they later came, arrested and detained him. They kept him for so long and eventually released him. A few days ago he was again arrested and detained. What I am hearing is that NNPC was using his tank farm for storage and they are alleging that some of the products have been sold. Go to court. This is no business of government represented by DSS or EFCC. What I heard is that because he gathered lawyers to go to court that is why they have detained him again. This is the case that should go to court. If he had misappropriated oil placed in his care he should answer for it in the court of law. Capital oil is claiming N16b from NNPC; and NNPC is claiming N11b from Capital Oil. How is this a national security issue. The Buhari policy of pull Igbo down is affecting many Igbo investors.

President Buhari has been sick for six months now. To what extent has his sickness rubbed off on good governance and what is your advice on what should be done?

This is not an area in which I am strong enough. If somebody is sick I sympathize. Buhari is sick. I pray for his recovery. I have heard all kinds of things. Some people were even saying things unthinkable not deserving of anybody who knows God. But the problem is that when he is not working as the president some people are working in his name. Those people have no legitimacy to work, they are using the powers of the President, without authorization. But how do you know it is without authorization? They will say the President gave this directive. If it occurs to the president that because of his being unwell and not able to function well, he knows what to do. But I don't want people shouting on him.

You remember during Yar' Adua's time he was the one that advised him to resign.

Well your brain is younger and fresher than mine. I didn't remember that he asked Yar' Adua to resign. If he did, what goes around comes around. He should do what he preached. I was telling some people that if it is the will of God for him to contest in 2019, no man born of woman can stop him. That is where I stand. Buhari should do the right thing. He should not be pushing the South-east out of Nigeria. That is wrong judgment on his part. In fact he has committed many impeachable offences because our constitution provides for federal character but has flouted it countless times.

Did anybody challenge him?

I was in the media shouting, instead of correcting it, they sent some people after me with some carrots. For a man like me, I don't care. God is in charge of my life.

Were you intimidated?

They were trying to intimidate me. They came to my house while I was out at night enjoying Christmas in my village. By 11pm when my family and I retuned in a convoy, we saw some military people in my compound. When I came back I went upstairs thinking they had brought a VIP to me, I found nobody and rushed down to meet the soldiers but they zoomed off blasting their sirens. Another time, I was to chair an event at Awka in honour of Ojukwu and the police and military scattered the people. Then I came back to Abuja and made some noise. One good thing for me was that when they combed my track record as permanent secretary, governor and special adviser to president and found nothing, somebody suggested that they put something on me but I understand that Buhari himself shouted and said "no, don't do it". I was very, very happy to hear that. But until he gives the SGF position to the South-east he has not started making amendments. Let someone fault me on anything I have said on radio, television or print media. If they find one lie from me, I am prepared to surrender.

How do you look at the performance of EFCC?

You see, the anti-corruption crusade of Buhari is selective and it is not good. You know those who are corrupt and you are working with them. It is not being pursued effectively. Selective injustice is injustice and selective pursuit of corruption is not war against corruption. Lamido Sanusi made statements that are true. Now, he is being investigated all round, because he said the truth. By being selective, corruption is being fed.

With deep insight you have how do you see a post 2019 Nigeria?

I stand with the west - Afenifere, Yoruba Unity Forum etc. At the Summit attended by 2014 confab delegates recently, we heard the decision of the west that they will not participate in the 2019 election if restructuring was not done. I think there should be interim measures. What are we talking about? Go back to agreed Nigeria. Agreed Nigeria is federal. It was four regions but now you can use the six geo-political zones. The 2014 confab attended by critical representative of diverse groups in Nigeria, that conference attended by the best brains at that time in the country, that conference that reached decisions through consensus and only few voting occurred, suggested the creation of 18 new states after a thorough evaluation of what is happening all over the country. Now, with 54 states, it becomes compelling to have the zones as federating units, with due attention to adequate provisions for the states.

Is that the interim measure you are calling for?

That is a solution to our problems but it cannot be implemented by the executive who don't believe in it. Buhari does not believe, but Atiku believes. Many people from the North-east and North-west believe. The entire South believe. Don't mind what Osinbajo is reported to have said. I don't know who told him to say that. I think it is not from his mind. And I forgive him. He said he does not support the way they are talking about restructuring. He cannot be different from all Yoruba people, all the Igbo, the entire South-south and, all the middle belt, and he alone is different. We are going to restructure Nigeria whoever likes it or not. I love this country; I want to be part of it. And nobody who thinks in the long term and who wants justice can certainly walk away from Nigeria, which can be restructured and with justice made to prevails.

15

TRUE FEDERALISM, CITIZENS' RIGHTS
AND
NATIONAL UNITY

A Keynote Speech By, Okwadike, Dr. Ezeife

At Ojukwu Ceremony of Tributes/Presentation of the Book: Dim Chukwuemeka Odumegwu-Ojukwu: A Man of History, on this day, 14th June, 2012.

INTRODUCTION

The man who has been mourned, like no human ever had, and perhaps none ever will, continues to attract tributes from far and near. I congratulate Aka Ikenga, the foremost and most focused Igbo group, for continuing the celebration. I expect Aka Ikenga, to make permanent, the celebration of the greatness of Ikemba, by instituting an annual activity in his memorial, whatever else any other groups may do. Brothers and sisters, things are changing and in the desired direction. In 2011, the Igbo dumped all their "eggs" in Jonathan's basket, it was a singularly solid united action. It might not have been known to many that it was the anticipation or expectation of that united action by Nd'Igbo which triggered similar actions from some other zones especially, Southsouth and Middlebelt/Northcentral. The burial of Ikemba provided another evidence of our progressively speaking with, approximately, one voice – another solid united action. Our reactions, so far, to the turmoil in Nigeria, have been truly united: the concerted efforts to resist reprisal attacks and the spill of innocent blood on our soil; the fervent pressure to resist the experimentation with Ogbunigwe in any mosque, and show the difference; is another. Any Igbo who is still basking in excessive individualism is anachronistic and very unwise. The truth is that, "when the come comes to become" or when it is important, we unite. We may have no leader to follow, we follow good ideas - follow what makes sense. The average Igbo is well equipped to judge.

The Igbo have a new resolve, new bases for united action. And what are these? The Igbo has resolved to improve the lots of the talakawa's and other down trodden Nigerians. We have resolved to rebuild the Nigerian middle class. We are committed to promoting the economic development and growth of Nigeria, and decided to, remarkably, raise the welfare of Nigerians. We are bent on returning pride to the institution of the family, through ensuring that every child born to a family is brought up and well taken care of by the family; the pride of manhood and fatherhood must be revived everywhere in Nigeria, by ensuring that every father wants to, and is in a position to, feed, shelter, clothe, educate and train every member of his family. These are among the great gifts which the Igbo have and have, in unity, decided to make to the rest of Nigerians! Nd'Igbo are unanimously saying that they don't want to monopolize: our achievement motivation, our aggressive pursuit of welfare, our hard work and industry, our pursuit of education, our egalitarianism and social mobility. We want the process of cultural assimilation to disseminate these traits or attributes to other Nigerians and show them the secret of success. Happy and contented people do not kill, they do commit suicide for any purpose.

Yes the dramatic improvement of the welfare for all Nigerians, is the primary and abiding motivation for an Igbo Nigeria President from 2015. The Igbo themselves will merely derive the psychic satisfaction that there is conscience in the society which gives rise to some fairness. The opportunities for such cultural assimilation and dissemination will be maximized by that development. Yes, it is time for maximizing economic development, growth and overall welfare in Nigeria. The days for "suffering and smiling" in Nigeria are numbered. It is suffering that brought Nigeria where she is today. Nigerians will, for the first time, know true happiness. This is the mission of Igbo Nigerian President. Think! This is mission easily achievable.

In this connection, the question is asked: what if the incumbent president wants to go for a second term? For about a year now, I have been making the point that it is not the interest or role of the Igbo to hound Jonathan out of office. The way I see it, we should play a game of co-operation with Jonathan, never a game of competition or conflict. And what does this mean? It means that the Igbo should approach the corporate campaign for President as if we are already late. We must, as a people, start meeting the various geo-political zones and the various ethnic groups, to negotiate for their support. We should do this for about a year before looking for individual candidates. Of course, Jonathan may also step-up his campaign for reelection. The game of co-operation will be played as follows: at the critical point, we should meet with Jonathan and his people to examine the prospects. If the prospects are such that Jonathan can win, without damaging the democratic structures he had helped develop, we should, obviously, support him; if, on the other hand, the prospects do not favour him, we should persuade him to support us. This is the game of co-operation and it is optimal!!!

Ladies and Gentlemen, where are we? Sorry, forgive me, I am

dealing with a totally different topic. Our topic is "True Federalism, Citizenship Right and National Unity", and, to that, we must turn without, any introduction.

TRUE FEDERALISM, CITIZENS' RIGHTS AND NATIONAL UNITY

The search for additional military/political power, for larger market, and the need to eke out some acceptable unity in the face of diversities, are the propulsions for political integration in the form of a federation. Now, what is "True Federalism"? It is either the structural arrangement of the federal set-up, which satisfies the aspirations of the nations or groups in the political arrangement, or it is mere verbiage. The elements that will make for satisfaction or lack of it include, fiscal arrangement, degree of real or respected autonomy of component units, looseness or tightness of the central grip and even the constitutionality of actions of the various units etc. Where there is no respect for the provisions of the constitution (like when some Nigerian governors were, some years ago, being hounded for incarceration, or when the Federal Government engages in arbitrary allocations and actions) it would be meaningless to talk about whether the federalism is true or false, whatever the letters of the constitution. The consensus among Nigerian commentators is that the "Nigerian variant of federation does not represent true federation" (Prof Dipo Kolawole); "Nigeria is a country where the conditions precedent to a federation predominate but the successful practice of federation has become a mirage" (Prof Akpodiete). Ample historical reasons are given: contributions by the colonial masters, deviation from the schemes of our heroes past, military coups and the inherent unitary command system of the military, military-strategy-induce creation of states in 1967, further unreason in military creation of states and local governments. I must add to these the basic fact that leaders of Nigeria, especially, the military leaders, have shown no craving for the economic development of the largest black country on earth, whose manifest destiny should be to constitute the rallying point, big brother and leader of Black and African persons on earth. Our political leaders were instead over engaged with politics of emotion, tribality, religiousity, and negative exploitation of all bases of pluralism.

I agree with a majority of knowledgeable Nigerians who believe that Nigeria needs restructuring. The rest of this paper will be devoted to why and how to restructure Nigeria. But first, we must deal summarily with the more controversial issue of "Citizenship Right"

Federalism And Citizenship Rights And National Unity

It is claimed for federalism, that it is a device for reconciling diversity with unity. I doubt that political scientists have given adequate thoughts to this claim. Among the diversities are included: ethnic nationalism, economy, religion, geography/ecology, language, religion and ethnicity. If a solution should exist for ethnic differences, can citizenship right diverge from indigenship right? Can a federating unit, or a geo-political zone, have a right to impose indigenship rights different from citizenship right given by the county – the federation. If not, in what way can federalism be said to make for unity in diversity, where the factor of diversity is ethnic? It does not, and this is not a theoretical matter. The majority ethnic groups in Nigeria seem to be comfortable with citizenship rights which recognize that a settler who was born in, or has lived in, an area for some (long period of) time, and performs all his/her civic duties etc, should have equal rights with the indigenes, including the right to vote and be voted for. Some minority ethnic groups in Nigeria think differently. And this has led to a serious breach of unity and peace. If those minority groups had proclaimed their terms at the point when, "We the People of Nigeria, make and give unto ourselves this constitution", they would have had every right for their stated terms of membership of Nigeria. But there had never been the opportunity for such proclamation. Similar problems arise from diversity of religion. We must recognize that there are no clear cut solutions and be ready to re-negotiate with various parties if the opportunity arises! A non-indigene may be allowed participation in some elections but not in others. References to the conditions in other countries do not solve the problems.

RESTRUCTURING NIGERIA: WHY AND HOW

Again, why the great outpouring of emotions for Ikemba? And why is it likely to endure?

How many people think ahead by one day? One week? One month? One year? So far, how many years have passed since Ikemba proffered his solution for the Nigerian problem. The problem and its solution are both becoming only more glaring today? It is becoming increasingly clear that whenever we summon the courage to solve our problem, that solution must be Ojukwu-solution of generations ago! Of course, if now we don't act fast, we may forget it: medication, except chemicals for embalming, is not for the dead. Any wonder we continue to talk about the visionary Ikemba.

The Summary

A. Why Restructure?

1. Politico-Cultural Considerations

Keeping Faith with our Heroes Past and the Original Order of Things. The arrangement made by the founding fathers had more political thoughts to them than what followed their exit.

2. Permanence of One Nigeria/ Accepting Our Manifest Destiny.

If we accept that God's purpose is for Nigeria to be the rallying point, big brother and leader of Black and African people's of the earth, we must restructure Nigeria for economic development and growth. There are clear internal and external threats to the permanence of one Nigeria. Restructuring by way of making the 6 geopolitical zones the federating zones will reduce some of the threats.

3. Peace, Unity and Stability.

It is believed that the proposed restructuring will make for greater peace. For example, making police a zonal matter already has the potential of reducing tensions which arise when police personnel from other tribes are policing outside their tribal areas.

4. Reversing Military Political Unreason.

The existing political structure of Nigeria bears the imprint of unreasoned emotional military political decision making.

5. Reducing the "Izing" Tendencies.

Some are hoping on "izing" Nigeria. Some fear that Nigeria may not resist "izing" and that an ized Nigeria, with her size and position, may make world management quite difficult. Their chosen solution is to break up Nigeria. They predict their wish and are doing things to make it come true – self-fulfilling prophecy – that is.

Military unitary command system.

Reduction of Ethnic Tension

There is a restraint arising from the recognition that you are in another person's zone. You do not vehemently insist on your rights.

Economic, Commercial And Ecological Considerations

1. Constraints on Corruption

People do not feel as pained when allocation from Abuja is looted. Let the people feel more that it is their money, for example, if they paid meaningful tax. And as they get more used to the system and appreciate that the son of so and so is squandering what they have a right to a part of.

2. Issues of Viability/Economies of Scale

Power, water, transportation and ecological projects respond to economies of scale. Both the 1994/95 and the 2005 Conferences condemn the 30-state and later 36-state structure as unviable. Today, only Akwa Ibom, Bayelsa, Delta, Rivers (all based on oil money) and Lagos are viable.

ENDC, NNDC, WNDC were all instruments of competition among the regions. It was meaningful to compete!

B. How to Restructure?

1. National

The Six Geo-Political zones become the Federating Units

3. Southsouth, Northcentral(Middlebelt) Northeast Zones

In the zones occupied by the minority tribes, a definite effort is needed to make most people feel relevant in the scheme of things. Distribution of power between the states and the local governments should depend on particular areas. But those ethnic groups which cannot amount to a local govt. must understand there are limits. This is however not at all the general case.

1 The Federal/Centre May remain fairly strong even as it operates constitutionally.

a. National Army
b. Unicameral Legislature
c. All Usual Federal Functions Plus Eco/Environmental and National Emergency Concerns
d. Country Diplomatic representation Zones

Zonal Police controlled zonally. No State Police. Lower Police personnel to be posted to their language areas but not to their towns. Zonal Military Command shared with the centre.

Special Appeal to Brethren

Federalism true or false, we have voted, with our feet, for One Nigeria. This has implications including:

Special effort on our security situation at home.

"Thinking Home", development and investment-wise. Applying pressure on home governments to co-operate for power, water, transportation and other infrastructure. Rebuilding the foundations for economic growth and development, reducing exposure to shame, ridicule and defeat by respecting some basic customs and desisting from doing some key things out of base!

The Bones are risen again! Take the message to all Markets: Eke, Orie, Afo', Nkwo'!! And to all Churches, Obu Ofo, Orthodox, and Pentecostal!!!

16

BAYELSA STATE
17TH ANNIVERSARY PUBLIC LECTURE

(Okwadike, Dr. Chukwuemeka Ezeife)

Transparent and Accountable Leadership in Nigeria

THE CASE OF BAYELSA STATE (30 09 13)

I thank Governor Dickson and the good people of Bayelsa State, for inviting me to this Anniversary Lecture. My gratitude is heightened by the fact that this gives me a very good opportunity to pay my respect to whom respect is due. Governor Dickson is fast becoming a national hero as a peace maker. The national assignments given to him were discharged successfully and creditably. He made peace where others failed. The reward for good work is more work. Nigeria needs peace and we look up to Governor Dickson to intervene everywhere - assigned or not assigned, invited or not. Nigeria is in danger – somebody who "was not born- to-rule", is in power, and he must be denied, even, his constitutional right to second term!! We must understand this root cause of the problem we face, we must sympathize with the aggrieved people, even as we must not allow injustice to take root. And we must not be so provoked as to endanger the gem, Nigeria, which our God Almighty has given us. Everybody knows who would lose most, should the unthinkable happen.

Today, we see convincing evidence, that efforts to make Nigeria ungovernable, through Boko Haram violence, has actually failed. Do you know that the Nigerian Railway is operating – running - from Lagos to Kano, and may soon begin to run from Port Harcourt to the North. Are you not noticing improvements in your electricity supply? If you did not listen to the Government's Midterm Report on the Transformation Agenda, you must have observed, first hand, that Jonathan is performing, even though his government is not informing, on his performance. With whom do you compare Jonathan on Presidential performance? Which President had faced determined efforts to making the country ungovernable, under him? If we help put a bag of salt on somebody's head and make heavy rains to follow the person, do we have a right, at the end of the rain, to ask how much salt is left in the bag? Yet this bag, carried by Jonathan, appears quite full, indeed. Now, you are to judge, whether Boko Haram has succeeded in making Nigeria ungovernable, by Jonathan.

Why is he succeeding? Jonathan is a tool in the hands of God to implement God's design for Nigeria. Jonathan's tolerance, cool headedness, fear of God, and respect for people, and their constitution, have neutralized Boko Haram violence. In the same way, the present political phase of the turbulence - the political Boko Haram, recently unleashed, which may end in the merger of many old are new parties – all without a definable ideology and all mostly one-sided, will also fissile out. We, Nigerians, must learn to accept, and submit to, the will of God for our country. It is the will of God that Nigeria must remain one, restructured to make things work, developing into a world super power, and so raise the dignity and respect of all blacks on earth. **Our country is blessed!**

> **Climate:** no extremes - no tornadoes, no hurricanes!!
> **The Geophysical Structure:** very stable - no volcanoes, no earth quakes!!
> **Material Resources:** In plant and animals, abundance; In minerals and other materials the ones we know already are surplus; there are many we have not yet discovered!!
> **Human Resources:** many talents from many tribes!!!

Our country is great, and was designed by the Almighty God, Himself, for unsurpassed greatness. **Nigeria needs peace! Governor Dickson must deploy his great gift in conflict resolution, to save Nigeria.**

Sorry, we are to talk about Transparency and Accountability. Yes! But if we do not get the centre right, there is no way we'll know the circumference!!

Transparency and Accountability in Government: General Statements

Scholars and practical political commentators and analysts, extol the merits of Transparency and Accountability in Government operations. Sometimes Transparency and Accountability are treated as twin attributes or virtues of democracy. What is transparency? A material is said to be transparent, if it can be "seen through". The opposite of transparent, in this case, is opaque . With regard to institutions or organizations, transparency refers to the openness in activities and operations. A government is said to be transparent if information about its activities is generally accessible to the public, that is, if the civil servants are open - and will freely give requested pieces of information to the public.

Definitions, Comments, Assumed Merits of Transparency and Accountability in Government
Definitions:
Government is transparent where there is openness of access to government information – where the public / civil

servants, are open to citizen's request for information.

Transparency requires openness, communication and accountability. The government should operate in such a way that the public sees, easily, what activities are undertaken by it, how the activities are performed, the cost, and the beneficiaries!

Merits of Transparency. The Following merits are claimed for transparency and accountability: Transparency in Government:

- is a virtue of democracy.
- will strengthen democracy and promote efficiency and effectiveness.
- promotes accountability and information dissemination on government activities.
- by promoting two-way information flow or information feedback, elicits greater co-operation from the people.
- reduces the difficulty and cost of re-electing/returning performing elected office-holders.
- is widely regarded as an important pre-condition for economic and fiscal sustainability, good governance and overall fiscal rectitude.
- creates an everyday participation in the political process by media and public.
- Accountability increases confidence in Government and motivates the people to support the Government, as well as, pay their taxes and perform other civil duties.

Why Do People Crave for Transparency?

The people are interested, and want to know:

➤ The sharing or allocation of the resources available to Government among the people, by LGA, by Senatorial Zones and by various publics and sectors.

> Government patronage and the beneficiaries: contracts awarded to foreigners, nationals and indigenes (and which indigenes)
> Employment distributing, and its fairness.
> Levels of salaries/wages, also the earnings of legislators and other political office bearers, relative to the levels outside the Government.
> Who is getting what from Government? How fair? What is there for various publics?
> Debts and Borrowings of Government.
  How indebted the government is, especially, foreign indebtedness. Some level of debts and, especially, foreign debts and borrowing, can tie the hands of future generations, and their governments and may render the achievement of the current Government unsustainable, and therefore, a fluke.

Vehicles for Transparency

- Town Hall Meetings, in down-to-earth reporting, questions and answers.
- Periodic Press Meetings/Briefings, where the press ask questions on any issues, and can, with Freedom of Information, ask about, and publish on, any issue,
- Press Releases.
- Special Development Reports: Half yearly, or yearly reports, covering infrastructural, educational, social and political developments among others.
- ICT. As information technology spreads to, and become used by, the people, the government should design on-line systems of informing the people and getting their responses.
- Competition among Ministries on transparency, accountability efficiency and effectiveness.

Means for Transparency.

- Budget: Planning, Implementation and Results.
- Physical Targets of the Budget
- Financial Provisions and Allocations in the Budget

- Achievements of Physical Targets (Implementation)
- Budget Reviews and Mid-course Corrections
- Budget Accountability Report, including half yearly physical and financial Report
- Releases on the progress of the budget.

Commentators on Transparency and Accountability are united is stating that public engagement enhances government effectiveness and improves the quality of decisions in governance. It is, however, necessary to state that openness has its limits: in foreign dealings, in customs and excise matters, in all manners of negotiations, even in some very mundane activities of government. Openness and secrecy are thus often in contention. There must be a balance which must be tilted in the direction of people's right to know - if nothing is clearly endangered by that right.

Transparency and Accountability
The Dickson Model

Accountability and transparency are good in themselves, even though the duo can be fake or sterile, or both fake and sterile. The State Government which promptly signs and issues monthly accounts in many newspapers, may, indeed, not be the most transparent and accountable. If you ask an investor about his global or ultimate objective, he may tell you that "the bottom-line is profit or profitability". Isn't the bottom-line for the governed, simply, *his/her welfare?* The welfare of the governed is, I posit, the bottom-line for effective governance. Sterile transparency and accountability may be there while people wallow in poverty, ignorance and disease. If welfare can be maximized or optimized and, in addition, there is transparency and accountability, then we have the best government. How do we achieve this?

What I propose, here, as "The Dickson Model "of Transparency and Accountability in Government

Operations", involves the peoples' participation and collaboration in Governance. It requires only the assumption that people know what they want - what is good for them – in some, if not, in most areas of their interest.

Central to the Dickson Model is the idea of "Peoples Council", at the State and Local levels of Government. The basic role of the Peoples Council is to participate, to a limited extent, in budget making, at both the Local and the State Government Levels.

At the Local Government Level, the Peoples' Council, in collaboration with the Chairman and Councilors and officials of the Local Government, define the needs to be met by the budget proposals. What does each sector of the economy and society require? At first, the collaboration may look like "brain storming" sessions, where every participant is free to mention the needs he/she feels must be confronted with the year's budget. The Peoples Council may end with participation in setting priorities for the budget policies, programmes and projects - leaving detailed work on the final budget, to elected and appointed members of the Council.

The principle and practice are the same at the State Government Level. In both cases (Local Government and State Government Levels), while the Peoples' Council will be involved in the half yearly evaluation, and the post mortem of Budget implementation, including necessary midcourse corrections, the final actions, including all aspects of budget implementation, are left to the elected and appointed officials of the level of government. The Peoples' Council should also participate in making long-range, - perspective – plans.

How is the Peoples' Council to be composed? It goes without saying that representatives of principal stakeholders and publics should be involved. At both levels of Government, the elected and appointed officers of the Government shall be the permanent members of the Peoples Council. Members appointed from outside government, shall include representatives of: manufacturers - mini, medium and giant enterprises; farmers and fishermen; the academia –

teaching staff and student leaders; religious organizations; the apex traders organization; labour unions; employers' organization; the media; and other publics/stakeholders, which have need to know, and are deemed capable of contributing positively to the effectiveness and efficiency of governance. No great elaboration is required here. It needs only be emphasized that non-government members of the Peoples' Council should appreciate and respect the limits of their involvement, and not seek to meddle in day to day activities of government. They should know, clearly, that they cannot affect who wins what contract from the government.

It remains to adumbrate the collaboration and co-operation between State and Local Governments, necessary in efficient and effective governance. The state and local governments should work out detailed measures and methods of collaboration for effective service delivery to the people. The bases of the collaborative effort include these three major situations:

(1) Every state road passes through Local Government Areas.

(2) Every state power line passes through Local Government Areas, and

(3) State water lines pass through Local Government Areas.

In all the above, the Local Government Officials are more likely to know about the developing problems before the state Government officials. As it is rightly said that a "stitch in time saves nine" it becomes necessary, and should be possible, to work out systems of effective co-operation and compensation which enable the Local Governments to promptly maintain state Roads, state Power and Water Lines!

All these enhance transparency and accountability. They do more. They enable the Government to be, not only open and accountable, but also to achieve the bottom-line of governance: *the welfare of the governed.*

Let me end by telling you, fellow Nigerians, fellow Easterners, that we may survive as Igbo, we may survive as Ijaw, as Ibibio etc; they may survive as Idoma, Tiv, Hausa, Yoruba, etc. We and they can survive as large or small ethnic nationalities, but, what is best of all, and so God seems to have designed it, not Lugard and British imperialism, who were merely used by God as tools, is that we survive as one, permanent Nigeria, restructured for efficiency and effectiveness. Yes! Restructured, so that Nigeria becomes a country, where things work!!!
May God use Governor Dickson and his ilk to save Nigeria!

Yours for Nigeria as a Super Power!

Yours, Adopted *Egbesu*! (at *Sagbama*, about a decade ago)

17

"BORN-TO-RULE" PHYCHOSIS KILLING NIGERIA

Chief Dr. Chukwuemeka Ezeife, former governor of Anambra State, is now a delegate at the National Conference. In this interview, he speaks on defected PDP governors, insurgency, state creation, federalism and other matters. Some excerpts of the interview were first published in Daily Trust last week. Here is the full interview.

From: Daily Trust, Thursday, May 22, 2014.

By Francis Okeke

A LOT OF DELEGATES HERE ARE VETERANS OF PREVIOUS CONFERENCES, WHAT DO YOU THINK OF THIS CURRENT CONFERENCE?

I am one of the many or few who ardently called for this conference. In Uyo when we were on a political summit, I wrote a committed, passionate appeal to Nigerians to pressure Mr. President to recognize himself as the focal point of the people's sovereignty and convoke this conference. It wasn't two months after that, the conference was convoked. But the principal reason it happened so fast is that we found

174

David Mark, the Senate President supporting the same thing.

Why does anybody call for this conference? Only so that we can have Nigeria as a permanent feature in this world. We don't want the breakup of this country. I love Nigeria passionately and when I say things as they are, some people in this country think I am working against them. When I say things as they are, many of my friends from the north begin to say I am turning an enemy but you see if we don't change things, we can't have Nigeria as a permanent feature of the world. So, what this conference is about is ensuring the permanence of one Nigeria.

YOU SAID WHEN YOU SAY THINGS AS THEY ARE, YOUR FRIENDS, ESPECIALLY FROM THE NORTH MISCONSTRUE YOU. WHAT ARE THESE THINGS THAT YOU SAY?

You see, the Generals were mostly from the north. They restructured Nigeria. From making it 12 states to making it 19 states to 21 states to 30 states to 36 states was the work of northern generals. In this process, one zone, the Northwest has 7 states. One zone, the Southeast has 5 states. In the process, Kano and Jigawa have more local government than the entire Southeast; it is not a matter of geographical mass; no. Governance is about the welfare of the masses, the person and not square miles. But because they were in power, they favoured their places causing structural imbalance in Nigeria. When I was governor, Babangida in his government wanted us to give phrases to describe our various states; Edo said the state is heart of the nation. I called Anambra home for all. Now it has been changed to Light of the nation, it is alright, I prefer home for all because we from Anambra make home everywhere and our own home should be for all.

That psychosis of "born to rule" is what is killing Nigeria now; from there we have found opposition to Jonathan as candidate for PDP, from there Buhari contested for President and Buhari told supporters and everybody that he must win; if he doesn't win, it must be rigging. Some other northern people whom you know, many of them said if Jonathan wins, they will make the country ungovernable.

CAN YOU NAME ONE OF SUCH PEOPLE?
I don't know; many of them. The government knows them. Then the result came out, Jonathan won and it was bloodshed. Bloodshed all over Nigeria; youth corps members wiped out, Igbos in the North wiped out, even some people attacked the emirs as symbols of feudalism. It wasn't long after they stopped killing people as a result of the 2011 elections that Boko Haram picked up. Boko Haram started, we asked the President to declare state of emergency, and he didn't until after more than a year.

DID YOU WRITE TO HIM?
We didn't write to him, we made a suggestion. So, in the process, some people started anticipating 2015 to make sure since he has won now, let's stop him 2015. Tinubu and Buhari merged their parties, now it has become APC. Atiku joined them in spirits. Seven governors, six Muslims and one Christian said they are breaking out of PDP. That is the first leg of Political Haram. Boko Haram had been there, and then political haram started with PDP governors breaking up and forming new PDP.

WHY DO YOU CALL IT POLITICAL HARAM?
Yes, that is the political wing of Boko Haram; that is the political counterpart of Boko Haram. The objective is the same: stop Jonathan. Whether it is Boko Haram or whether it is anything else, or even what they call cattle rearers, all of them are targeted at stopping the one who was not born to rule who happens to be ruling and therefore the country must be made ungovernable for him and the members of the society must would be made tired of him that blood is flowing. But who is causing the flow of blood; the person who is killing people will turn around and say oh, the President is not worthy of ruling because blood is flowing

under him, who is shedding the blood, themselves who are saying it.

IS THERE ANY EVIDENCE TO THAT EFFECT?

What evidence do you need? Somebody told you I will make the place ungovernable through his extensions of power and you are talking about evidence. There has been consistent move towards the same objective. From the result of 2011 elections and what came out of it, then Boro Haram, then Political Haram, then Cattle Haram.

AND NO ONE HAS BEEN ARRESTED?

Yes, no one has been arrested. It is a matter of style; another person would have put people in prison and killed many. But I like the godly, I won't say Christian, but his (Jonathan's) godly way of getting things done, praying to God, hoping people will change their mind and do the right thing.

FROM THE SCENARIO YOU CREATED, HOW WILL THE CONFERENCE TACKLE THE ISSUES THAT YOU HAVE RAISED?

Now, there are limits to posturing;

> *"It wasn't long after they stopped killing people as a result of the 2011 elections that Boko Haram picked up. Boko Haram started, we asked the President to declare state of emergency, he didn't until after more than a year".*

Posturing is like what the Yorubas call Shakara. There are limits to posturing. I am Igbo; I will say Nigeria is not important to me after all I am in China, I am in Russia, I am all over the world, no, that is Shakara. We the Igbo have voted with our feet for one Nigeria and we want one Nigeria to continue forever. We can go to other places but we already have developed Nigeria. We know we are enjoying Nigeria, we marry Nigerian women, Nigerian men marry our women, we developed Kano, we developed Abuja, we developed Lagos, we developed all over Nigeria to the extent that the Hausa man says if you get to anywhere in Nigeria and you don't find the Igbos, park and go, the place is not fit for human habitation. This is the Hausa man saying so. So, if Igbo say they don't mind if the country collapses, they are lying, that is Shakara.

What about Hausa Fulani? The North is the reason for the amalgamation of Nigeria. The British were spending money, balancing the budget, bringing money to the North. In the South there was surplus money, they (British) wanted to stop spending their own money, so they amalgamated the North and the South because of resource gap-deficit in the north and surplus in the south, now the gap is wider. If a Hausa-Fulani tells you we don't care if Nigeria breaks up that Igbos will go back and leave all the houses they have built for us, it is called myopia, short sightedness. The resource gap today is much wider than in 1914 when amalgamation was done. So, the North saying they are not interested in resolving the problems or in permanence of Nigeria is Shakara; posturing, fake posturing. Therefore, their long term interest is the same as Igbo's long term interest. The permanence of one Nigeria is what should be the long term interest of the North.

Look at the West; Yoruba. Today, finance, they get am, commerce, they get am, industry, they get am, much of importation of fuel which is a profitable business, they get am. Yes, the West may have had their constitution for Odua, national anthem and everything made ready to be independent but the market of Nigeria holds them together. It is in the long term interest of the West to exploit the largest market in Africa and grow than to go and have one small Odua country and pay tax to come into Nigeria, pay duty to export into Nigeria and have a lot of problems not being Nigerian.

Tell me, is it Nasarawa Toto, is it Edo, is it Ibibio, if they look at their interest in the long term no group of Nigerian have interest in the breakup of Nigeria. Therefore, we think the conference is convoked so that we begin to understand ourselves. In the first two days it was like war; one emir said that he can go to Cameroun, his brothers were there, he said when the country breaks up, he has somewhere to go, and many others don't have anywhere to go. Shortsightedness, political myopia may make some people think that it doesn't matter if Nigeria breaks.

The small gain you are making short term; throw it away for the bigger things. Igbo people are going to make this country very developed. It is in our blood, it is not the matter of helping people. We made mistakes when we allowed small children to be roaming the streets in Kano and we sent our own children to school. It would have been better for us to pay their fees; Almajiris. In the process, when there is strife, they are given N200 to kill us. If we had developed them as human beings like we developed our children, they will not be available as raw materials to shed blood. Now, Jonathan is doing it; I don't want Almajiri schools to concentrate on Islamic Studies, these boys and girls must be prepared to face today's economy. That I very much support.

Why the conference, to give Nigeria a chance to become a super power and to obey God. Nigeria is in this conference in effort to obey God. Many people don't know why Nigeria is here to obey God. Nigeria was created by God using the instrumentality of British imperialism but Nigeria was created for a purpose. What is the purpose? To wipe out the shame of slavery from black man who share colour with Jesus. How does Nigeria develop and clear the shame of the Blackman? By developing into a super power among the nations of the world. Then people will look around like they look around now and see China and Japan, they will look around now and say, oh, these black men, they have caught up with everybody. They are now super power.

Doing that will raise the dignity and respect of the black man everywhere the black man is. We are also the greatest concentration of blacks on the face of the earth. So, our manifest destiny, which is another way of saying God's purpose for us, is to develop into a super power, raise the dignity of blacks and African people and finally wipe out the shame of slavery from our faces. We cannot do it if we don't have peace, unity, justice and equity. If we are not in peace, look at Borno State; is it where it used to be? It is going backward; if this thing continues, Nigeria as a whole will be going backward. That is not how we can raise the dignity of blacks and African people. The purpose of the conference is not just to keep Nigeria ion the map forever but also to answer God's purpose and desire for Nigeria. Look, God prepared us for what he wants us to do; look at your country, the climate is fantastic, it doesn't have extremes. There is no tornado, no hurricane, no cyclone, and no extremes of anything. That is your climate. Then look at the resources God gave you with which you achieve your purpose. Material resources; how many minerals do we have, do you know? Even the ones we know, what is the deposit of oil in Nigeria? Nobody knows. For all that matters, Chad area, Bauchi, Sokoto, every part of Nigeria may be pregnant with crude oil, then gold, silver diamond; all kinds of gemstones. Then animals, plants; in the north, parts of the north like Gembu, Jos, we produce apples. What can't we produce with genetic engineering in Nigeria? Nothing. Animals are surplus. If you come to human beings, God gave us many talents from many tribes. So, God's design for Nigeria is for unsurpassed greatness, abundant resources. To realize God's design for Nigeria is the purpose of National Conference.

YOU SPOKE ABOUT "BORN TO RULE" MENTALITY, DISPARITY IN NUMBER OF STATES IN THE GEOPOLITICAL ZONES AND THE RESOURCE GAP. WHAT DO YOU WANT TO ACHIEVE IN THIS CONFERENCE AS A DELEGATE FROM THE SOUTHEAST?
We don't want number of states to be any problem, anywhere, anymore. Instead of that, we just say we have not

these infeasible 36 states as federating units. We will have about six geopolitical zones as we now have as federating units. We can even double it and say 12. We arrange each zone and get two out of a zone which eventually becomes 12. Therefore 6 or 12 geopolitical zones.

HOW DO YOU FUND THEM?

How are the 36 states funded? There will be continuous funding as it is now but there will also be every effort made in every state to produce what the state can produce and have serious internally generated revenue. The people who are producing oil are not saying go home all of us who are not producing oil and get nothing from oil; no. They are not saying so. They are just negotiating for higher money to be given to them. In the past it was 100%. Whatever you were producing you got 100% of it but eventually it became 50%, today it is 13%. In fact, it was one percent. So, if you give them 25% and then go and make effort in Anambra; industry or agriculture, you get more from your own resources. We are feeding from the north now, if well organized, they will get more and export from Nigeria to other countries.

PEOPLE ARE TALKING ABOUT SINGLE TERM FOR POLITICAL OFFICE HOLDERS...

(Cuts in)... I believe in single term for political office holders because it is more efficient. If you go there, you want your name to be immortalized. You work without people harassing you, without going for second term and bribing left and right and killing people even. Six years is alright.

SOME PEOPLE ARE SAYING THERE IS A HIDDEN AGENDA IN THIS CONFERENCE...

(Cut in)... tell me what they say is the hidden agenda.

THEY SAY IT IS A PLOY BY ESPECIALLY SOME PARTS OF THE SOUTH TO ELONGATE PRESIDENT JONATHAN'S TENURE.

Okay, that does not make sense but I can give credit to people that look far in the future. Now, the possibility they are referring to maybe my own papers where I said between this National Conference and 2015 election there may be a clash and what do we do if there is a clash? For me as an individual, I will have no qualms allowing incumbent office bearers to stay one more year or even two in order to get the country properly planned, a constitution that will lead us to where we want to go instead of rushing to crises 2015 election.

WHAT OF THE LEGAL BACKING?

No legality can produce the quality of membership we have in the National Conference today. This is the best representation of Nigeria, best representation of the sovereign people Nigeria. No election could have produced them and they are best suited for nursing Nigeria. Look at me, I ran for President two times; I never crossed a certain point. I quit politics when I turned 70, so, I am not a member of any party. I cannot run for any office now and many people in the conference are like that. These are the best people to produce a new constitution for Nigeria; these are the best people to plant trees that will provide shed for where they don't need to take shed. They, not being interested in what position they would hold in the system that they are constructing, are in the best position to construct that system. So, those of us who are old and who are said to be in the departure lounge, death can come anytime, we are the people who have no conflict of interest. For example if you take anything we are doing to the National assembly, National assembly people have conflict of interest. Clearly, one of the things we want to decide is whether it will be bicameral or unicameral system. If it is unicameral, either Senate or House Representatives will go; conflict of interest. Beyond that, we say, will it be full time or part time? Conflict of interest; how do you ask a person who is on full term to change to part time and you give him such decision to make? It won't work. Even the structural imbalance, those who have advantage will go and lobby so that there will be no change. What we are doing in the national conference must have the support of everybody to be of any use. We were talking about 75%, 70%, two third majority (voting modalities for the National Conference); nonsense. A constitution is like this, you take it to the people on referendum, "Yes or No?" If I am from anywhere, I will tell my people to vote No if I am not carried along. So, we must produce something that everybody accepts in the National Conference in order to happily go to the people in the referendum to say vote Yes.

DO YOU THINK THREE MONTHS WILL BE SUFFICIENT FOR THE NATIONAL CONFERENCE?

In my view, even with the raw materials available, it is not enough. A minimum of six months is necessary and we can still do so and have 2015 elections in six months. Why it is feasible at all for six months is that 1994 conference the result is on paper, 2005 conference, the result is on paper. In fact, for that one, I was the chairman power sharing committee, one of the strongest and toughest committees and we reached consensus. Not majority; consensus.

WHAT ARE THE KEY ITEMS YOU WANT CONFERENCE TO ACHIEVE IN TERMS OF RECOMMENDATION?

More meaningful, large federating units. Unicameral system, part time legislature, police as zonal matter not state, with a national police also. Go back to parliamentary system or at worse, have a hybrid of parliamentary and presidential system. Of course the military remains one. Drastically unburden Federal Government and then achieve fiscal federalism. These are the major issues. I may have not mentioned some major issues, but these also are the major issues. When you get them, you get Nigeria moving.

WHAT DO YOU MEAN WHEN YOU SAY MORE MEANINGFUL, LARGER FEDERATING UNITS?

Larger, meaningful federalism means using the six geopolitical zones as federating units or expanding them. Because of problems we see in various parts, restructure them into two per zone, therefore you have 12 geopolitical zones. Fiscal federalism means that the bulk of funds don't go like today to Federal Government because of reducing the responsibilities of the Federal Government, you correspondingly reduce the funds that go to it.

PART III

**SELECTED WORKS OF DR. EZEIFE
NIGERIA - ECONOMIC SOLUTIONS**

18

THE STRATEGY FOR SUPPLY OF PETROLEUM PRODUCTS TO THE DOMESTIC MARKET

(Okwadike, Dr. Chukwuemeka Ezeife)

Only a few months after **Dr. Goodluck Jonathan** took office as President, the price of petrol in my village, Igbo-Ukwu, tumbled down to the official price of N65/litre – to the price in Abuja. That had not happened in the last, more than, three decades! And my village was not alone; it happened all across Nigeria and has largely remained so. Diesel (AGO) and Kerosene (DPK) have not fared as well because petrol is by far noisier. Driven from Petrol (PMS), forces in the Petroleum Lobby (mafia) are now exploiting people with manipulations in the supply and distribution of the other products. This, too, can be stopped.

This achievement of President **Jonathan** gives me the guts to renew my proposal on the "Strategy for the Supply of Petroleum Products to the Domestic Market." I made this proposal to President **Obasanjo**, even after I had left office as his Political Adviser. He appreciated it, instantly implemented the aspect that affected the price of Kerosene, and, unusually, wrote to thank me. I discussed the proposals with the late President **Yar'Adua**. He showed great appreciation but not in many words. He left Nigeria not long after. But even if he had not travelled, the very powerful and multifaceted Petroleum Lobby would have tried to kill the proposal.

A. THE PROBLEMS

The observed problems include:

1. Under-production from the existing refineries
2. Non-development of new refineries – many years after 18 companies were issued with preliminary licenses for new refineries, we do not know of one which has commenced production.
3. Tying domestic prices of petroleum products to the world market price of crude oil destabilizes the domestic economy with strikes and threat of strikes.
4. Cost of doing business in Nigeria is high and very high petroleum product prices in Nigeria is like strangulating the economy with a product we produce, whose price we should use as instrument of economic policy. Most OPEC countries subsidizes petroleum product prices.
5. High subsides are paid on imported products, often not well monitored, not well defined and can be misapplied.

Many of the problems, especially, (1) and (2), are connected with how the domestic market is supplied.

B. THE SOLUTION

The solutions proposed include:

a. More efficient and effective performance of the existing refineries.

b. Government encouragement of new refineries by private investors.

c. Creation of new refineries with a view to exporting refined products, and

d. Efficient and effective supply of the domestic market.

Only the Proposal for the Supply of the Domestic Products is summarized here.

The simple proposal has the following elements.

i. We estimate the crude oil equivalent of the total demand for domestic petroleum products: petrol, diesel, kerosene etc. This maybe *guestimated* at 450,000 barrels of crude oil per day.

ii. This quantity of crude oil is allocated to, a slightly restructured, PPMC which becomes the Supplier of Petroleum Products to the domestic market. The PPMC is slightly re-organized to become a production and marketing company. The cost per barrel of crude oil, to the PPMC, is agreed for a term of, at least, one year.

iii. The refining of 450,000 barrels of crude oil per day is the responsibility of the PPMC, and it implements that through, using the local refineries and contract refining overseas.

iv. All supply of petroleum products to Nigeria is controlled by the PPMC from whom the marketing companies source products.

v. The cost of refining, local and overseas, are combined and added to other costs, namely, cost of crude, movement/distribution, to arrive at the cost of products to the PPMC.

vi.   The prices of products to the Nigerian user are set for, at least, one year. If it is found that the cost of ex-PPMC (cost of crude, refining cost, movement and distribution plus fair distribution margin), is less than existing market prices, some percentage may be added as government revenue.

SOME MATTERS ARISING

ON CONTRACT REFINING ABROAD

After studying what is possible, the PPMC may use the major marketing companies, if at all necessary, to organize contract refining of crude abroad. This carries the risk of retarding the development of home refining capacity, which risk would be much reduced by the PPMC directly giving out the contracts. Contracts refining abroad is, of course, a temporary measure pending the expansion of the domestic capacity.

ON SUBSIDY

The issue of subsidy is greatly classified. There being no direct importation of refined products, no subsidy is paid. Any subsidy will then be on the cost of the crude to be refined by the PPMC. No matter how this is handled, it will be clear-cut, and clean. And the true subsidy will be a very small percentage of what is claimed as subsidy at the present.

ON OPEC QUOTA

Nigeria must lead in making the case for OPEC quota to be based on export (of crude and refined products) and not on total production. In any case, the size of Nigeria can be used to justify special treatment of crude devoted to domestic consumption. With the quota situation, the opportunity-cost case for subsidy weakens. If there is no opportunity to sell all you can produce, you cannot sustain the classic argument for opportunity-cost subsidy on internally consumed crude oil.

ON THE PETROLEUM LOBBY

There is no open confrontation with the Petroleum Lobby. Things take their natural course. The same policy covers petrol, diesel, kerosene etc and there is no reason why the experience with any should be different. Over time, people will learn to live with normal profits.

I humbly submit that this is a vast improvement on the existing circumstances. It can be seen through.

genuine service to the people, integrity and patriotism, which are the foundation and pillars of a good society, must be re-engineered and re-activated in Nigeria!!! Nigeria must survive!

19

DIVERSIFICATION OF NIGERIAN ECONOMY

A Sine qua non for Sustainable Economic Stability and Growth

(Okwadike, Dr. Chukwuemeka Ezeife)

(Protocols)

Ndi-eze na adi ndu rue mgbe ebighi ebi- na ha fu ife ha ga eri. Ndieze no n'ebea fulu ihe ha ga eri. Indeed I am proud of you. After reading the title of the topic which you assigned to me, which is: Diversification of Nigerian Economy: A Sine qua non for Sustainable Socio-Economic Stability and Growth, I felt like saying simply: Amen! Because it is the simple truth. Our country is currently suffering from the consequences of violating that principle. I became very proud that our traditional rulers are educated enough to set PhD thesis topics. Of course you have academics among you. Congratulations!!!

What Is Diversification?

The base word is "diverse", which means "various", "different types" "multiplicity". Diversification of the economy is, therefore, the creation and operation of diverse, or multiplicity of economic activities! At the individual level, we talk of multiple sources of income leading to income sustainability. However a robust single source of income can make a person's income, sustainable. For an Economy, however, no single economic activity can lead to sustainable economic stability and growth; if for nothing else, because of the word change. In the economic zone, the only constant is, change!! Something can change from being of great value, to being close to useless. We have witnessed what is happening to coal; crude oil is in line for the same fate. Iron is still valuable, but not as valuable as before the advent of plastics. There in insurance in numbers.

Economic Diversification and Nigeria

Nigeria, thy name is diversity, or vice versa! In human resources, Nigeria is very diverse – many talents from many tribes: some are manipulative and diplomatic, some are long range in thinking/planning, some are gifted with aggressive achievement orientation, some are copyist or "Sidon looks" etc. but it is when we come to non-human material resources: plants, animals, and minerals, that the diversity of Nigeria becomes really dizzying and blinding. This is saying that God, the Almighty, endowed Nigeria, with stupendous diversity of resources, and each known resources is available in abundance. Yet, not all, and possibly, not even a majority of the minerals have been known or identified. If it had not been that the Nigeria man, in politics, has been messing up God's design for unmatched greatness for the country, there is no way the current and increasing level of suffering and welfare misery in Nigeria can be explained or understood.

Oil Money and Economic De-diversification in Nigeria

What made Nigeria retreat from economic diversification when oil revenue became significant? Ultimately, it was principally corruption and poor economic management. Our politicians focus on, not serving the interest of the people but, as Donald Trump, the Republican candidate for

President of the USA has said, they focus on carting away the wealth of the country, and dumping such wealth in foreign Banks. It was, therefore, the failure of man – the failure of leadership, the failure of economic policy, perhaps starting seriously from the military leaders that resulted in the de-activation of the economic diversification in Nigeria. There is no deeper explanation. The Nigerian economic agents were really not involved so much in the oil sector. Only a small percentage of the labour force was involve in oil-related economic activities. How then, did the discovery of oil and the increasing earning from oil mining discourage activities in the other areas of the economy? Surely, before the dominance by the oil sector, the Nigeria economy was fairly diversified. The groundnut pyramids of the past, our palm oil export which attracted our present major supplier of vegetable oil to come and take palm oil seeds from us, (efforts were made to produce palm wine for export), our export of semi-processed hides and skins, tin and columbite, and our once virile textile, soap and drinks industries, all evidenced Nigeria's achievements in the area of basic or nature-based diversification of her economy. Basic or nature-based diversification refers to diversification based mostly on natural resource endowment. Advanced or knowledge-based diversification is not based on natural resources of a country but on the level of her education in areas of science and technology. An example of such advanced economic diversification is what is happening in the Israeli economy which is not based on the availability of natural resources.

The advent of increased earnings from crude oil provided opportunities for unearned income for many Nigerians. These sources of income came through commissions on oil sales, allowances, corruption through over-costing of government projects, bloated employment of civil servants and even the number of local governments and states, these and other types of unearned income were made possible by earnings from the oil sectoer. The pursuit of income from non-oil economic activities eased and governments, at all levels, depended basically on oil money, rather than promote the growth of internally generated revenue. What is worse, poor government economic policies and corruption led to steady decline in the supply of electric power and in the levels of other economic infrastructure. The evidence of this decline can be seen in the fate in Nnewi, which used to be called the Taiwan of Africa. Nnewi, today, has some economic activities but they are nothing near the levels reasonably projected, from its earlier trajectory.

Promoting Again Economic Diversification in Nigeria

Ndieze! You are not, really, interested in lamentations of our past failure but in how to ensure, through diversification, the stability and growth of our economy.

For this, power and other economic infrastructure, especially, water and transportation, science and technology education, are the most important ingredients. Yet the Federal Government of Nigeria has clearly shown serious inability to provide these key requirements for sustainable economic stability and growth. And, the four States that can fund the development of these infrastructures are, like the rest of the States, too small to do so efficiently. This is because economies of scale are important in creating power and major economic infrastructural facilities. What to do? This seems to be one compelling reason to make the six geopolitical zones in Nigeria, the Federating units. That way, each of the units (zones) will be large enough not only for the development of the necessary economic infrastructural facilities, but will also be in a position (that is, large enough), to do so quite efficiently (at reduced unit costs). There is the problem of differential motivation for economic development among Nigerian groups who, also, have differential access to national political power.

Diversification in Agribusiness

It remains to comment on area of diversification. The greatest potential for diversification is in agribusiness – the cultivation and processing of agricultural produce: seeds, leaves, wood and others. With regards to seeds, the clear model is cocoa. Today Nigeria produces very good quality cocoa seed, parts of which are processed in the country to pure natural cocoa powder. Many Nigerians may not know that we are about leading the world in this pure cocoa production. There are many such seeds to process for the world market. The export of raw cocoa, beans, raw cashew nuts, raw shear nut, palm kernel nuts, sesame seeds, pumpkin seeds, and seeds similar to these, should be discourages and banned in due course. In this and other agribusiness sub-sectors, perspective plans should be developed to bring about effective planned diversification, and exportation. Reports from Anambra State Government indicate that our common vegetable like Onugbu, Ugu, Utazi, Nchuanwu, Oha, Ewedu, and the like, can be exported to raise foreign exchange. The case for pineapple export is confirmed by a Mexican firm which left its country, bought land in Enugu State for growing pineapple, and has made, at least, one profitable export run. The firm's economic calculation is as follows: since it would transport the pineapple for 14 hours from Mexico to Europe, and only 6 hours from Nigeria, and, the Nigerian soil is not inferior to the Mexican, it is bound to gain by cultivating pineapple in Nigeria. This compels us to open our eyes and study, critically, today's international agribusiness, to see where we have the potential to participate. From these, it is clear that we can reverse the negative trend in the Naira exchange rate, if only we'll study and aggressively implement necessary economic diversification measures.

Diversification and General Strength of the Economy

As with the agribusiness sub-sectors, so it is with other sub-sectors, but our comparative advantages in agribusiness are greater! In both cases, there is need to do a thorough study and perspective planning. Diversification helps sustain economic stability and growth. We should also consider measures, which not only support diversification, but also strengthen the overall economy. It is necessary to examine the overall cost of production, especially, the cost of manufacturing, in Nigeria, and possibly find ways to reduce it so as to raise our ability to compete in the world market. Some years ago, some industrial establishments were wiped out in Nigeria when imports from China entered the Nigeria market at less than their costs of production. This is why we must think of using what we have to get what we need. We should consider using the pricing of petroleum products to bring down our cost of manufacturing. The pricing of petroleum products is singularly suitable for this purpose because it affects virtually every economic activity in the country. To achieve this, the importation of refined petroleum products must not be done by private importers. Otherwise a lot of money will be required for subsides. We should estimate the quantity of crude oil which can meet our domestic requirement for petrol, diesel, kerosene, and other products (making allowance for leakage to neighboring countries). This quantity of crude oil is dedicated to domestic market- to home consumption. It is processed, by contract, in Nigeria or with arrangement with foreign refineries. The prices of products are set low to bring down our cost of manufacturing and enhance our competitive position in the world market. It may be the policy to always recover the refining costs, including transportation. We can set the product prices as we consider reasonable – without reference to international prices! This does not only increase diversification, possibilities, which makes for greater economic stability and growth, it also strengthens the overall economy and strengthens the naira on continuing bases.

Advanced Diversification

Diversification of economic activities in Nigeria should be taken to its advanced stage at which it is no longer dependent mostly on resource endowment (but is footloose). For us, this may not be so urgent, yet globalization creates all kinds of opportunities. The internet provides trading and other economic activities for the "digital". Indeed meaningful foreign exchange can be earned from internet businesses.

Tourisms

Finally, we must plan to exploit the potentials of tourism which can be a major source of foreign exchange earnings. We do have diverse sites! And focusing on tourism, forces improvement in internal or domestic security, which helps the economy!

Ndieze, unu ga adi! Please pray for our people pray God to lead our President to the right path- the path to the welfare of the people and the negotiated unity of the country!! And pray God to reveal to those who say they are opposed to political restructuring, the long term interest of their people!!

PART VI

SELECTED WORKS OF DR EZEIFE
IGBO – THOUGHTS & LECTURES

20

IGBO LEADERSHIP

(Okwadike, Dr. Chukwuemeka Ezeife)

By lacking effective leadership, the Igbo people are seen as disunited, yet the Igbo are basically more united than any of the other major groups in Nigeria. The Igbo have been out of central government power for more than 50 long years, yet they still do thing together, to a large extent. They answer the call of Igbo leaders, and are not openly as disorganised as their opponents desire them to be. After 8 years of Obansanjo rule, the North was virtually in pieces and were only brought back together by Obansanjo's third term bid. The Yoruba display apparent unity but the existence of Yoruba Unity Forum evidences the disunity of the Yoruba. We doff our hearts for Yoruba control of the Nigerian press which adds to their appearance of unity.

Yes, these are true but the Igbo must make the strong move to create effective leadership and unity. The saying "Igbo Enwe Eze" has meaning when applied to dictatorial leadership by one person, one Eze - one man as the leader. Igbo individualism and republicanism cannot co-exist with one man autocratic leadership. In the traditional Igbo society, leadership was in the hands of the "Nze na Ozo" who swore to the oaths of truth, righteousness and integrity. The oldest titled man took the symbolic leadership position. He relayed or confirmed decisions made by the leadership group within the Nze na Ozo. To create a modern leadership, Igbo need to emulate, to a great extent, their traditional leadership model. This is what we need to do now, this is what we must do - design a leadership system as close to our tradition as possible. We must indeed realize that the very strict code of conduct imposed on the Nze na Ozo - are, indeed, in some respects tougher than the biblical code. Of course, it is doubtful that the strict and stern code imposed on the Nze na Ozo can be fully honoured today - assuming that they were ever fully honoured. The selected members that constitute the leadership group must be trusted, very much respected and honoured by the people - this is very essential.

The Leadership are responsible for the good of Nd'Igbo: their respectability, dignity, prestige and honour in the nation and the world. The Leadership shall perform duties in all matters affecting the Igbo: giving more backing to some Ohanaeze decisions, maintaining Igbo traditions and values, working on issues referred to it by the Ohanaeze and by other apex Igbo organisations like the Councils of traditional rulers at home and in Diaspora and such bodies, giving decisions on authentic Igbo values and traditions and influencing modern and traditional leaderships among the Igbo.

THE SUGGESTION

We need Collegiate Leadership which is the only leadership our people had known and accepted. By the way, the position of Ohanaeze will not be in conflict with the Collegiate Igbo Leadership because the two bodies have, to a large extent, different assignments. As we go on, it will become clear that the new Collegiate Leadership is, not at all, in conflict with Ohanaeze. How do we set up the Collegiate Leadership?

There are five Igbo states and two other states in which there are significant Igbo presences (Rivers and Delta). Three persons may be selected from each of the five states and one person, each, from Delta and Rivers.

apex Ib

Persons to be selected must have the following attributes or characteristics:-

1. Tough minded persons of strong will, character, self-pride and convictions, the kind of persons who may refuse food even while very hungry. Persons who will never "sell out".

2. Persons who must no longer be interested in the pursuit of elective or appointive political offices - and should be of such age and exposure that the persons strength of character is well known to his people.

3. Persons who are reasonably satisfied with their personal achievement, so far, in life, that they are no longer trying to impress people.

4. People who are so committed to, and even so consumed with, Igbo Interest, that, should their personal interests clash with Igbo interests, they will have no difficulty in jettisoning their personal interest.

5. Persons who are well known for integrity, truthfulness, trustworthiness and good judgement.

6. Persons who, not only have all the above characteristics, but are also, clearly seen by their people to possess them.

The selection process will be dominated by the people's perception of the persons and may, in some cases, be confirmed by secret research by knowledgeable people.

The selected persons will be subjected to oath taking in their states and also at   central Ecumenical Service organised at our *Obi* - Enugu.

It is most important that Nd'Igbo should have such confidence in the leaders that the decisions and actions of the leaders are not questioned. Such decisions and actions include matters of discipline. Indeed, the Igbo Collegiate Leadership should develop a strong Disciplinary Arm to ensure that Igbo decisions are respected and enforced.

21

NDIGBO AND THEIR ROLE IN NATION BUILDING.

National and Diaspora Integration Arena for Igbo Aspiration (Ndiafia Development Forum)

This topic is pregnant with "ifs" and it is best to tackle it by expressly clearing the "ifs" I interpret the topic as Ndigbo and their role in building Nigeria what comes to mind is whether the topic is referring to the Nigeria of yesterday or the Nigeria of today and of tomorrow.

I pray the Almighty God opens our eyes and hearts and our sixth senses.

(A) to see, perceive and appreciate the real truth about the state of our country, Nigeria! We can, on the positive side, see the unmatched greatness, designed by God, for One Nigeria, as the Super Power giant of Africa. And on the negative side, because of man's mess up, there exists the imminent danger of Nigeria's collapse, disintegration and going into extinction! May God uphold His Will and positive designs for Nigeria, and forbid the consequences of the mess up by man, colonial masters, and local.

The position I take in this paper is based on my strong hope and interest in the permanence of one Nigeria. Why this hope and interest? Let me repeat what I have been saying and write for many decades. Every group in Nigeria, large or small, will gain stupendously from one Nigeria that is made to work.

Among the larger groups, Igbo, Yoruba, Hausa cannot doubt that one Nigeria is best for them even though they are larger than some countries of the world. Of some smaller groups Gbagi, Urhobo, Ijaw, Ibibio, Fulani, Kanuri etc. Their gains from the permanence of Nigeria especially, their potential gain of being part of an eventual Super Power nation, cannot be overlooked or downplayed.

The crisis - urgent, make or break, Nigeria one and make her to work. A Nigerian from the Fulani stock said, in effect, that the North is ready for the disintegration of the country, as the situation in the country seen to be crying for a break up, unless we can go back to Nigeria as it was at Independence. Some people, wrongly and myopically, saw this statement gas a negative with regard to one Nigeria. It is indeed a positive statement and provides a good basis for keeping Nigeria One. The statement did not end with "The North being ready for Nigeria's break up. It ends with a positive suggestion of going back to what I understand as Pre- 1960 days!!!.

Contrary to the statement of some people who made restructuring sound like a big grammar, restructuring is indeed Prof Ango Abdulah is alternative to disintegration. It is, going back to the agreed Nigeria" of Pre-1966, namely, a Federal system based on regions the 1960 to 1963 constitution as Federating Units.

Federating and regional are there in the achieves. Of course, they will need some adjustments.

A major adjustment is the addition of the 18 new states carefully assessed and approved by the 2014 National Conference. By the way, this brings the number of states to

54 plus Abuja sometime treated as if it were a stated. One does need to be an economist to seen the infeasibility of operation 54 Federating Units. No anachronistic feelings of inferiority, complex can justify 54 Federating Units. The fear of going back to Egypt is based on ancient history the circumstances of which have drastically changed and or, reversed it make sense to adopt the six geographical zones, which has been there for decades, as the Federating Units. The states in, each zone, must work out and agree on the zonal constitutions. Such zonal constitutions may have features like federal constitutions. It depends entirely on the states.

I can now confidently, proceed with "Ndigbo and Their Role in Nation" with the understanding and hope that the Nation is One Nigeria restructured with justice preventing for things to work.

(B) Ndigbo And Past And Current Development of Nigerian

Future Development The Igbo achievement motivation remains unchanged. But the impact of the direction statement that" one builds where he lives" must be reduced!

Yes, this motivational statement has led to the contribution to the development of every nook and cramy of Nigeria by Nd' Igbo. The percentage of modern buildings in any part of Nigeria belong to the Igbo, must be very high indeed. Nd'Igbo has contributed immensely in the social and economic of every part off Nigeria indeed. In education, many of today's non-Igbo educated Nigerians attended schools, build by Nd'Igbo outside Igbo- land; in economic activities non-Igbo people have emulated the Igbo and there is more competition between the Igbo and the indigenes in some activities, formerly, though to bed Igbo monopolies. The competition often lead to seeing conflicts which must be discouraged it is, indeed, the greatest contribution of Nd'Igbo to the Development of Nigeria that some non- Igbo

Nigerian have and are emulating Igbo achievement motivation economic activities and methods and other.. This is way Nd' Igbo is contributing to the foundation to development of Nigerian as A Nigerian Super Power among nations - giving her population and geographical sizes.

The contribution of Nd'Igbo to the building of Nigeria has largely been to the detriment of the development of Igbo - land. And there is no reason why it should be do or remain so that is why the in augural statement I gave as Governor of Anambra State is titled: " Think home" In that statement I called our people to invest in other parts of Nigeria but to invest also in Igbo land ("Anambra"). Thinking hone and investing to build a strong South East economy is now overdue.

On the future of Igbo contribution to nation building, it is necessary to point to the existence of a document titled Igbo - Strategic Roadmap, should the South - South see the document and appreciate and like it, it can be reworked and titled SESS strategic Roadmap where SEDD stands for Southeast and Southsouth.

It remains to make suggestions to improve relations among Nigerians as they engage in Nation Building. On Igbo and the rest of Nigerians:

It is clear that the Igbo did not set out to make his hosts jealous or unhappy. He does, in the open, whatever he gains from, leaving it open to anybody to emulate. And, as stated above. The emulation is on , but in some cases it is creating unhealthy competition.

(C) God and good men, know that One Nigeria, effectively resurrected, for justice to prevail and things, to work cannot be to the detriment of any group in Nigeria. No! By God, not all!!! On the contrary, it will usher in explosive growth in peace and tranquillity, enabling Nigeria to become a Super.

(D1) The Igbo must now actively pursue friendship with their host communities; plant a variety of enduring seeds in the host communities; respect the customs and traditions of the host communities; use the town union system, which they have everywhere, to educate new comers to know and respect the dos and don'ts of the host communities. We must blunt our forwardness or audacity, with some diplomacy and studied silence. Of course, no individual Igbo chooses to behave the way he does, by himself; it is a matter of up-bringing, not much of personal choice . I became Igbo , On Arrival, Not by choice. So did everybody from every ethnic group of any size.

Like the Igbo, many other Nigerian groups must introspect. The Fulani needs introspection most, as their superiority psychosis, is really getting out of hand. How fair and reasonable is their "quit notice" to an autochthonous group, like the Igbo.

(D2)The Igbo, like other successful groups in Nigeria, do whatever they do for economic success in the open, not in secret. The Yoruba, the Kano Hausa, the Kanuri, the Ibibio and many other successful groups in Nigeria are all using, or applying, learnt behaviour, or knowledge, which other groups can also learn or emulate. The greater the number of groups which assimilate achievement motivation, the greater the welfare and happiness in Nigeria.

(D3)Fellow Nigerians, it is time to break with our past of recriminations, jealousy, hatred and blind selfishness. Time to resurrect Nigeria. We must become our neighbours' keepers. Time to be concerned about fairness to all concerned. No longer should we turn blind eyes to the discriminations against, or the marginalization of, other groups in Nigeria. The octogenarian, Chief Edwin Clark, is leading the way to the New Nigeria of neighbours' keepers.

Nd'Igbo must continue to mend where they " but this must

no longer be at the expense of the home from. we make better appreciated contributions to national if our home base is a major component of a Super Power nation.

22

2012 AHIAJOKU LECTURE, OWERRI, 23RD NOVEMBER CHAIRMAN'S OPENING STATEMENT,
by Okwadike, Dr Chukwuemeka Ezeife
For Nd'Igbo

TIME TO MAKE PEACE, UNITE, MAKE FRIENDS

Other Peoples' Attitude to Nd'Igbo

The book of Ecclesiastes reminds us, in style, what should really be obvious: that there is a season, a time, for everything under the sun – under heaven. For the Igbo, now is the time to make peace - time to make friends - within and without. It is time to unify and integrate. It is time to court the friendship of other Nigerians. For those in Diaspora, or outside Igbo land, it is time to make friends with our host communities. To make peace, to make friends, we need to understand the basis of the attitude of other Nigerians to us, (the Igbo). It is not just other Nigerians, indeed, it is the attitude, to us, of other peoples of the world, with whom we come into close relationship. Igbo slaves, in the epochs of slavery and slave trade, were seen and treated differently from other slaves – they attracted higher prices but there were slave masters who

211

would not have them, at all. Their *"eji ndu eme gini"* (what is the use of life without honour?) disposed them to suicide. What motivated a white author to describe the Igbo as, "a people before whom the white man feels inferiority complex"? Why do Yoruba describe Igbo as people who swallow stone without water? Why do the Igbo cause envy and resentment among other Nigerians?

The Bases of the Attitude

The method of progressivism, which suggests **putting** oneself in the other person's **position, in order to** understand and appreciate the other peoples' point of view and attitude to us, becomes handy here. Imagine that some "strange" person comes, apparently empty handed, from an unknown village, very distant from yours. The stranger starts with carrying your "night soil" or doing other mean jobs. Later he sets up a kiosk, where he sells some "articles". The stranger goes on to, over, not too long, a period, develop a viable big business, and proceeds to build a mansion in that your village, where you have only a hut. He forms the habit of sitting in front of his mansion, in the evenings, exuding more confidence than even the original owners of the land - than you!

If the story ends there, what would be your attitude to that erstwhile stranger? Yes, this stranger leaves you with your culture and tradition, including your religion. He installs his practices in your village, among his people and makes no effort to introduce you to his ways, even though he opens if you knock. He takes off to his village, at some of his home festival periods. What would be your attitude to this person? What, if he adds some bad mouth to the situation, always insensitively boasting of his successes? Reader, be honest! Yes, you would start with shocked admiration. Some tinge of envy and jealousy may creep in overtime, and these may mature into resentment and, even, open violence!

The Price of Extra-Ordinary Success

Does the above appear familiar? For the Igbo, it is time to make friends of our host communities! Time to, seriously, endear ourselves to the other Nigerians!

The bases of the problems of Nd'Igbo in Nigeria and in other countries is founded in Igbo culture and child upbringing. The strongest propulsions to success are buried in the Igbo language and idioms, and in the contrasting roles of mother and father in preparing the child for adult life. Succeeding where others do not, or making it by far more than others, ignites the fire of envy and sometimes resentment on the part of those others. Matters get worse if you are insensitively noisy about your success or you are boisterously flaunting your wealth. The Jews understand this story very well – and so do the Berbers.

The Ingredients of the Success

Igbo egalitarianism with associated upward social mobility, which makes parents pray for their children to be greater than they, and makes the masters pray for their apprentices to overtake them in achievements, combined with a number of Igbo cultural traits or attributes, including achievement orientation, fast acculturation, persistence – the never say die attitude – aggressive industry, tenacious application of hard work, competitiveness and the confidence that comes from *onyekwe chi ya ekwe,* which enables man to harness the creative powers of God who made him in his image and likeness etc, all these, make the Igbo hugely successful anywhere they go. And their huge successes left unmanaged, breed resentment towards them. It is time to device or design ways to manage our success in ways that will endear us to our host communities. It is time to make friends of other Nigerians.

Will Nigeria Continue to Make Progress Backwards?

Nigeria has not gained like she should from Igbo successes,

in spite of such successes being showcased in every nook and cranny of the country, by a people who have voted with their feet for one Nigeria, a people who came back to Nigeria after their apparent rejection and resumed the development of every part the country, as if nothing had happened. Why is the potential cultural assimilation not working for Nigeria's development? There is a cardinal reason why *the talakawa* and the downtrodden Nigerians in parts of Nigeria may not wish to emulate the Igbo: other Nigerians are developing the habit of looking down on the Igbo, rather than emulating them. This is because, especially after the civil war, the Igbo are seen as a people excluded from political power. And as things stand in Nigeria today, with monumental corruption and the adoration of the god of crass materialism, only political power seems to count!!! And the evidence of Igbo exclusion from power is so glaring!

Igbo Exclusion from Political Power
Of the ethnic tripods, on which the country stands, only the Igbo has not supplied an elected Chief Executive Officer of the country. Again, of the six geo-political zones of the country, only the southeast, home of most Igbo, has not supplied a President of Nigeria. The corruption that is fueled by oil money, combined with the apparent death of conscience in Nigeria, has weakened values, especially the value of hard work. And so, Nigeria grows backwards, remaining in the kindergarten, while those that started the development race with her, are far into the tertiary levels. It seems to be the case that, as long as the Igbo remains down politically, for so long must Nigeria remain down economically, worsening the problems of *Boko Haram*, and all dimensions of insecurity deriving from poor economic performance. And some people like to keep it that way! *Tufia!!!*

23

CORPORATE CAMPAIGN STEATEGY
FOR IGBO NIGERIAN PRESIDENT

(Okwadike, Dr. Chukwuemeka Ezeife)

The mission is to sell to Nd'Igbo and other Nigerians, the idea of an Igbo Nigerian President. The campaign will initially be only corporate – that is, undertaken by Nd'Igbo as a people, as all Igbo make effort to sell the idea of Igbo Nigerian President to themselves and to other Nigerians. Thus, no individual candidate is expected to initiate this effort. It is obviously in the corporate interest of Nd'Igbo to produce, for the first time, a Nigerian President who is Igbo. It is therefore not a burden to be left to individual candidates. The corporate campaign, which may be undertaken by a Foundation (***Ntonana Ndozi Igbo***), may go on for a substantial length of time (perhaps up to two years) before the unveiling, or the emergence, of the individual candidate(s).

It is important to state here that the Igbo do not see it as their role to hound President Jonathan out of office. We take over at the end of Jonathan Presidency. (This raises the issue of Jonathan wanting a second term. Political wisdom requires that we play only a game of cooperation, not of competition or conflict, with the President. We should, indeed, make haste to be quite ready to take power in 2015. Jonathan, on his part, vigorously pursue his succession bid. The game of cooperation requires that, at some critical point, the two parties should meet, as friends, to analyse the prospects. If Jonathan can win fairly we should support him, otherwise he should be persuaded to support us). The fact is that, at the end of Jonathan Presidency, whether it ends in 2015 or after, each and every one of the six geo-political zones in Nigeria, except the Southeast, shall have provided the Chief Executive Officer, or President, of Nigeria for more than five years. Ironsi, from Southeast, ruled for only six months, was murdered, and buried with more than one million Igbo: who died in the pogrom and in the long civil war.

Selling Igbo Nigeria President to Nd'Igbo

Most Igbo will readily appreciate the psychic satisfaction (benefit) derivable, by them, from the emergence of the first Nigerian President who is Igbo, even though the Igbo do not expect the emergence of a brother of theirs as Nigerian President to enhance the level of their material welfare, except in so far as this results from general improvement in the economic environment. Indeed, the Igbo will not want an Igbo Nigerian President to do anything special to improve their economic wellbeing. On the contrary, they will frown at any such attempt because they do not want to be denied the joys of their individually merited achievements. They do not want their achievements to be credited or attributed to favours from anybody. To demonstrate that they are no second class citizens, that the rulership of Nigeria is not the birthright of any Nigerian group, to the exclusion of others, and their concern for faster development of the Nigerian economy, are the only motivations for Igbo pursuit of a Nigerian President who is from their stock. Nd'Igbo will therefore readily buy the quest for Igbo Nigerian President. The challenge may be in their readiness to pay the price. The greatest challenge facing the Igbo in this connection is their believing that they are capable of generating the required unity of purpose among themselves. But this they can easily confront with the Igbo traditional belief in how the Universe works. This is encapsulated in the creed, *"onye kwe chi ya ekwe"* which is similar to saying that mighty forces (indeed, the Universe) aid in the implementation of a worthy goal which man conceives and believes. The Igbo must achieve greater unity among themselves. And, they can! This is quite ease and may even seem effortless, when the challenge is major and clear enough. With singleness of purpose, the Igbo buried their Ikemba, with greater pomp and honour, than had any man, born of a woman, been buried before, and quite possibly, none will ever be. Before that, acting in unism dumped virtually all their "eggs" in Jonathan's electoral basket. The areas requiring immediate attention are:

1. Anambra and the Rest of Igbo

Small cultural differences between Anambra and the rest of Igbo are causing serious misunderstanding and resentments. Anambra Igbo have a different cultural practice, from the rest of Igbo, with regard to verbal behavior concerning respect to seniors/elders. This is mostly in methods of address or name calling. An Anambra father or mother takes no offence when his children call him/her by his/her given name, like; Okeke, Okafor, Okoh, Nwafor, Nneka, Adamma. This is abomination or gross insult among some Igbo, especially, of Imo and Abia. Persons from these states and some other Igbo areas where the practice is different, take it that Anambra persons are deliberately rude and insulting to them and they hate it. An Imo person or Abia person will add the prefix "Dee" or "Daa", respectively, in addressing an older person and must never call parents by their given names. It is, first, necessary to spread the knowledge that this is clearly a cultural matter, that the Anambra person intends no offence, and that the Igbo from outside Anambra are reacting in line with their own cultural practices and not unnecessarily taken offence. Fortunately, things are changing gradually. Anambra people now say: Nneanyi, Nnaanyi, Nne Joy, Nna Emeka. It remains to develop a prefix to attach to the name of someone who is significantly older than one (3-5 years older). Why not all Igbo adopt the "Daa" and "Dee" or Anambra design a prefix of respect for elders, like "Oka m". This is not all. Anambra people are accused of being too loud, often boasting of their achievements and successes without being sensitive to the feelings of other people around. The town unions, especially outside Igboland, have work to do.

2. Ebonyi and the Rest of Igbo

Ancient grudges about domination and marginalization are causing strains and stresses in the relation between Ebonyi people and the rest of Nd'Igbo. Indeed, it has been delaying inter-state co-operation in the Southeast. In the long past, the rest of Southeast developed faster than Ebonyi – indeed, really, Abakaliki, **in** modern economic activities. The town of Abakaliki was dominated by non-indigenes and they controlled the levers of economic powers. Add to this the perception that eastern regional government appeared distant from Abakaliki people. They were not well represented in the civil service. This led to the development of a feeling of marginalization among Abakaliki people. Persons of all Ebonyi state appear to have imbibed this attitude. But this is something of the long past. Today, the opposite is the case. Ebonyi is now a state run fully by Ebonyi indigenes who control every element of the social structure, especially, the polity and the economy. What is more, Ebonyi indigenes now dominate and control rural Igboland, and many urban areas too. They are in charge. They are in every economic activity, they have massively intermarried. But the old leaders of Ebonyi state are still remembering the era of their being dominated by other Igbo. This is causing a problem and must be recognized, addressed and buried for the good of Igbo unity. The past must be kept in the past. Any zonal association or government must be based on a constitution, which the states of the zone must freely negotiate. Of course, the device of "Federally Administered States" may be provided, even though it will not take long before such states realize their folly and beg to join their zonal formations.

In unity, the Igbo must agree, to buy into, adopt as article of faith, and **work** for the actualization of the idea of a Nigerian President who is Igbo. Nobody is going to "dash" the position to us. We must first internalize our craving for the position so that **Chi anyi** and **Chineke** will intervene. Thus, we need to reach the Igbo anywhere they are to accept that an Igbo Nigerian President is important to their psyche, and crave for it, **onye kwe, chi ya ekwe**. One way is to temporarily change how we respond to **Igbo Kwen!** Let it now be:

Igbo Kwenu: Anyi ga achi
Igbo Kwenu: Anyi ga achi
Igbo kwezuenu: Anyi ga achiriri.

Selling Igbo Nigerian President to other Nigerians
We must sell Igbo Nigerian President to other Nigerians but first we must make the effort to understand our past and present relations with other Nigerians, and the reasons for them.

I. Understanding, and Making Friends with Other Nigerians.

Making friends with other Nigerians, especially our host communities is most necessary. The Igbo man is not hated in Nigeria, he may be feared and envied (jealoused). These feelings (of fear and envy) are also quite natural and should be easily understood. An Igbo person comes to a non-Igbo town, that is, among another ethnic group, apparently empty-handed. Often he starts with the most menial of jobs, and soon begins to grow. He achieves great wealth, builds houses, lives and appears to exude greater confidence than even the original owners of the land. What more fertile soil can there be for jealousy. If that Igbo adds, as some often do, loud-mouth to his success, should resentment of him by members of his host community require any further explanation? There may also be the fear that he will upset the existing social system. Thus he arouses fear and jealousy and some resentment. What should the Igbo do in the circumstance? It is only fair to think of our being the **horse**, "if we were the horse". (The story is told of a horse keeper who came out of his house, looked and finding no horse in the stable, entered the stable picked up, chewed some hay and asked himself, "if I were a horse which way would I go"). The Igbo should ask himself, "If I were an average indigene in this community, what or how would I think about this stranger that is me"? The proper reaction for the Igbo is to understand the problem and make friends with members of the host communities, discover and respect the dos and don'ts of the communities, try to reduce the resentments by making philanthropic and other sacrifices to appease the hosts, and very importantly, be careful with the tongue. Of course, in verbal behavior towards the hosts, the Igbo should realize that they are susceptible to being seen as arrogant – the arrogance that comes with success. They should therefore behave accommodatingly. Clearly, the death of Ojukwu has shown that the Igbo is not hated, he may be feared and envied. Really, we must not stop thanking other Nigerians for the huge outpouring of emotions at the death of Ikemba and the contributions made by every group of Nigerians to the success of his burial.

The marketing of Igbo Nigerian President to other Nigerians should emphasize the benefits to other groups of Nigerians of a Nigerian President who is a thorough-bred Igbo. These benefits arise from some obvious factors and some factors that are not so obvious, like:

I.   Igbo and One Nigeria
The Igbo have voted, *with their feet,* for one Nigeria, have made home of everywhere in Nigeria, and are busy developing everywhere in Nigeria. Of all ethnic groups in Nigeria, the Igbo have greatest vested interest in one Nigeria,

even, in spite of Nigeria/Biafra conflict occasioned by the pogrom. In consequence, an Igbo Nigerian President must be interested in fairly even development of everywhere in Nigeria, if he/she is to satisfy his/her Igbo brothers/sisters who are everywhere in Nigeria. An Igbo Nigerian President will therefore govern for all without discrimination. For the same reason he/she will be the best custodian of Nigerian unity.

II.   For other Nigerians, an Igbo Nigeria President will affirm their sense of equity justice and fairness. This will boost patriotism. Of the tripod that makes up Nigeria, only the Igbo has not produced a President of Nigeria. As already stated, every one of the six geopolitical zones in Nigeria, except the Southeast, shall (by 5015) have supplied the Chief Executive Officer of Nigeria for more than five years. And every Nigerian of age knows that the civil war was imposed by Nigeria. For, by the pogrom, Nigeria declared her rejection of Easterners, and when those rejected did not reject themselves, but sought to build a world of their own, Nigeria changed mind and made war to keep Nigeria one!

III.   **An Igbo Nigerian President Should Lead to some Positive Elements of Igbo Culture Being Observed and Assimilated by Other Nigerians. Examples Are:**
(a) Igbo Egalitarianism and Upward Social Mobility
Nigerians need to develop their economy. This requires "all hands on the deck". Economic effort is not for the few and the rest of the people living off the few. In Igbo society, every man is responsible for his family: to feed, to house, to cloth and to educate/train. Igbo society extols upward mobility. The parent prays for the children to surpass then in achievement. The master prays for his apprentice to be "bigger" than himself. A Nigerian President who is Igbo is bound to lead to faster cultural assimilation in the area of self-efforts. No society in Nigeria today accepts a situation of a few stupendously rich, with the masses in abject poverty.

Youth restiveness, from OPC, Niger Delta Groups, MASSOB, kidnapping, Boko Haram, etc. are said to have arisen basically from the poverty, mass unemployment and the hopelessness of the youths – including educated youths. The Boko Haram is today being exploited by very strange bedfellows.

(b) Igbo Achievement Orientation/Motivation
The celebrated Igbo achievement orientation/motivation will rub off on other groups and this should quicken the pace of economic development. Individuals must make the effort to achieve economic success. One way this cultural assimilation works is this: with an Igbo as President, some non-Igbo may see the Igbo as "also born to rule". The positive compensating thought is that other Nigerians should engage in, or even invade, those areas hitherto considered as preserves of the Igbo. What Igbo can do others can do too. They too can succeed in commerce, industry and finance.

(c) Igbo Ethic of Hardwork-induced Success
This is seen in the consuming thirst for education, entrepreneurship, innovativeness, hard work, doggedness, focus, respect for all work, menial and others etc. This aggressive pursuit of welfare is the result of the combination of egalitarianism and achievement orientation/motivation and the belief that God created all of us equal, we are equal before God, Who has given each person the right and ability to pursue his welfare. These are good for the economic transformation of Nigeria. Independent Nigeria has been a failure in economic development under Hausa/Fulani and, to a great extent under, Yoruba leadership. The Igbo have made economic success of everywhere they have been in Nigeria. The emergence of an Igbo Nigeria President may signal the commencement of the actualization of that greatness which the world has known as only potential. With Igbo Nigerian President it will be Nigeria period in the sun – Nigeria's time, or turn, to shine!!! Economic welfare will reach all – including

the down- trodden and the abandonment of offsprings must end, a large middleclass will develop.

Thus, with Igbo Nigerian President, the poor gets rich, the rich gets richer and the gap between the rich and the poor narrows!!!

Ingredients of the Delicious Soup: The Logistics

There will be need for all manners of publicity: meetings (local and overseas) talks, travels, letter writing (to individuals, churches and mosques, town, state and country unions, student bodies, special publics : women groups, civil society groups, professional bodies), pamphleteering, saturation bombing in electronic and print media (cultivating media men, retainerships, press conferencing, features writing, special pages, the world wide web, internet campaigns, twitters, face books, blogs), special location campaigns: in motor stations, in buses, in markets, churches and mosques, bars and hotels, special events venues, through event planners, MCs, sympathetic organizers etc. We shall go to every zone and possibly every state. The publicity aspect is very extensive and expensive. And there will also be the need for, sometimes, costly investigations of the potential candidates. In terms of funding the demands must be very high. And the corporate campaign should continue even after the choice of candidate(s)

Yours for Nigeria as a Super Power!

24

FOR ND'IGBO: THE WAY FORWARD WITH ONE NIGERIA.

2013 Madona University Convocation Lecture

(Okwadike, Dr. Chukwuemeka Ezeife)

Protocols

Introduction

We the Igbo, have voted with our feet for one Nigeria and have invested in other parts of Nigeria more than we have invested in our home base – living perhaps too much, by our dictum: *Ebe onye bi ka ona awachi* (where one lives one mends). We were even forcibly prevented from building a world of our own when we were rejected. It remains true, however, that *emecha a chi ekweghi, asi ka abulu abulu, asi ka acha a acha a.* The way I see things, *odi ka chi oga ekwe.* That is why I have chosen to speak on: For Nd'Igbo: The Way Forward with One Nigeria!!!

One digression, I should let *ndi nwe ozu,* understand my politics. At the **Institute of International Affairs, Victoria Island, Lagos,** where I launched my book: **"Remarking Nigeria with Progressivism"** (in 1987), I told the Igbo and Yoruba, who dominated the audience, that: should they, the

Igbo and the Yoruba continue, as they were then, moving like parallel lines in Nigerian politics, they would remain parallel slaves in the system. *Onye aghogbulu ka agbalu. Onweghi ndu obuna Chineke nyelu uburu ka nke onyelu anyi. We* just have to be awake and alert. Onye aghugho nwua, onye aghugho enie ya. That explains to you, my role in the Abiola saga and my membership of Alliance for Democracy, even though, I was a founding member of the G-34, which formed PDP. I gave a similar message at Etinan, more than three years ago, at the funeral of ex-Governor Akpan Isimen. When called upon to give a tribute on behalf of ex-Governors, I said clearly that I brought no tribute, that I brought a bomb instead! After the unease, I proceeded to explode my bomb: "for as long as the Southeast and Southsouth continue to play lone rangers in the Nigerian system, for so long will they continue to eat frustrations. But, should the two zones speak, approximately, with one voice, what they ask of Nigeria is about what they will get!" Knowing this now, it will not surprise you that, on 10th August 2010, at Yar'Adua Centre, of the more than 20 Igbo "leaders", who met with the big wigs of the North, I alone, came out opposing the communiqué that gave Igbo support to the North for 2011 Presidential election, in return for Northern support for Igbo in 2015. I respect the views of my opponents, but nothing in my dream or imagination, remotely supports the supposition that a Northern President instead of fighting for 2nd, 3rd terms, and thereafter, life Presidency, would yield to the Igbo, the Presidency in 2015. But only God is Omniscient!

Sorry for the digressions, but I should also let you know that the Southeast, Southsouth and Southwest, under the auspices of Southern Nigerian Peoples' Assembly, have adopted a common position on the modalities for national Dialogue! Now straight to the topic!

Nd'Igbo: The Way Forward with One Nigeria.

Social processes have this characteristic that they seem to

possess limitless elasticity – it looks like you can keep pushing and stretching them without end. Yet they end up, sometimes, snapping – after reaching and passing their elastic limits! However, where the spirit of God is at work, involved or invoked, close to that limit of elasticity – close to the point of snapping, creative forces, corrective messages and salvaging ideas flood the minds of many at the same time – forcing rethinking, re-evaluation, change of mind and attitude, leading to crucial regenerative modifications or changes in direction! Is this the point at which we are with the situation of Nd'Igbo in Nigeria today? Are regenerative ideas evolving from many minds? Is this the reason for the call by the Madona University? Is it also behind the big call by the Southeast Development Association? Is this the essence of the planned, January 2014, Igbo Colloquium? A movie that is about to be released, seems to rehearse the Igbo problems and their possible solutions so intensively. The author claims divine inspiration. He may be right. His ideas are great and emphatic; the look too meritorious to have come by mere chance. And the time is most apt!

Yes! Our problems are many and varied: the ones we created for ourselves, the ones other peoples brought on us, and the ones divine favour to us generated against us from other peoples. If we are not summary, we may have to be driven out by the owners of this hall before even making a dent on the topic.

I choose to summarily speak on our problems and prospects, under the following sub-heads: The Bad and Ugly, The Good, Great and Glorious, and The Way Forward.

The Bad and Ugly
How are the mighty fallen are and the weapons of the war perished? Are the Igbo, before whom the white man confessed inferiority complex, and most Nigerians adored in awe, are today, scorned and despised - the wretched of the country? It may not be quite so. But the once highly envied, is

today scorned. Or, is the scorn only relative to level of the former envy. They are blamed for many things! They are blamed for blaming themselves! One accomplished Middle Belt politician declared that nothing made him more angry than hearing some Igbo bemoan or regret, their decision to go to war, rather than celebrating the courage of that decision and their ingenuity, inventiveness and tenacity, which converted a proclaimed "three – months police action," to almost three years of all-out war, even, with major foreign powers fighting on the Nigerian side! Our women are said to be ten for a Kobo, in contrast to an epoch when it was said that some men would avoid washing hands after shaking Igbo women. There are these major issues in the **Bad and the Ugly:**

1. The great and celebrated Achievement motivation/success consciousness, of our people, now without the foundation supporting values, ethics and social control, has turned to a very serious problem: we have become money mongers, stopping at nothing to "succeed". Our people are dying in their thousands in the Sahara and Kalahari deserts; in the Mediterranean Sea; they are dying of burst drugs in their stomachs; dying as factory hands in strange lands; they are dehumanized in Libya; they are congested and dying in the prisons of China, Japan, South Korea and even South Africa. Cheating has become confused with trading and, fakery is not frowned at; we have moved from Hoo Haa, the truth and honesty, to copying other peoples and talking from two sides of our months. Some Igbo men, though yet very few, have started begging in urban Nigeria. We are even learning to run loose nuclear families, where we were well known for our closely knit extended families. And the idea of not effectively planning for tomorrow has caught the fancy of a few.

2. We are killed for religious beliefs, economic successes, we are even repatriated from our mother land — the land in which, of the major groups, we are the only autochthonous!

3. Our traditions are grossly desecrated with even traditional weddings being celebrated in strange lands. Are some not even being buried where ever they happen to die?

4. The Igbo-enwe Eze republicanism and apparent leaderlessness is on the ascendency. So are centrifugal forces, and the excessive individualism, caused partly by the *Ibenne* Taboos broken during the civil war, which made angry relations *take off* to anywhere, at all, at the end of the war. It remains a major problem.

5. The trading of inter-generational blames is on the rise: the young say the old have ruined their future and are not showing the right way. The old blame the youth of mannerlessness, consciencelessness and holding nothing dear, except their self-interest, most of which, they see, as perverted.

The main ugly problems are still stinking: the abuse of achievement consciousness, copying the worst from other Nigerians and foreigners, the un-cleansed *Ibenne* Taboos and the blood of the un-mourned and un-buried dead shrieking to high heavens from various areas. There is the specially bad case of **"One Man Nigeria Ltd"**, which is threatened by the Plazas, Malls, Shoprites etc. The last Governorship contest in Anambra State has capped the horrors: the cast was the poorest, party men from other states carted away billions of naira from Anambra on the pretext of candidate selection. Our Lords Justices, who have turned to their Lord's injustices, had their field day. It is possible that the bottom has been hit. The elasticity has reached its limit. An upturn seems inevitable, because we are a people blessed by God. Time for us to make up with our Lord God!

The Good, Great and Glorious

Do we have anything to celebrate? Shut up anybody who tells you we don't!

1.   Show me that group of Nigerians, who have been out of central power for about half a century and still maintains half as much unity, cohesion and coherence as the Igbo. Look around, don't be myopic. Don't look Westwards because their tight grip on the Nigerian press media squeezes water out of political, rocks for them, and they have controlled central power. Think of the North! Be objective! What has happened to the "born-to-rule mentality". When I was naming Anambra state "Home for All", Sokoto state chose "Born to Rule". Can we trade the excessive individualism, born out of our republicanism and egalitarianism for their assumed conformity? Four tributaries are feeding the Boko Haram river. The fastest flowing, has its source in the social structure of Hausa/Fulani. We should kindly approach our Northern friends, show brotherly understanding, and appeal to them to look into the long term and find that, like us, they should give up fads and join the train for the permanence of one-Nigeria. They should not be the ones to rock the boat. The other people, with whom they are dealing, know the truth. They can distinguish between ignorant boast, from positions based on building on sandy foundation – short term advantages, that, if pushed too far, may lead to long-term ruin. They should also remember their association with, and the support they received from our heroes past, and their sabotage of our heroes present, and recalculate matters and relations. Odua may be an attractive idea but it is a poor route to take where there is a clear chance of so transforming Nigeria that things begin to work and the large and mighty market for commerce, finance and manufactures lies sprawling at Yoruba feet. No Nigerian group, large or small, can walk away from an effectively transformed Nigeria, feeling triumphantly! With the Igbo in Nigeria, the leadership of Africa, and over some chunk of the rest of the world, is open to this country.

2.   Should we not celebrate the foresight of our leaders and the resilience of our people? No transformation of Nigeria can really be great and effective if it totally ignores the Aburi Accord! Positive ideas are already bursting from various Igbo minds. As we peep into the New Transformed Nigeria, we catch the glimpse of the Golden Age of the Nd'Igbo – the Igbo Union Days – returning with advancements.

3.   Our King-making Role: We can claim, without qualms, the responsibility for making Jonathan the President of Nigeria and thereby sowing the seed for the permanence of one Nigeria, which is now about to be effectively transformed to make things work.

4.   We are, so the World Bank States, the highest developed rural Africa. Imagine what will happen if we think home and pay greater attention to investing in our home land? Of course, we must think home, but we should also remember that the resources that built the most developed rural Africa was earned from outside that area.

5.   In every area of Nigeria, we are the most populous group after the native indigenes. Consider the potential it holds for the good governance and rapid development Nigeria.

6.   Our sons and daughters are making waves at the frontiers of technology in foreign lands, this is well known.

7.   Only the Igbo, of all African, Asian and Australian peoples, are given the honour of recognition for contributions made to the building of the United States of America. This honour is institutionalized in an Igbo Village in Virginia.

8.   Our tolerance of political disaster must end with the chaos of 2013 Anambra gubernatorial election!

9.   Tell it loudly and tell it everywhere: the Igbo are God's gifts to Nigeria. Is there any place the impact of Igbo developmental, commercializing, civilizing, motivational zeal and efforts have not reached? Is there any such place in Nigeria? "Anywhere you don't find an Igbo, leave the place in a hurry, it is not fit for human habitation", so say some indigenes!

The Way Forward

The Way Forward for Nd'Igbo should include the following considerations and institutional efforts.

1. **Internal Integration**
    a. **Anambra Vs Igbo.**

Anambra people must learn to be less mouthy or boastful, and know that respect in addressing (calling the names of) seniors and elders, is expected in the cultures of other Igbo. That is why *"Da a"* or *"De e"* are used. Nd'Igbo in Diaspora may consider instituting Councils of Traditional Leadership, with the chairman, who shall be *Ochi/Eze* Igbo, should stay in office, if healthy, for a maximum of 10 years, and the position should rotate among the Igbo states in the area.

b. **Ebonyi Vs Igbo.** The Government of Ebonyi state should commission a study of rural and urban Igboland to discover which states' people dominate others. The study should confirm the more than complete reversal of the former dominance of Abakaliki town by other Igbo. It is, however, now known that the Governor of Ebonyi State is not an obstacle to some levels of Eastern Integration. The Zonal Government, which the governors may take turns to chair, may take the form of some loose Common Services Arrangement. It is a matter of agreement among the states. In the extreme case of disagreement a, category, called Federally Administered States, may be created.

2. Boasting Ohanaeze as the apex effective umbrella organization. Current undermining of Ohanaeze should stop. Whatever are the residual problems can, and should, be sorted out

3. SEPA: A Federated, all-inclusive, Igbo political body, should be created under the auspices of the Southern Nigerian People's Assembly, just as the Southsouth has SSPA and the Southwest is making efforts to bring groups under Yoruba Unity Forum, and possibly form SWPA as an arm of the SNPA.

4. Creating, and Swearing in *"Okwu Muo Nd'Igbo"*, A small body of about 15 persons, each of whom should be

70years or above, each sworn not to fight for political office, elected or appointed, and each committing, in open church ceremonies, ending an Ecumenical Service in Enugu, that where personal interest clashes with Igbo interest, personal interest must be extinguished! This body should pronounce on major issues affecting the political leadership of Southeast states. Its decisions cannot be ignored by anyone without consequence. *Olugo na Omume!*

5.   Minimum Integration in the Southeast Common Services, should include Zonal Police, Transportation, Power, Water, Ecological Problems, Security, and the Reversing of Property and activity locations in favour of the Igbo Home base.

6.   Time to Exploit our spread in Nigeria by

1.   Making friends with host communities. The Town unions must educate new arrivals on the dos and don'ts of the host communities and lead in deliberate efforts to forge relations with the leadership of the host and the other peoples in the area.

2.   Igbo Corporate Interests and persons, should, through philanthropy, give back some of their earnings to host communities. Almagiri problems should no longer be allowed. Those children should join our own children in Schools. Necessary individual and Town Union efforts should be encouraged.

3.   We should make Deliberate Efforts to cultivate relationship of agape love across ethnic and religious lines.

4.   Where possible, Igbo Schools in Diaspora should be revived.

5.   We must Return to our Good old Social Values:

The churches, schools, clubs, Town Unions etc should endeavour to revive ethics and good values, including respect for age, position, and good reason. Sources of personal wealth should be clear before ever a person is concerned for honours in church or society. We should also encourage the return to solving Igbo problems in good old Igbo ways, where fair.

6   We must learn to invest together in joint Ventures, which should outlive the founders. One man business is doomed in this day and age.

7. It remains to regret that what makes us Igbo is not really in our blood, but in our culture and up-bringing, which includes our language.

Maximum efforts must be made to keep Igbo up bringing alive and well.

CONCLUSION

Brethren, Sons and Daughters of Igbo land, Great members and friends of the **Madona University,** the bones shall rise again!! The bones shall rise again!! Please join me to shout it: THE BONES SHALL RISE AGAIN!!! How fast they rise depends on you and me!

May God forgive us our sins!

God bless Madona University!

May God turn his smiling face on us!

God bless Nd'Igbo!!!

God bless Ndi Nigeria Nile!!

Yours for Nigeria as a Super Power!

25

BIAFRA: INJUSTICE CAN MAKE IGBO REPUBLIC POSSIBLE –EZEIFE

Interview on The Sun Newspaper, 23rd April 2018

By Jeff Amechi Agbodo, Onitsha; Vincent Kalu

Former governor of Anambra State, Dr. Chukwuemeka Ezeife, has said injustice against South East zone can make Igbo republic possible.
Ezeife said there are more indications of discrimination and inequities against the South East geo-political zone even without mentioning Python Dance or the whereabouts of the leader of the Indigenous People of Biafra (IPOB), Nnamdi Kanu.

Ezeife warned that if the present administration fails to correct the wrongs against the South East zone, then, Biafra may become an inevitability, if the Igbo are pushed to the frustrating point of asking the question, 'what is life worth?

He made the remarks at the weekend, while speaking on the topic: "Political discrimination and inequity issues in national development," at a seminar organised by the Diocese on the Niger, Anglican Communion. He said among the six major protocol offices in government (President, Vice President, Senate President, Chief Justice, Speaker and Secretary to

Government), none is held by a person from the Southeast, just as nobody from the zone attends the National Security Council (NSC) meeting.

He prayed that God should plant in the mind of President Muhammadu Buhari, the idea of emergency restructuring of the country, stressing that it is the surest way to keep Nigeria one.

"How do we, from the South East zone, react to the president's declaration for second term? Do we join the heavy political noise against it? I really doubt if the idea of second term came from the president. Even if he has it in mind, the most promising and effective action to take is to run to God."

"The Bible says 'the heart of a king is in the hands of God'. Let us pray God to manage or manipulate the heart of Buhari to realise the unreasonableness and dangers of this second term. Let Buhari's mind, resolutely, reject that idea. But, we should remember that God allowed Buhari to take over the presidency of Nigeria.

"Buhari should convene a well constituted emergency sovereign body, with all necessary powers, including the power to take necessary actions, should he run out of time on the basis of the present time table or arrangements. The raw materials for the body are down and, seriously, we don't need more than six months to accomplish the task," he said.

Ezeife said restructuring is the enduring and effective solution to rampant political discrimination.

"Restructuring takes persecution power from the centre. Each region cares for her people's interest, so, exposure to the whims and caprice of the central authority is greatly reduced.

"Should Buhari urgently and effectively restructure the country, his name will be indelible in the story of Nigeria, and all future generations will be singing his praise," Ezeife said.

Meanwhile, a group, Biafra Nations Youth League (BNYL), has called on President Muhammadu Buhari to forget his second term ambition in the interest of the country.

Reacting to the declaration of the president to seek re-election, the group called on him to concentrate his efforts to see how he can turn around the fortune of the country before the expiration of his tenure.

A press statement signed by the group's leader, Princewill Obuka-Richard, emphasised that though the constitution allows him to seek reelection, it will be counterproductive to go on with his ambition, given the tensed situation in the country.

"Yes, we know that the President Buhari has the backing of the constitution to seek reelection, but, if he is a true patriot, he should bury that ambition and work harder to improve the country before the end of his tenure, next year."

"The polity has been overheated for some years now, and his coming back may not help matters," the statement said.

The group called on the president to recognise the region known as Biafra, and queried why politicians from the South East and South South zones have not been able to present the position of the regions to him, saying, "all we want is for him to recognise the region known as Biafra and respect the demands for her independence and we will extend a hand of friendship to his government, as that would be his greatest achievement.

"Some politicians from South East and South South have refused to present the position of our people to President Buhari; that we are not concerned with his re-election, but in recognition of Biafra.

"Buhari's government will be one of the best in the world, if Biafra is recognised. Achieving that is not difficult, all we just need is recognition and we will be glad that Buhari's government becomes the first to recognise us."

The group also threatened to attack herdsmen if the government continues to keep mute, while they endlessly massacre people and destroy communities.

Meanwhile, BNYL leader has paid tribute at the funeral of the late Biafran Army Commander, Col. Joe Achuzia in Asaba, Delta State.

26

OPEN LETTER TO NORTHERN ELDERS

WITH REFERENCE TO THEIR LETTER TO THE PRESIDENT

(Okwadike, Dr. Chukwuemeka Ezeife)

1. The Northern Elders' letter was before the President's trip to China. Now, I call on all Nigerians to congratulate President Buhari on the China Agreements. He got the confidence, interest and support of the very sagacious leaders of China. Of course, we should know that China signed the Agreements out of clever self interest, not out of altruism! We must, therefore, be careful with the implementation of the Agreements, to achieve a win-win result, otherwise, China may win as we lose! I call on every Nigerian to also pray God to redirect our President to the right path, for economic progress, people's welfare and socio-political calmness. Buhari's success is success for us all!!!

2. I must state my dismay and protest against the use of the eloquent, elegant, and very intelligent, gentleman Amb. Maitama Sule, as signatory to the Northern Elders Letter. It is a desiccation of the one symbol of One Nigeria from the deep North - a person seen by many as a personification of One Nigeria. Why didn't they use Dr. Junaid Mohammed, the

irredentist deep Northerner, who appears to be disdainful of other Nigerians.

3. I salute the courage of the Northern Elder's in pointing out some of the critical negative factors responsible for the rapid decline of the Nigerian economy (the collapse of naira, serious loss of values in the stock market, unprecedented suffering of Nigerian people etc) within less than one year of President Buhari's leadership. Your letter also implies the inaccessibility of the President for advice by those who should know. Many will agree with your call for: (1) immediate establishment of an Economic Management Team; (2) raising the "quality of advice and support the President requires"; (3) the President "to conclude the appointment of key officers and advisers"!! The Northern Elders did not add that these officers and advisers may not all be available from Daura or even Katsina. They observed the "evident weakness and gaps in skills, competences, experience and (even) integrity". They also appear to believe the "allegations that Boko Haram still has substantial presence in many Areas near Maiduguri and other towns and villages. They were doubtful about the "quality of intelligence, and integrity of the leadership of the Armed Forces". These are good points coming from a friendly direction and must, therefore, be taken seriously and handled with the urgency they deserve.

4. I find it unnecessary to point out the weaknesses of some points made in your letter. The main claim that the North is "short changed" in capital budgetary allocations is an empirical matter. You "studied" the budget and must have noticed the dominance of the three zones of the North, especially the Northwest in budgetary allocations. It may be a matter of how much more the North must have, in excess of the South, for the back-bone North not to feel short changed. On the claim of Southern dominance in recurrent expenditure, I am sure you know that not all recurrent

expenditure is personnel emolument goes to the South, according to you. Recurrent expenditure includes operational and logistics costs of Governance - the oiling of the machinery of Governance. For example, the trip to China, to Saudi Arabia, Abu Dhabi etc., contributions to OIC and Saudi-sponsored Anti- terrorism fund, payment for power, fuel, stationery etc, are all recurrent expenditure. They are not paid to the South. On the North being the back bone of Buhari's Administration, it should be noted that the backbone of anything, or body, or an administration, should be an asset not a liability - or a leakage. The North takes, by far, more than it contributes to the coffers of Nigeria. Neither in funding, nor in expertise, can it be said that the North is the backbone of a Nigerian Government. Or, did they mean that the North voted for Buhari most. That is in the past, even if it is the truth. What about the West, from which Buhari is not. We cannot talk of the North as backbone and at the same time lament about "poverty in the North increasing relative to the rest of the country.... a serious threat to the region and the unity and survival of' our dear country. Another point is your recommendation on IPOB. The Law you mentioned includes: respect for court decisions, human rights, right to self determination, which the United Nations has removed from the internal affairs of a state. The Sun Newspaper summarized your recommendation to Buhari as to "crush" IPOB. How mature is this? I hope that good sense will prevail.

5. Answering some of the issues raised in the Elder's letter is like chasing rats while the house is burning. The Fulani North does have the right to, and should advise, their son, on winning ways: in politics, economics and social relations.

The Current Issues On Which The Elders Should Advise The President Include:

(1). Neglect of the Southeast/Biafra.

Buhari takes action that makes non-pretenders in the Southeast feel exposed to gross inequity, injustice as unfairness, marginalisation, discrimination, not seen as full-fledged Nigeria nationals or not qualified to hold the highest office in the land etc.

Some of these actions include: (i) not including, even one, Southeast person, in the President's first 40 appointments, (ii) the withdrawal of the appointment of an Easterner at Nimasa three days after announcement, something similar happened at another very major national organisation, (iii) failure to appoint a Southeast person to even the sixth and least protocol position in Government in a six-geopolitical-zone structure (the position of SGF), (iv) no Igbo person in the National Security Council, (v) packing dangerous Boko Haram prisoners to Ekwulobia, in Anambra State, and leaving them there for very long, in spite of massive protests from all and sundry, (vi) not giving enough key ministries to the Southeast persons, (vii) spilling the blood of Eastern youths - at Aba Onitsha and many other places, (viii) the impunity in not respecting the rule of law but keeping Nnamdi Kanu in detention after a court of competent jurisdiction had ordered his release on bail, (ix) body language of undisguised hatred for a part of the peoples one had sworn to be fair to and to protect. (x) There is also the recent case of handcuffing Mr. Metu, while other accused persons, whose cases were more heinous, were swaggering into the court. It has been asserted that the body language of the President gave the officials the motivation to do that, hoping, by that, to please the President.

In the way, some military persons visited my village compound night of 29th Dec. 2015 - the day the Punch

241

Newspaper published an interview in which I said that Buhari is pushing the Southeast out of Nigeria. This is what Biafra is about - a reaction to unfairness's, injustices and inequities against the Southeast by the President. Why Biafra now?

(2) DSS Authoritarian Dictatorship and Ethnic Bias.

As recently as Saturday the 16th of April, 2016 the DSS stopped a book launch at the Women Development Centre, Awka. Their reasons: (i) The book launch honours Ojukwu, (ii) Okwadike, Dr. Ezeife CON and Dr. Pat Utomi have spoken in favour of Biafra Agitators, therefore, they should not have been included in the programme for the book launch. In spite of my efforts reaching the Commissioner of Police and Director SSS, Police and Soldiers matched to the alternative venue - the White View Hotel, and dispersed the crowd who had to run for dear life. The impression is strong that the DSS is the power behind the AK 47-touting Fulani Herdsmen, especially after their unsubstantiated allegation of a shallow grave in Abia State. It is not in the long term interest of Nigeria, nor of Fulani in Nigeria, that the Herdsmen maraud Nigeria, rampaging, raping, killing, sacking and taking over farm lands. And it cannot be in the long term interest of Nigeria that farm lands are taken over by with AK 47 or through a Grazing Commission under any ill conceived Grazing Law - whether or not members of the NASS can be sufficiently induced to approve the proposed law. Since this is an issue concerning land, *nso ani* will not allow that - especially for southern legislators. We should not institute a source of permanent conflict which a law on Grazing Reserve will represent.

CALLING ALL NIGERIANS

Nigerians: Northern Fulani, Northern Hausa, Other Northern Groups; Yoruba of every Shade; Southsouth Peoples, Igbo nine; we are playing - toying - with the gem God gave us! The truth is, if Nigeria is organised for things to work, and this is easily possible, starting with some of the recommendations of 2014 Conference, or simply adopting zonal structure of government, no group can work away from Nigeria, smiling!! It will appear that those who need Nigeria most are toying most with her survival!!! Yes! Although today Nigeria seems to be a comprehensive failure.

Reasonable persons believe that God has a special purpose for creating Nigeria - even though He used the instrumentality of British Imperialism to bring her about. What could be God's purpose for creating Nigeria? It seems clear that God intended Nigeria to be the big brother and rallying point for all blacks. And God's bounteous resource endowments on Nigeria must be to enable her achieve that Manifest Destiny, which has to involve Nigeria developing into a Super Power among nations, thereby raising the dignity and respect of Blacks on earth. To wipe away the shame of slavery from the faces all of Blacks, has to be the ultimate Manifest Destiny of Nigeria. And God endowed Nigeria with every ingredient she needs to develop into a Super Power among nations.

What has been the result? So far, it has been colossal failure, unmitigated! The Nigerian humans, especially the men, are working tirelessly to mess up God's design for our country. The main cause of the total failure of Nigeria is monumental corruption which has saturated every element of the social structure. Far from raising the respect and dignity of Blacks, Nigeria has become the generator and accumulator of shame to all Blacks. And it has now come to the stage that all Blacks are being suffocated with shame emanating from Nigeria.

Yes, we Nigerians have failed in our Manifest Destiny, and have no basis for continued existence, except as a totally changed country!!! We must become the opposite of what we are now. There must now be zero tolerance of corruption in Nigeria. No half measures can do it!! Zero tolerance must be zero tolerance. We must achieve success in re-making

Nigeria!! Because the Almighty God, who gave us this mission and gave us the where withal to achieve it, does not change. Man can try and appear to succeed for a time. But man cannot permanently mess up God's design. It must be Operation Total Clean Up. **Away** with all corrupt institutions! **Away** with all existing political organisations and parties. **Away** with all agents of corruption. Away with untruths, deceit and lies. No more sacred cows! No more untouchables! To keep Nigeria clean to achieve her Manifest Destiny, is a task we must commit to.

May I take this opportunity to condemn bad mouthing by my people; the comment on the Northern Elders letter attributed to a Biafran advocate should indeed properly be called unprintable. We gain nothing senselessly antagonizing people. There is superior wisdom in making friends with our neighbours and host communities. We gain, not lose by making friends with other Nigerians.

27

WE MUST "BEGIN AGAIN"

Dr. Chukwuemeka Ezeife

Sun Newspaper 20th November 2016

By Onyedika Agbedo

Former governor of Anambra State, Dr. Chukwuemeka Ezeife, is a busy man on the political terrain even though he has taken the back stage and joined the league of Nigeria's elder statesmen. His activism on the turf is rooted in the fact that he is ever at home with trending political issues in the country and is hardly left out of any national discourse. With his Igbo kinsmen moaning of marginalisation under the incumbent administration of President Muhammadu Buhari, he has constantly spoken against the development without minding whose ox was gored.

Off the beat, however, Ezeife is an avid reader of books that keep his mind in form. "Reading is what I enjoy very well. I read all kinds of books including books on different religious faiths, fiction, history and autobiographies. I have read the Qur'an for about four times," Ezeife, who is a practicing Christian, noted.

He noted that the variety of books he reads expands his worldview and makes it possible for him to easily understand other people.

He said: "The books I read have made it possible for me to understand other people. In fact, if you give me connection and wealth, I can turn the world around. It is a big claim but it is something I can do. Given the chance, I can remove religious bickering from the world. I can remove religion as a problem from the world and make peace amongst all kinds of people. And that is what God wants us to do. It is total misunderstanding for people to be accusing, fighting and killing each other and making the other person to be unhappy. That is not what God intended."

Ezeife explained further: "For example, I am a Christian. But did I choose to be a Christian? I was a Christian on arrival. Musa, who is a Muslim, was a Muslim on arrival. We did not choose to be either Christians or Muslims. We all became either Christian or Muslim based on the culture or religion we met at birth. Whatever you meet when you come is what you accept and it is difficult to change. "The day I was born into my father's family in Igbo-Ukwu, there was no single Muslim there. If you go beyond Igbo-Ukwu to the whole of Aguata Local Government Area and even the entire Anambra State, there were no Muslims. So, I was Christian on arrival and so was Musa. Where you are born to a large extent determines the culture or religion you practice. If you are born into a family in Kano, your chances of being Muslim are very high; the chance becomes even higher if one is born into a family in Sokoto. So, we as creations of God, do we have the right to question other people's faith? The way we became Christians on arrival was the way other people became Muslims on arrival and only God could determine that. Do we now question God?"

The elder statesman, therefore, called for a reorientation among Nigerians. He submitted: "Nigeria has failed socially, politically and economically. The foundation for our failure is in monumental corruption, which has eaten deep into every element of our social structure. The only way out is to eliminate corruption by cleaning up Nigeria. We have bagged a 'B.A' as a country. The 'B.A' means "Begin Again" and we must begin again. We must fight corruption; we must remove all the institutions that created corruption. We must do away with APC, PDP, APGA and all the political parties in the country today and begin again. When we do that, we must make sure that anybody who wants to go into politics in the country is doing so with the aim of serving the people and not to serve himself. If that is done, we will begin to found a new nation, which will be able to accomplish its manifest destiny. God has a purpose for creating Nigeria and I suspect that that purpose is that she becomes a super power, big brother and rallying point for all Blacks. That is Nigeria's manifest destiny. But from the way we are going, we have already failed. Nobody should be pointing at any person. We failed collectively and must rise collectively and fight to liberate Nigeria from corruption and allow her achieve her manifest destiny."

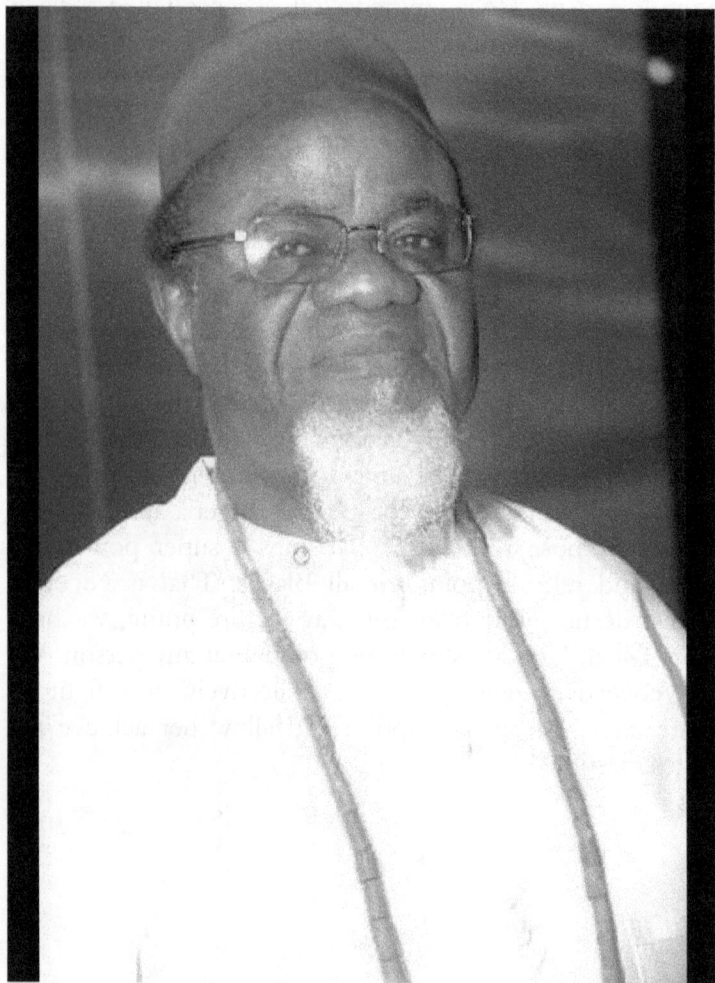

PART V

CONTRIBUTIONS:
NIGERIA – DEMOCRACY & STATE OF
THE ECONOMY

28

DEMOCRACY AND GOOD GOVERNANCE: IS THERE A NEXUS?

Nwosu M. Eze, MBA, CFA, FCNA, DEd, PhD.
National Institute for Legislative & Democratic Studies, National Assembly
Tel: 234-803 328 0224, E-mail: mail4eze@yahoo.co.uk

Abstract

This paper examines the concepts of democracy and good governance with an assessment of their dynamics and the mechanism of their workings towards the realization of a viable political system of a country. It pays more attention to the relationships and effects that exist between the variables and their boundaries with regard to their elements, contending that, for good governance to be achievable in a country, the elements of democracy are significantly necessary conditions and if democracy becomes an adopted ideology, such a governmental process must definitely guarantee the needed good governance. Determining the nexus between democracy and good governance and ensuring that the dividends of democracy expected to reach the grass-root at all levels of administration has become a subject of debate in most jurisdictions. The author argues that, where this expected process becomes a mirage, then, such a government ideal is wishful, not credible, popular and legitimate, and cannot serve the people's interests. The paper recommends that where exists a political system that lacks credible elements and principles of democracy vis-à-vis good governance such a government is deemed unpopular.

Keywords – *Democracy, Good Governance, Element, Necessary, Condition.*

1.0 Introduction

Democracy as a term is viewed from three principal contexts: concept, ideology and system. **As a concept**, it is a terminology or word in the dictionary of politics, used for interpretations and explanations of issues, and hence, it is commonly used even by a layman on the street or in the household. **As an ideology**, it is a thought conceived as a practice and which is upheld by a group or a society or even a state or nation, determining the pattern by which a governmental system flows to give the excitements and the contentment that the ruled desire. **As a system**, it is a process or mechanism which explains the political life and culture of a people within a country where the principle of the "General Will" as postulated by Rousseau is upheld or where 'society' is preserved as the property of all in the words of John Locke. These three contexts could help to establish whether there is a nexus between democracy and good governance.

The need for government has been central to human society ever since social order became a necessity. However, this process becomes more complex just as societies also become more complex devising different patterns by which administration of justice, equity and respect for human dignity and liberty are carried out and realized.

In relatively equitable societies like indigenous peoples, the distinction between those who govern and the governed is the least. In feudal village communities, which are largely agrarian, structures of hierarchy are often stronger and rigid. So, governance is functional and it is integrated with culture and tradition into the social settings of a given people for observance of rules, significance of roles and how these roles are taken up by individuals in determining power relations.

Since governance establishes social and political order and the means by which that governance is carried on daily is 'government', the latter becomes the machinery by which the "Will" of the country is formulated, expressed and realized. This government and its process as noted already, takes various forms and embraces different ideologies such as democracy, autocracy, plutocracy, technocracy, oligarchy, aristocracy and other "cracies" we may think of, depending on the society in question. The one that has become most popular worldwide today or widely talked about since the beginning of the cold war, the decolonization process and the regime of the global powers via the United Nations Security Council (UNSC) is "Democracy". This is further orchestrated by the way any leader in the contemporary global system does wish to be seen as a democrat or a regime that does seek to be described as democratic even when such a regime is dictatorial in sense. To this end, the world has continued to witness an astronomical increase in the activities and growth of mass organizations that seek to demand for more acceptable and refined means of governing through protests and violence from their respective regimes which appear more undemocratic and not liberal.

The Arab spring of the 2010 till date is a good case, some portions of which have taken the forms of terrorist movements and insurgencies where the regimes in power apply force to quell them, but, only to aggravate tensions of ignominious destructions. The Syrian, Egyptian, Yemenis and Tunisian, even Libyan cases are clear instances in this respect. These mass protest movements are yielding more catastrophes which have become one of the foremost challenges of the twenty-first century that the international community is now seriously grappling with to contain in averting a probable third world war. Today, the world is not at ease with the activities and bestialities of Islamic fundamentalists and democracy extremists in their respective domains around the globe, such as those of the Boko Haram in the North-East and North Central of Nigeria, the Mali-

North Maghreb fighters, the Palestian-based Hamas, the Muslim brotherhood insurgents of Egypt, the Lebanon's Hezbollah group, the ruthless Taliban of the Afganistan-Pakistan, the Separatists of the Eastern Ukraine, the M23 Rebel Group of the DRC in East Africa, the Colombian Rebel Fighters waging wars against its government for many years now and worse than useless are the beheadist ISL fighters of Iraq and Syria, let alone the Syrian based insurgents themselves fighting to oust the already unpopular Yasser-Al Assad regime, with the backing of the western powers, claimed to be the crusaders of western democracy.

The argument here is that, while democracy movements inspired by western capitalist oligopolies came to nurture its good for the liberalization of governance, it is not without its drawbacks in sparking-off unnecessary tensions that have resulted into mass killings and wanton destructions of properties globally, believed to have resulted into global economic distress and political stalemates ravaging most world countries as highlighted above. The worsening situations have been helped by the lack of patience, dogmatism and rigid principles maintained by the rulers of affected countries, especially those of the third world, Africa in particular. It has also been worsened by the inordinate ambitions of some rulers who are bent on holding on to power, even in the face of total defeat and alter rejection by their people. More calamitous in this case is the neo-colonialist postures of the power politics of the western powers led by America in their bid to control the global economy and dictate the tunes, and this they have been achieving through various devices e.g. planting puppet governments that protect their interests and/or conspiring to overthrow those ones that are blocking those interests through sponsoring of internal mutinies, strife and disgruntlements that heap coals of unrests, often times on issues of human rights and welfare matters. They also achieve this through their multinational companies and their agencies which engage in sharp business and financial practices that have adverse consequences on the development and growth processes as well as the political stability and internal security of their host countries.

What cannot also be ignored as a cause of the degrading state of democratization process in the globe today is the rise in the number of failing states of the world, especially the third world countries and how this has made many of them to succumb to western power politics pressures as a result of over-reliance on the latter and the disparaging underdevelopment of their own economies. Though, a few developing nations like the small Gambia in West Africa tend to challenge this power bloc, by raising world attention to the devices of their actions in terms of lack of respect for what can be termed 'international democracy' and non-respect for the sovereignty of other nations under article 2 on the principles of the United Nations Organization, by using available forums to articulate their feelings on this and how the global powers should allow equal level playing ground in international politics and governance as well as peaceful means of resolving major internal and international crises. While this development is however welcomed in order for balance of power to be ensured in international politics and global governance, what, to this writer sounds more effective and far-reaching is the ability of developing and other underdeveloped countries of the world to be self-reliant and self-sufficient, while guaranteeing political stability and sustainability through practice of good governance and observance of the rule of law in their respective domains, which is believed to douse tensions of democracy agitations that attract external attentions. Once this is done all the stakeholders in the making of governance including the opposition and the civil society groups in the country as well as the general populace will be able to find peace in the home administration for collective efforts towards development and national security. This will enable and guarantee international diplomacy to be played on the basis of mutual respect for each other and in the spirit of interdependence.

1.1 Democracy and its Origin

Democracy is an existential concept which lives with man from creation or the natural instinct of man when Charles Darwin discovered man's nature and described it as animalistic because he lived an individualistic life where he was free but all the time in danger with another man. He could be killed at any time by anybody or anything or another animal because nothing like law protects him except by "self-defense". Order was later restored into man's existence as a social animal which transformed and bequeathed on him a political life as popularized by the great Aristotle, (the Political Philosopher of Greek).

The need for order and justice, equity and respect for human dignity and liberty heralded governance, governance brought various forms of governmental systems, several of which had been practiced before the emergence of modern democracy.

Modern democracy also known as the representative government evolved or had its root from the Athenian democracy of the Greek city states when the direct democratic principles were in practice, where decisions were undertaken by all in the society. It was first practiced in Athens barely two thousand and five hundred years ago before extending to other parts of the city-states and its environs. This form of democracy was called the classical democracy.

However, with the revolutions and explosions recorded in population, development and growths, the direct involvements' process was gradually discarded in favour of the indirect or representative model.

Democracy is a set of Greek words, that is, "Demo" meaning

'the people' and 'Kratia' or 'Kratein' implying 'rule by the people'. The two words now combine together to mean 'DEMOCRACY' which means "the rule by the people". This perhaps necessitated why the great Abraham Lincoln of the United States of America describes the term as the ... "government of the people, for the people and by the people". This was so, because it was a form of rule where everybody was directly involved to partake in the decisions that concerned his own affairs. He was not represented by anybody except 'self'. From this perspective, principal elements of the direct democratic governance could be said to include recognition for equality of mankind, irrespective of class, position, and roles in societies. They also included political participation, respect for human liberty and freedom and of course equity in economic life.

In his Comprehensive Government for West Africa, Anyaele, (2005; 35) describes democracy as a system of government in which all qualified adult citizens share the supreme power of the state directly or through their elected or accredited representatives.

Appadorai, (1983) in his Substance of Politics posits democracy as a system in which the people exercise the governing power either directly or through their representatives periodically elected by them. He stresses this form of government as one which expresses the popular will on basic questions of social direction and policy, economic, equality, fraternal feeling and political liberty. Appadorai maintains that the content of political liberty is indeed the indispensable minimum for democracy requirement, which means it is the element that determines the right of every man to partake in governance through decision – making process, expressed as the popular or the general will.

Omotosho (2008), in his seminar paper, University of Lagos on "Democracy and Constitutionalism": The Makings of Good Governance in a State describes democracy as "a

257

government by consent of the governed or by the approval of the people upon which governing authority is exercised".

According to Maclver, (1965) as cited in "Democracy, A Political Culture Alien to Africa" by Ikotun, (2010: 20) "Democracy cannot mean the rule of the majority or the rule of the masses"

To Maclver, this was the manner in which democracy was interpreted by the Greek philosophers, at a time when there was no representative system or any party system. He stresses that true democracy occurs when leadership recruitment procedures are subjected to 'polls' where people are liberally allowed under the law to choose who represents them in decision-making process.

Heater defines democracy as essentially a method of organizing society politically, saying, there are five basic elements that determine if a community is democratic (Heater, 1964: 114). These elements he lists as equality, sovereignty of the people, respect for human life, the rule of law and individual human liberty. Heater emphasizes the importance of the ballot which is one man one vote as central in the makings of governance that respects human value, irrespective of differences in wealth, religion, education, intelligence and roles in society, arguing, it is when all these are respected that a society can justify its democratic governance.

1.2 Democracy and Good Governance: Is there a Nexus

This paper looks at the extent of nexus that exist between democracy and good governance in a country.

In attempting to look at this or figure out the element of democracy in good governance, it is imperative to explain what the concept of good governance itself is about in brief. In our introduction, the word governance was explicated by linking it to a process that brings about social order and political control through administration of law.

Good governance implies an administration that is sensitive and responsive to the needs of the people and believed to be effective in coping with emerging challenges in society through framing, implementing of appropriate laws and measures and the realizations of the results of such administrative procedures and measures. It includes strict rules of accountability and transparency, which center on community groups and individuals, based on a notion of rights as inherently compromising duties, bound by generally accepted norms and institutional enforcements.

Within this broad conceptualization of good governance are two distinct positions, first, the one articulated by the World Bank which conceptualizes good governance as competent and judicious management of a country's resources and affairs in a manner that is open, transparent, accountable, equitable and responsive to people's needs. The second, which argues that governance is 'good' when it serves not just any public interest but that of the most poor, the deprived, under-privileged and marginalized people in society.

In the 1994 Report on Governance by the World Bank as stated in the Good Governance Resource Book, (2004)... "Good governance is epitomized by predictable, open and enlightened policy- making that is transparent, a bureaucracy imbued with a professional ethos, an executive arm of government, presumed accountable for its actions and a strong and formidable civil society participating in public affairs and all behaving under the rule and ethics of law".

According to the United Nations Development Programme (UNDP), (1997), governance is the exercise of economic, political and administrative authority to manage a country's affairs at all levels. It comprises mechanisms, processes and institutions, through which citizens and groups articulate their interests, exercise their legal rights, meet their legal obligations and mediate their differences. (GGR, 2004: 7). So, in the same vein Economic and Social Commission for Asia and the Pacific (ESCAP) posits governance 'good' only if efforts are made to minimize corruption, take on board the views of minorities and the voices of the most vulnerable sections of society in decision-making, stressing that good governance ought to be responsive to the present and future needs of society, lest the democratic elements in it will be made irrelevant.

For the European Union… "In the context of a political and institutional environment that upholds human rights, democratic principles and the rule of law, good governance is the transparent and accountable management of human, natural, economic and financial resources for equitable and sustainable development". It entails clear decision-making procedures at the level of public authorities, transparent and accountable institutions.

ESCAP identifies eight major elements of good governance as:-

    (i) A process that is participatory in nature, meaning, there should be political participation at all levels where people are involved or carried along in the decisions of their own affairs,

    (ii) Consensual in nature i.e. bearing the consent of the people governed,

    (iii) Accountable,

    (iv) Transparent,

    (v) Responsive,

    (vi) Effective and Efficient,

    (vii) Equitable and all inclusive and

    (viii) Involving the practice of the rule of law. Just as the Commission on Global Governance observes that the sum of the many ways individuals and institutions, public and private, manage their common affairs is what is regarded as good governance, so the Office of High Commissioner of Human Rights (OHCHR) sees and assesses it as the process by which public institutions conduct public affairs, manage public resources and guarantee the realization of human rights.

OHCHR opines, good governance is good when it accomplishes all its elements as stated, in a manner essentially free of abuse and corruption and with due regard for the practice of the rule of law.

The Commissioner affirms further that the true test of 'good' governance is the degree to which it delivers on the promises of human rights: civil, cultural, economic, political and social rights.

Experts and resource personnel in good governance have identified three major components to governance. These they name the process, the content and the deliverables. The process they explain as encoding factors like transparency and accountability, the content, they claim includes values such as justice and equity and the deliverables they identify as the accomplished fulfillments and deliveries of the process and values of governance where the basic necessities of life, especially those of the 'weak' in society are met for them, through effectiveness and efficiency of state apparatuses in a manner that is most dignifying and humane.

Governance is good and practically human and acceptable for standard rule only when the three components of process, content and deliverables are inherently present, institutionalized and sustained, in any modern state. From the foregoing and given all the characteristic components and elements of good governance, as well as those enumerated in our introduction in regard to democracy and its elements, it suffices to say that there is a clear nexus between democracy and good governance.

Good governance is therefore established as a process for poverty eradication, development and human rights' issues with attendant features of transparency, accountability, equity, respect for the rule of law, justice and love for one another, equal opportunities for all and level playing ground in politics, aimed at building trust and confidence for good neighborliness and harmonious co-existence within the social relations and polity.

Democracy on its own part is being viewed as a governmental process that allows for liberal rights of choosing representatives or the acceptable credible standards of organizing elections for people to choose their leaders willingly without any form of intimidation, victimization and deprivation and believed to be ethical, refined and constitutional for a viable, veritable democratic governance process. At this attainment and growing liberal governance, government in a state becomes more purposeful, just, desirable, non-corruptible, fulfilling and all-inclusive.

1.3 Summary and Conclusion:

This paper has assessed and analyzed, with the use of historical-descriptive survey, intuition and intellectual guides, concepts of democracy and good governance, to determining the nexus between them and how they cannot be practiced without the need of each other for an established political order which would guarantee a country as truly democratic and observance of good governance process in building a viable polity within humans social relation.

The mechanism and functioning processes of democracy and good governance in an adopted political system are examined.

The paper maintains that it is in this process that a genuine practice of good polity can thrive to meet people's oriented government. Should this be absent, the state could be assumed to be practicing authoritarianism or absolutist oligarchy. In a true democracy and good governance process, individuals will realize their best 'selves', peace will attain, order will reign, development will thrive and there will be general contentment and lessened controversies over issues.

1.4 Recommendations

If democracy is to be practicable and be free from any form of mockery and pretense and for good governance to be genuinely observed, practiced and realized in the national interests and for national security toward nation-building, the various elemental factors entwining both concepts of democracy and good governance as processes for the making of a viably-credible government must all be respected and preserved in a country.

Leadership recruitment process, in particular, must be highly organized and executed to leverage qualitative, non-parochial political culture and non-corruptible political class. Corruption must be institutionally addressed by using the apparatuses of the country and self-discipline to tackle it in all ramifications.

Leaders must be disciplined, patriotic and committed to national values and ethical rules. This is the problem in most emerging democracies like Nigeria and most developing countries. Indeed, party politics must not be turned to money politics but a career-making program, believed to be non-corruptible but service-oriented.

This means that our leaders and politicians must have to stop seeing politics as a means for amassing wealth at the expense of the electorate that vote them into power. They should see politics as a service to the nation and pursuant of national interests through a vibrant, but liberal external relations.

Political practitioners and other stakeholders within the polity must be able to define interests by separating self-interests from national or state interests, be able to position the latter to reflect popular wishes for a veritable nation-building. The rulers must respect constitutional law and other laws of the land by guiding against abuses that can alter peace, growth, development and prosperity.

Above all, the electorate and the general public through the activities of the civil society groups and social activists, especially those of political parties and the pressure/interest groups, should realize the need for obedience to law that governs all, while engaging in dialogue whenever issues generate and resolving for consensus in order to deal with tensions and anarchy, which is not in the interest of all in a country. With leadership-followership partnership, people's patriotism and sense of identity, governance process and the entire state are made strong, consolidated and sustained for the good of all and sundry.

References

A UNDP Policy Document (1997), Good Governance and Sustainable Human Development in Good Governance Resource Book (2004), Action Aid India Publications in "Books for Change" Karnataka Projects, Bangalore, India.

Anifowoshe, R. et al. ed. (2005). Elements of Politics, Sam Iroansi Publications, Lagos, Nigeria.

Anyaele, J. U. (2005). Comprehensive Government for Senior Secondary Schools. A. Johnson Publishers Ltd; Lagos, Nigeria.

Akinbobola,A.(2005),International Organizations in Anifowoshe, R.et al (2005) Ed; Elements of Politics(2nd Ed;), Oxford University Press,UK.p.309-447.

Appadorai, A. (1983), The Substance of Politics, 11th ed. Oxford University Press, New Delhi. P. 131 – 137.

Enemuo, F. C. (1992). "The Resurgence of Multiparty Democracy in Africa. What Hopes for the Downtrodden?" Nigerian Journal of International Affairs, Vol. 18, Number 2. Pp. 29 – 30.

Enemuo, F. C. (2005). Democracy, Human Rights and the Rule of Law in Anifowoshe, R. et al. (2005) ed.; Elements of Politics, Sam Iroansi Publications, Lagos, Nigeria. P. 141 – 152.

Gareis, B. S. (2012), The United Nations: An Introduction, Palgrave Macmillan.

Garner, R., Ferdinand, P. and Lawson, S. (2009) Introduction to Politics (2nd Ed;), Oxford University Press, UK. p. 309-447.

Heater, D. B. (1964). Political Ideas in the Modern World, George G. Harrap and Co. Ltd; P. 117.

Held, D. (1996). Models of Democracy (2nd ed.). Cambridge: Polity Press.

Held, D. ed. (1993). Prospects for Democracy. North, South, East, West, Cambridge: Polity Press, P. 15 – 16.

Hurd, I. (2012), International Organizations: Politics, Law, Practice, Cambridge University Press, UK.

Ikotun, A. (2010), Democracy: A Political Culture Alien to Africa? Focus on Nigerian Experience, Nuga Litho Productions, Lagos, Nigeria. P. 19 – 58.

Maclver, R. M. (1950). 'The Ramparts We Guard'. The Macmillan Publishing Co; London.

Odinga, R. (2008). 'Democracy and the Challenge of Good Governance in Africa'; Lagos, The Guardian Newspapers, 14th October; P. 9.

Omoruyi, O., Schlosser, D. B., Sambo, A. and Okwuosa, A. (1994) ed. Democratization in Africa: Nigerian Perspectives, Centre for Democratic Studies, Vol. 2.

Omotosho, O. F. (2008). "Democracy and Constitutionalism". The

Makings of Good Governance in a state. Seminar Paper Presentation at Unilag, Akoka, Lagos for M.Sc; Programme.

Omotosho, O. F. (2014), The Electoral Process in the Gambia: "A Giant Stride in the Makings of a Viable and stable Political System". ICON, Canada Journal Publications (http://www.globaljournal.ca/englishpapers.html).

Omotosho O. F. Democracy a Necessary Element for Good Governance and Good Governance a Necessary Element for Democracy "A Symbiotic-Relational Assessment" http://www.stclements.edu/Articles/Democracy-a-Necessary-Element-Full-Article.pdf

Ozor, F. (2014). Democracy and Popular Right to Revolution: Lessons from the Arab World; Veritas, Academic Journal of St. Clements Education Group. Vol. 5, No. 2. ISSN 2307 – 2806.

Parasuraman, S. (2004). Good Governance Resource Book. Action Aid Publications, Books for Change Publications (Karnataka Projects, Bangalore, India).

Ray, L. J. and Kaarbo, J. (2008), Global Politics (9th Ed;), Houghton Miflin Company, NY.

Roskin, M. G., Cord, R. L., and Jones, W. S. (1994); 5th ed. Political Science: An Introduction, Prentice-Hall International Inc; USA. P. 60 – 94.

United Nations Economic and Social Commission for the Asia and the Pacific (UNESCAP). "What is Good Governance?" http://www.unescap.org/huset/gg/governance. http://www.egg.ch/welcome.html

29

BUILDING DEMOCRACY IN THE CONTEXT OF POVERTY

By Dr. Louis Nwabueze Ezeilo, PhD Leeds

Louis is a member of the Institute of Chartered Economists of Nigeria, the Economic Network of the Higher Education Academy, United Kingdom and the Research in Development Network (RiDNet) of the University of Leeds, United Kingdom. His interests are highly focused on the issue of poverty and how to create an inclusive environment for a better economic and human development in Nigeria.

The problem of poverty remains one of the most challenging issues in our world today. Poverty as a global problem affects continents, regions, nations and peoples in different ways. It has been reported continuously that Nations in sub-Saharan Africa, South Asia and Latin America are currently with the highest level of poverty and consequently with the lowest level of socio-economic development. Besides, they are often described as characterized by the highest level of social insecurity, violence, unrest and low standard of living. Nigeria is not an exception in this case. Poverty has become a protracted menace in the country. It is more worrisome that despite possessing rich natural resources and huge amount of resources committed to poverty alleviation programmes, the problem keeps aggravating, and more people are experiencing poverty instead of escaping it. In its findings, UNDP (2015) describes Nigeria as a country with very low human development, especially in terms of health, welfare and education; and ranks her as one of the poorest countries in the world, further justifying the UNDP's (1998 and 2001) past description of the country as being increasingly worse off today than it was in the 1980s.

All formal activities designed with a view to reducing the rate and prevalence of poverty in the country seemed to have yielded unconvincing results. For instance, several poverty alleviation programmes in Nigeria as initiated by both the Government and Non-Government Organisations , and with the purpose of reducing poverty, have been found to be unsuccessful. Although the primary aim is to reduce the incidence of poverty, these programmes seemed to have served as means for draining the national resources and increasing the scourge of poverty. This could be due to factors such as the pursuit of parochial interests, corruption, dishonesty, diversion or mismanagement of resources. In situation like this, it becomes difficult if not impossible to build a formidable democracy as well as achieve a sustainable development. Hence the question: Can we build democracy and development in the context of poverty?

We briefly explore on some key factors that should be given attention so as to build a stronger and formidable democracy and development in Nigeria.

Exclusion of one's opinion from public policy-making.

Opinion exclusion in the making and implementation of public policy is a specific case of social exclusion. The institutional structures and practices such as culture, religion, amongst others, play a role in the social exclusion present in a given country or community. The issue of exclusion from public policy-making is rampart in Nigeria. According to

Narayan (1999), social exclusion includes all the institutional and societal processes that prevent certain groups of people from engaging fully in the social, cultural, economic and political life of the society in question. The UN (2010) explains that social exclusion and poverty "stem from discrimination on the basis of race, ethnicity, gender, inequality, unbalanced rural/urban development, unequal distribution of assets or unequal access to services, persistent conflicts and instability, often resulting from long-term exclusion" (p. 67). The main focal issue of social exclusion everywhere is the powerlessness of those who are being excluded.

It is obvious that non-recognition of people's opinion is believed to have largely characterized the Nigerian society. Is been a case of no dispute that Nigeria is seen as a country where people's feelings or opinions do not count when designing policy, and our government does not seem to reckon with the opinions of ordinary man on the street. Given the significance of opinion in the design and implementation of public policy, and the desire of the majority of people to seek opinion recognition, the inability to achieve this objective could be described as being detrimental to democracy and development.

Marginalization also plays an important role in the context of poverty and democracy. Marginalization in the context of Nigerian environment means a situation whereby a geographical region (despite its huge natural resources and human capital development) is denied adequate infrastructural development, key political positions or appointments, adequate political representatives, and important role in national decision making. A denial of these factors can render such a region or community poor and makes mockery of democracy.

Brain drains

This is also another area of interest if we want to place democracy and development in the context of poverty. According to 'Nigeria Demographic and Health Survey 1999' as published by National Population Commission (Nigeria) (2000), the poor economic base and political instability of the country have driven out many skilled professionals. Nigerians are found in almost all countries in Europe, America and Asia and majority of those migrating are experts in various fields. Reasons adduced to this could range from bad economic policies to poor remuneration.

America, England and Canada are not better off than Nigeria in terms of natural resource endowments, but these countries have got what it takes to organise, manage and distribute their resources equitably to a reasonably good extent. In most of these countries, everyone in every areas of life is responsible and accountable. All sectors of the economy are well organised and managed. Professionals put in their best and are paid what is commensurate with their efforts. The reverse is the case in Nigeria, where resources are mismanaged by a select few, people in public offices are not responsible and accountable and the rule of law thrown to the pit. Professionals in the different sectors of the economy especially health and education are treated poorly. In this type of precarious situation, many of these professionals opt to travel abroad in search of a better working condition and this grossly affects our democracy and development.

Though there may be counter arguments that brain drain is a measure for addressing domestic poverty, the impact on the economy and human capital development of Nigeria could be significantly negative and higher than the financial benefits from the remittances (Agaptus, 2011; Muhammad *et al.* 2012. (See also Dodani and La Porte (2005) on the impact of brain drain on the developing countries).

Lack of knowledge and information

It is obvious that when you don't have information, you don't know where your rights start and end and the only way a person can be liberated is by getting enough information about his environment. Britz (2007) defines a lack of information as a "situation in which individuals and communities, within a given context, do not have the requisite skills, abilities or material means to obtain efficient access to information, interpret it and apply it appropriately. This is further characterized by a lack of essential information and a poorly developed information infrastructure" (P. 194). By *'essential information'*, Britz (2007) meant information that is needed for survival and development with regard to the basic needs of an individual or a community. This *'essential information'* is seen as a public good, which from an economic perspective is a good that is non-exclusionary and open to all without payment (Parkin *et al.*, 2012). Lack of information is seen as one of the greatest challenges facing the world today, especially Third World countries, which, if not given attention, might have a negative effect on the cultural, economic and socio-political development of a nation.

When people lack the needed information, they are powerless and are regarded as poor (Harande, 2009). Knowledge and information are important in every society. A graduate, who is unemployed, may continue to be out of job owing to a poverty of information. The amount of information at the disposal of an individual may be a function of a person's social network and location. Development and democracy are highly hampered when one needs a job and does not have job-market information due to geographical factors and lack of social networks. Moreover, one is powerless in terms of not being able to access information in a globalized information-driven world, where information and communications technologies play an important role.

Interestingly, Floridi (2001) explains that the causes of a lack of information should not just be narrowed to a deficiency in ICT, but also to cultural and linguistic diversity, low levels of education, un-affordability, unavailability and inability to apply and benefit from the information. This may apply to Nigeria, where there is cultural and linguistic diversity, and where the level of literacy is still wobbling. People are not able to afford social, political or legal information, as well as not being able to derive the necessary benefit from information.

Educational attainment is a key distinguishing feature in the context of democracy and poverty. Through education, intellect, skills and experiences are developed. When people have low educational qualification, they are regarded as being poor, because they might not be able to articulate their ideas and thoughts on certain issues, especially those that pertain to their rights. This emphasizes the importance of education over other things. In Nigeria, many families cannot even pay school fees for their children. As a result, they have had their children sent out of school or forced to withdraw from school, due to inability to pay school fees. In this case, these children are denied access to knowledge. This situation tells a lot about the issue of human capital, as economic prosperity and functioning of a nation depends on increasing physical and human capital stock, of which education is one form. Accordingly, there cannot be an effective democracy and development without adequate knowledge, information and education.

Peace and security

Lack of peace and security is not something that is new to every Nigerian. Since the days of independence, Nigeria has experienced many forms of conflict, leading to a severe lack of peace. There are so many regions and states in Nigeria where there are no peace and security. Some regions lack peace due to insecurity arising from the 'Boko Haram' insurgency in the North-East of Nigeria, the militants in the Niger-Delta of the South-South, and some other minor ethnic and community clashes caused by political power tussles, religious intolerance amongst others. In some region, the Fulani herdsmen are terrorizing and killing innocent people, destroying structures and farmlands, thereby depriving people of their sources of income and livelihood.

Insecurity affects socio-economic activities and all social institutions. This occurrence has made life short, nasty and brutish, almost like Hobbes' "state of nature" (Murray, 2003). Due to these incessant attacks, houses are burnt, people live in fear and stay without shelter, their economic tools are destroyed (creating material poverty), and schools are destroyed denying hundreds of students quality education, as teachers migrate from troubled regions in search of jobs. This institutional anomie caused by lack of peace also affects quality of health and access to health facilities as hospitals are destroyed in the face of these violent attacks and riots, thereby impoverishing the people further. It also reverses economic and human development and makes a mess of democracy (see for example Battman, 2010; Stewart and Fitzgerald, 2000). Faleti (2012), reasons that once there are entrenched conflicts, the available scarce resources, which ordinarily should be channeled towards social and human development, are diverted for other purposes. Apparently, lack of peace inhibits human and national development. Families, communities, societies and nations where there are wars and conflicts are seen to be backward as far as human and national development are concerned and there is no way democracy can thrive in such a nation.

Denial of freedom

We cannot build democracy where people are denied of their freedom. There is a connection between freedom and poverty. Sen (2008) summarizes his perceptions of poverty thus: "...ultimately we have to see poverty as un-freedoms of various sorts: the lack of freedom to achieve even minimally satisfactory living conditions." (p.xiii). He continues to describe lack of freedom as when individuals do not have the opportunity to choose; when one is not given the opportunity to be what one wants to be or do what one wants to do or even develop one's initiatives and potentials. Sen (2009) gives two reasons why freedom is very valuable: "more freedom gives us more opportunity to pursue our objectives..., it helps us to decide to live as we would like and to promote the ends that we want to advance. It is concerned with our ability to achieve what we value. Freedom leads us to the process of choice itself, in that we are not being forced into some state because of constraints imposed by others" (p. 228).

In Nigeria, there is the case of denial of freedom of association between the poor and non-poor. The poor are sometimes not allowed to participate in the political, and sometimes even in the civic life of the non-poor. This is seen as political poverty, buried not only in lack of choice, but also in denial of power to participate in political activities. This view indicates the social exclusion of individuals from social networks, and therefore highlight what Sen (2009) describes as the roots of capability deprivation, where individuals and groups of people are excluded from taking part in the political and social life of the community. Political freedom and social freedom are two out of the five types of freedom enumerated by Sen (1999a).

The lack of political and social freedom brings to limelight the issue of social capital formation, which is a relevant strategy for poverty reduction in the pursuit of democracy and development. According to Oyen, (2002), social capital is based on the formation of informal and formal network structures around certain kinds of human needs. These network structures according to him could be heterogeneous in terms of being open to a wide range of individuals or be homogenous in terms of accepting only people of the same kind. In this sense, the questions worth asking here are: Do the poor have the same kind of networks as the non-poor? Are the poor allowed to join the networks of the non-poor? The answer to these questions is negative, and this non-participation in both political and civic life has been termed political poverty (Oyen, 2002). The basic reason behind this according to Oyen, (2002) is that poverty does create a time constraint which reduces participations that are organized around non-profit activities. As a result of this, the networks of the poor are mostly found to be connected to strategies for survival. Thus, it becomes very difficult if not impossible to build a sustainable democracy in situation like this.

Gender poverty and child abuse

The existence of the social isolation of women and insensitivity to children is a known enemy towards building democracy and development. This is a form of social exclusion based on gender inequality and children's rights abuse. Gender inequality is viewed to be prevalent among various societies and is usually characterized as male dominance. Women, it has been argued, suffer from disrespect and are subjected to treatment that leaves them with low self-esteem as well as lack of confidence (Holmes and Jones, 2010). Setting different standards or roles for men and women in the society, which influences how each sex is treated by their parents, is seen as a dimension of poverty that requires much re-orientation and sensitization. There are some jobs or social activities unavailable to these women, such as, participation in government and leadership in the town or community union. It is very rare to see women holding the top positions in the government. This is not only peculiar to Nigeria but pervasive in many countries. This, Allanana (2013) argues, might be as a result of cultural, religious and socio-political reasons. In some societies, women are forbidden from participating in certain economic, social and political activities.

With regard to cultural practices that inhibit the rights of women, it's been observed that in most parts of Nigeria especially in the South East, some cultural practices restrict women from inheriting their parents' properties. Fayomi, (2012) calls this discrimination, intimidation, exclusion, marginalization and stigmatization of women by their men counterparts (see also Ayoola *et al*, 2001; Ali-Akpajiak and Pyke, 2003). Interestingly, there are also some forms of discrimination against women coming from religious institutions. It is observed in some northern parts of Nigeria, where Islamic religion is practiced, most women are not permitted to come out and engage in trade like their counterparts from other parts of the country. No wonder, our incumbent president from the Northern part of Nigeria referred to his wife some time ago in 2016 as belonging to the kitchen, which was massively attacked and criticised by so many Nigerians. This situation worsens the plight of women in those areas and keeps them in perpetual impoverishment and does not in any way promote democracy and development

On the other hand, child poverty is also present in Nigeria which basically is rooted on the abuse of children. Child abuse is a deprivation which most children undergo globally. It will be recalled that the 'Convention on the Rights of the Child' (CRC) in 1980 met and defined the basic rights of children. These included the right to survival; the right to protection from harmful influences and practices, abuse and exploitation; the right to develop to the fullest; and the right to participate fully in family, social and cultural life (UN 1989). In Nigeria, it is very obvious that most of these rights are not given to children. A good example of the abuse of these rights is how children are used by their parents to make money by sending them out to the streets to hawk and beg, thereby denying them the opportunity of going to school.

Some of these children end up becoming criminals or victims of rape, kidnapping or trafficking (also see Ajani, 2008; Ikejiaku, 2009). Some become fatally unprotected and malnourished (UNICEF, 2007; UNDP, 2009; Cimpric, 2010). The end result of all this is reproduction of poverty which hinders democracy and development.

Religious Institutions

It is no longer news that most men of God in their preaching encourage laziness which leads to poverty. Nigeria and most African countries are currently experiencing another form of slavery through Pentecostalism. Most people are now mentally and scientifically incapacitated, others do not believe in themselves again. Ingenuity and creativity are relegated in the lives of some people due to the preaching of these neo-Pentecostal men of God. In Nigeria, most of these pastors and men of God encourage their members to sleep in church 24 hours every day in the name of one crusade or another. Our Nigerian pastors and men of God have forgotten that most of all we enjoy today and most of the good things reshaping our world today are fruits of the creativity, ingenuity, efforts and dedication of several people who devoted their time working in every part of the world. Most Nigerians have now developed a new mindset of becoming millionaires by just sleeping in the church and believing the false utterances of these pastor and men of God; that God is going to bless someone who puts his hands in his pocket and offers whatever he brings out of the pocket or someone who uses the remaining money in his account to sow seeds, or someone who rushes out to drop cheques at the altar. This is wealth without work which is one of the deadly sins of the world today as propounded by Mahatma Gandhi. Our pastors always talk about one John who got a job he was not qualified for. What does that tell you? If someone got a job, he was not qualified for; is it not corruption and bribery and there is nothing that encourages poverty as corruption and bribery. This may be argued as one of the reasons Nigeria is where it is today.

What then are the implications of the above? We see the earth conquering us instead of us conquering the earth as the scripture stated. We see majority of Nigerians burying their talents. We see a God who abhors creativity, ingenuity, efforts and hard-work in Nigeria. We behold a new breed of generation of young people who are now lazy and dependent on God for a reward of mediocrity, insincerity and laziness. We see a situation where some people steal in order to pay tithe, sow seed and then be blessed by God. These utterances from many of these neo-Pentecostal men of God can arguably create rather than fight poverty in the country and situations like this impedes democracy and development.

Government policies, structures and resources

Government policies and political factors are also viewed as one of the factors that hinder democracy and development in Nigeria. Policy-making and implementation are two key sides of government practices. It shows how a government operates by capably carrying out its function. In other words, policy-making and implementation involve a clear identification of the policy plans, activities, programmes, projects, and well-thought out roles of the organisations/institutions that are responsible for these outcomes (Sambo, 2008; Maduabum, 2008). Sometimes Nigerian government make seemingly good policies, but the implementation is often poor coupled with corrupt and selfish actors and organisations/institutions responsible for policy implementation.

There have been serious constraints regarding the design and implementation of policies in Nigeria. According to Ajulor, (2013), many factors have been adduced to this, such as unrealistic goal setting, lack of participation from the beneficiaries, power imbalance, corruption and inadequate distribution of resources. For example, balancing power in Nigeria would entail a balanced distribution of resources and power among the various ethnic groups. Yet the reverse is the case, as power has been manipulated by the Hausa-Fulani hegemony since national independence. This group perpetuated their power at the expense of other ethnic groups through use of the military. Power and resources should be well distributed, rationalized and mobilized as this promotes democracy and development.

The allocation of one quarter (25%) of the nation's resources/budget to the national assembly is also not helpful to democracy and development. This is another form of colonialism, where people succeed themselves in office, amassing wealth at the expense of the development of the nation and individuals, thereby deepening poverty in Nigeria. The reason for this is that the political office holders in the country make elitist policies that protect their earnings and allowances, thus, giving them the opportunity to receive bogus incomes. Statistically, the members of the National Assembly are not more than 1000 individuals against a total population of about 180 million Nigerians. By implication, about 1000 individuals are sharing one quarter of the federal budget and leaving over 179 million people struggling by with the rest. This situation, where a few individuals by virtue of political appointments or political elective positions are made much richer than the rest of the millions of citizens in Nigeria, is grossly unfair. It results in negative envy, which has plunged many into killing, ritualism and occultism, in order to gain access to politics, where it is hoped they will be better off. In doing this, the government keeps on creating instead of fighting poverty and in this context, democracy and development are hampered.

The rate of unemployment in the country is on the increase. NBS (2017), recently reports that unemployment has hit

14.2%. This is attributed to government's insensitivity to job creation, which has made the youth to live without work. The rise in youth unemployment, together with frustration with governance, are arguably responsible for the incessant increase in the rate of crime and social unrest, such as 'Boko Haram', Niger Delta militancy, kidnapping and rape (Salami, 2013). The opportunity structure of the Nigerian society favours the elite at the expense of the poor. There is a rotation of the political leadership and the amassing of wealth at the expense of national development. This point becomes clearer when one considers the number of unemployed and underemployed in Nigeria. Employment is an important social and economic concern of any nation as it contributes immensely to the nation's economic growth. Statistical records available show that the youth constitute more than half of the approximately 170 million Nigerians today and are therefore most affected by unemployment (Doreo, 2013).

The focus of these views is that most Nigerians have now lost hope in the government. This is aptly seen in the low enthusiasm with which people turn out to vote. Agu *et al.* (2013), observe that voters' apathy has kept on rising in Nigeria from an 84% turnout in 1999, when the first democratic government was elected, to a 25% in 2007, when the next election was conducted. This diminishing trend, according to them, is observed in all the three tiers of government, showing lack of enthusiasm from the electorate. This of course is not healthy for democracy and development

On the systems of the Nigerian government, there is the view that, the introduction of a federal character principle (quota system) by the Nigerian government to create equal employment and appointment opportunities for all geo-political zones has indirectly substituted merit for mediocrity. Federal character principles emphasise the sharing of political appointments into public office, among others. Section 14(3) of the 1999 Nigerian Constitution provides that: "the composition of the Government of the Federation or any of its agencies and the conduct of its affairs shall be carried out in such a manner as to reflect the federal character of Nigeria and the need to promote national unity, and also to command national loyalty, thereby ensuring that there shall be no predominance of persons from a few State or from a few ethnic or other sectional groups in Government or in any of its agencies". The federal character principle is designed to result in provision and evenly distribution of social services among the various geo-political zones in the country, and no unit is expected to be unnecessarily discriminated against in the establishment of social services. However, this system seems not to have lived up to its expectation as it is viewed to have given preference to the less qualified candidates over the most qualified candidates under the guise of equal representation.

In Nigeria, due to these authority structures, people are no longer given opportunity because they are qualified, but because of where they come from and in this case, mediocre are used to fill political posts where they are not fitted in. The appointment of mediocre candidates may not help in the implementation of government policies, especially anti-poverty policies. This implies poverty perpetuation as caused by authority structures, which Jordan (2004) referred to as structural causes of poverty. According to Jordan (2004), structural causes of poverty refer to those structures that either in the form of economic, institutional or authority structure, tend to favour some groups of people over others, based on class, gender or race. In other words, the political and social networks determine what one gets rather than one's identity (Putnam, 1995; Adler and Kwon, 2002). Invariably, the lowly placed and less connected are more likely to be out of favour, and hence, may remain unemployed irrespective of the qualities they possess. Therefore, while many people may aspire to have the fundamentals of life, they are excluded from the distributive chains of favour, because of cultural factors, corruption, nepotism and tribalism or gender considerations. In this sense, unequal access to empowerment opportunities may plunge people further into poverty. Hence, the system of government in Nigeria retains the unconnected in low-quality or low-income employment, and ultimately keeps them poor.

Corruption

One of the major problems confronting Nigerians is political leadership and a culture of impunity. This is generally referred to as corruption and has been the major factor responsible for the poor growth of the Nigerian economy as well as socio-economic stagnation. The World Bank, in conjunction with the anti-corruption organisation known as Transparency International (TI), views corruption as an abuse of public power, especially public office, for the private benefits of the person holding office or for a third party (TI, 2003). Public offices can be abused through accepting, soliciting or extorting bribes, as well as through nepotism and patronage. Also private agents may use bribes to circumvent policies for private profit and competitive advantage (TI, 2003). Corruption is not limited to an abuse of public office and public power alone. Corruption gives birth to extreme poverty, distort democracy and hinders development. This is the case in Nigeria.

There is corruption in Nigeria and the culture of corruption has effects on poverty, democracy and development. A director of a government organization once told me that:

"The nature of corruption in Nigeria is called prebendals. Nigerian people divert resources into their pockets and call it personal share. In their view, there is nothing wrong with it. People steal money meant for the public and convert it to their own personal use. The money is for the master on the seat and for his clients. Clientelism is also there as one of the components of corruption in Nigeria."

The nature of corruption here is referred as 'prebendalism'. Joseph (1991) defines prebendalism as "an unremitting and unconstrained struggle for possession and access to state offices, with the chief aim of procuring direct material benefits to oneself and one's acknowledged communal or other sectional groups" (p. 75). The concept of 'prebendalism' was derived from Max Weber who used the word to describe the compensations paid by the feudal lords to individuals for their duties. In this sense, 'prebendalism' is seen to be attitudinal and a behaviour. This is then used to describe the nature of corruption in Nigeria, where most people, especially those in authority, utilize the power given to them as an opportunity to get rich or offer all manner of rewards to those loyal to them at the detriment of taxpayers. This is rather than use the power for the governance of the common good. These loyal parties are called the 'clients', and thus, 'clientilism' also contributes to poverty and undermines governance in Nigeria. Clientilism is explained as the kind of relationship existing between a person, who actually prebendalizes and the community or groups attached to his office (Joseph, 1991).

"Clientilism", is also linked with the character of the Nigerian state, and one can use what is called the 'Capture Theory' in politics to explain it. Accordingly, 'Capture Theory' in politics or in political science simply means, in the case of Nigeria, that there are two contending forces. These two forces are firstly, the people who want reforms and progress, and secondly, those who want the status quo to remain - they do not want changes. These latter groups are the 'clients' and they seem to dominate in Nigeria. Unless those who want reforms dominate those who want the status quo to remain (the character of the Nigerian state) then there will not be an end or a change in the character of the Nigerian state.

Furthermore, most people in Nigeria have frowned at the government's silence over the incidences of corruption in

Nigeria, thereby making life unbearable and miserable for the people as well as hindering democracy and development. The government of Nigeria has for long time and to a significant degree, been paying lip service to fighting corruption. At the inception of every government, there is always an agenda to fight corruption. For instance, the government of Goodluck Jonathan put forward the "transformation agenda" dedicated to fighting corruption and correcting the bad image of the country overseas. The success of this agenda remained a question yet to be answered, as TI ranked Nigeria as the 33rd most corrupt country in the world during the Jonathan administration, compared to Botswana which ranked 74th, the cleanest African country (Kalu, 2014). The current government of Mohammadu Buhari, since inception on May 29, 2015, has also embarked on a wide anti-corruption crusade prioritised as a major agenda of his administration, but the impact has yet to be internationally assessed, not minding the comments made by the former British prime minister, Cameron; that "Nigeria is fantastically corrupt".

The culture of corruption has further deepened poverty in Nigeria. All levels of government are charged with cases of corruption, caused mostly by a lack of accountability. Money laundering has become the order of the day, with some Nigerians engaging in this activity. This has necessitated the establishment of the Economic and Financial Crime Commission (EFCC). However, the promulgation of this act seems not to have been as effective as expected, as many people still involve themselves in money laundering. Despite the anti-money laundering laws promulgated by the federal government, it has been observed by some studies that most highly placed Nigerians, especially the political office holders and some religious leaders still engage in this act. They use this money to either buy expensive houses or embark on huge investment in foreign countries (see Okeshola, 2012; Abiola and Obasan, 2012). Close to two thirds of former state governors in Nigeria are facing corruption cases in the

EFCC. The EFCC on its own has abandoned its mandate to fight corruption, and thus became a toothless watchdog being used for persecuting perceived political enemies.

Failure on the part of government to fight corruption hinges on leadership problems in Nigeria, as most of its leaders are also corrupt. Hence, it becomes very difficult to fight corruption as most of our leaders are involved in it. Based on his experience on Nigeria and its leadership, the renowned writer, Chinua Achebe (1930-2013) noted that the causes of the major problems in Nigeria are rooted in bad leadership. Achebe (1983) argues that: "the trouble with Nigeria is simply and squarely a failure of leadership. There is nothing basically wrong with Nigerians. There is nothing wrong with the Nigerian land, climate, water, air or anything else; the Nigerian problem is the unwillingness or inability of its leaders to rise to their responsibility, to the challenge of personal example which is the hallmark of a true leadership" (p. 1). There is bad leadership in the government, religious institutions, various communities and societies in Nigeria. In all, corruption, alongside the bad leadership prevalent in all segments of society is the major problems that cause and perpetuate poverty in Nigeria and in this context, democracy and development are hindered.

Conclusion.

We have been able to discuss building democracy in the context of poverty. The government stands at the centre of our discussion. Government should be accountable, make, review and implement policies, listen to people and make political posts less attractive. There should be existence of a basic political order, political legitimacy, effort to enforce the rule of law and opportunity for popular participation, controlling of the recurring crisis in the country, provision of infrastructure among others.

The community's and the people's attitude have to change. There has to be an introduction of a Community Charter of Demand (CCD), which is a strategy employed by communities to commit political aspirants towards developing their communities. The charter of demands represents those areas of deprivation present in a particular community. With a charter of demands, communities hold leverage based on the 'political worthiness' of candidates. The community can ensure that candidates canvassing for votes are ready to meet the communities' demands should they get into office. With this, the likelihood of changing the attitude of those in political offices increases, as they may see a new set of communities who now understand their basic rights to demand things that can change their living standards as well as bring development.

Bibliography

Abiola, I. and Obasan, K. (2012), "Ant-Money Laundering Policy and its Effects on Bank Performance in Nigeria", Business Intelligence Journal, Vol. 5, No 2, pp. 367-373.

Achebe, C. (1983), The trouble with Nigeria, Oxford: Heinemann Educational Publishers

Adler, P. S. and Kwon, S. W. (2002), "Social Capital: Prospects for a New Concept", the Academy of Management Review, Vol. 27, No. 1 (Jan., 2002), pp. 17-40 Published by: Academy of Management.

Agaptus, N. (2011), Brain Drain and National Development in Nigeria, A PhD Thesis submitted to the Department of Political Science, University of Nigeria, Nsukka, Available online at: http://repository.unn.edu.ng:8080/jspui/bitstream/123456789/1219/1/ AGAPTUS%20NWOZOR.pdf (accessed on 25/05/2016).

Agu, S. U., Okeke, V. O. S. and Idike, A. N. (2013), "Voters' Apathy and Revival of Genuine Participation in Nigeria", Mediterranean Journal of Social sciences, Vol. 4, No. 3, 2013.

Ajani, O. (2008), "Gender Dimensions of Agriculture, Poverty, Nutrition and Food Security in Nigeria", NSSP Background Paper 4. Washington, DC: IFPRI.

Ajulor, O. V. (2013), Policy Implementation and Rural Poverty Reduction in Nigeria (An Analysis of the National Poverty Eradication Programme (NAPEP) in Ado-Odo Ota Local Government Area, Ogun State); 1st Annual International Interdisciplinary Conference, (AIIC), 24-26 April, 2013, Azores, Portugal-Proceedings.

Allanana, M. G. (2013), "Patriarchy and Gender Inequality in Nigeria: The Way Forward", European Scientific Journal June 2013 edition vol.9, No.17 ISSN: 1857 – 7881 (Print) e - ISSN 1857- 7431.

Ali-Akpajiak, S. and Pyke, T. (2003), Measuring Poverty in Nigeria, Oxfam Working Papers, Oxford: Oxfam Publishing

Ayoola, G. B., Aina, C., Mamman, B., Nweze, N., Odebiyi, T., Okunmadewa, F., Shehu, D., Olukemi, W. and Zasha, J. (2001), "Nigeria: Voices of the Poor: Consultation with the Poor", Country Synthesis Report, World Development Report, 2000/2001.

Bateman, M. (2010), Why doesn't Microfinance work: The destructive rise of local Neoliberalism: NY, Zeb Books, Northwestern University

Britz, J. J. (2007), "To know or not to Know: A Moral Reflection on Information Poverty", Journal of Information and science, 30(3) 2007, pp. 192-204.

Cimpric, A. (2010), "Children Accused of Witchcraft: An Anthropological Study of Contemporary Practices in Africa", Dakar: UNICEF WACRO

Dodani, S. R. and LaPorte, E. (2005), "Brain Drain from Developing Countries: How can Brain Drain be converted into wisdom gain?" Journal of the Loyal Society of Medicine, Volume 98, November 2005

Doreo, P. (2013), "The Nigerian Unemployment Challenge", Africa Report Features.

Faleti, S. (2012), "Poverty, Peace and Development in the Niger Delta", Paper Presented at PIND's Niger Delta Development Forum – Supporting Poverty Reduction through Partnership, Port-Harcourt, 21-21 November 2012.

Fayomi, O. O. (2012), "Women, Poverty and Trafficking: A Contextual Exposition of the Nigerian Situation", Journal of Management and Social Science, Vol. 5, No 1 (Spring) 65-79.

Floridi, L. (2001), Information ethics: An Environmental Approach to the Digital Divide, Philosophy in the Contemporary World, 9(1), (2001), 1–4.

Harande, Y. I. (2009), "Information Services for Rural Community development in Nigeria", Library Philosophy and Pracice, available online at: http://www.webpages.uidaho.edu/-mbolin/harande.htm (accessed on

20/06/2014).

Holmes, R and Jones, D. (2010), "Gender-sensitive Social Protection and the MDGs" Briefing Paper 61 London: Overseas Development Institute (ODI) available at: www.odi.org.uk (accessed on 20/06/2014

Ikejiaku, B. V. (2009), "The Relationship between Poverty, Conflict and Development", Journal of Sustainable Development, Vol.2, No.1

Jordan, G. (2004), The Causes of Poverty, Cultural vs. Structural: Can There Be a Synthesis? Available at: http://www.asu.edu/mpa/Jordan.pdf (accessed on 11/06/2014).

Joseph, R. A. (1991), Democracy and Prebendal Politics in Nigeria, Ibadan: Spectrum Books Ltd.

Justin, A. U. (ed.) (2001), Managing the Environment in Popular Neighbourhoods: A Manual for Action, Shelter Rights Initiative (SRI), Lagos, esc@srinitiative.org.

Kalu, U. (2014), "Nigeria is 33rd Most Corrupt Country-Transparency Int'l", Culled from Vanguard Newspaper, June 5, 2014, Available at: http://www.vanguarddngr.com/2014/12/nigeria-33rd-corrupt-country-transparency-intl (accessed on 13/06/2014).

Maduabum, C. P. (2008), The Mechanics of Public Administration in Nigeria. Lagos: Concept Publications Ltd.

Muhammad, A. H., Ashi Z., Tariq M., Syed A. H. N. and Faiz, M. S. (2012), "Factors Driving Brain Drain in Pakistan: An Exploratory View" Journal of Asian Business Strategy, Vol. 2, No.2, pp. 7-20.

Murray, F. (2003), "Leviathan: Thomas Hobbes", in "the Political Classics", Forsyth, M. and Keens-Soper, M. (eds.), Oxford: Oxford University Press.

Narayan, D. (1999), "Bonds and Bridges: Social Capital and Poverty" Policy Research Working Paper, Vol.2167.

Okeshola, F. B. (2012), "Corruption as Impediment to Implementation of Anti-Money Laundering Standards in Nigeria", American International Journal of Contemporary Research, Vol2, No 7, July 2012.

Oyen, E. (2002), "Social Capital Formation as Poverty Reducing Strategy", in UNESCO (2002) "Social Capital and Poverty Reduction: Which Role for the Civil Society Organizations and the State?" UN Summit 5.

Parkin, M., Powell, M. and Mathews, K. (2012) Economics; eight Edition, Harlow: Pearson Addison-Wesley

Putnam, R. D. (1995), "Bowling alone: America's Declining Social Capital", Journal of Democracy Vol. 6 (1995) 1, 64-78.

Sambo, A. (2008), "What is Public Policy?" in Anifowose, R. and Enemuo, F. (eds.), "Elements of Politics", Lagos: Malthhouse Press Ltd

Sen, A. (1999a), Development as Freedom. New York: Oxford University Press.

Sen, A. (2008) Foreword, in: Green, D. (2008) Poverty to Power: How Active Citizens and Effective States can Change the World, Oxford: Oxfam International, xiii-xvi.

Sen, A. (2009), The idea of Justice: New York, Penguin Books.

Transparency International Corruption Index (2003), Available at: http://www.transparency.md/Docs/TI_CPI2002_en.pdf (accessed on 12/06/2014).

United Nations, (1989), Convention on the Right of the Child, A/RES/44/25, New York: UN.

United Nations, Department of Economics and Social Affairs, (2010), "Rethinking Poverty" Report on the World Social Situation, 2010. Available online at: http://esa.un.org/unpp/ (accessed on 18/12.2013).

United Nations Development Programme, (1998), Nigeria: Human Development Report, Lagos.

United Nations Development Programme, (2001), Nigeria 2000/2001 Human Development Report: Millennium Edition, Lagos.

United Nations Development Programme, (2009), Human Development Report Nigeria 2008–2009: Achieving Growth with Equity", Abuja: UNDP.

United Nations Development Programme, (2015), The Millennium Development, Goals Report, Available online at http://www.un.org/millenniumgoals/2015_MDG_Report/pdf/MDG%202015%20rev%20(July%201).pdf (accessed 11-01-2016).
UNICEF, (2007), "Global Study on Child Poverty and Disparities" National Report on Nigeria to UNICEF, Available online at: http://www.unicef.org/socialpolicy/files/Nigeria_GLOBAL_STUDY_ON_CHILD_POVERTY_AND_DISPARITIES_smaller.pdf (accessed on 06/01/2013).

30

ARE MORE TOLERANT SOCIETIES MORE LIKELY
TO INVEST IN EDUCATION?

BY WILLIE EYO

Willie is a consultant reader and library developer, co-ordinator, peniel library (member: national action committee, on read campaign; (fme) and reading association of Nigeria)

INTRODUCTION

In order that a developing nation like Nigeria turns into a developed one, its education policy has to be re-engineered. The fact has to be realized that mere industrial development and increase in number of factories and industrial plants is not sufficient for national development. The country's future can be brightened by brightening the intellect of its budding citizens; that is, the students who are like clay that can be moulded in any desired shape for serving any purpose. All our institutions of learning have to play a pivotal role in this movement. Educational policy and progress have been revealed in the light of the goal of national development and priorities set from time to time. The comatose state of education in Nigeria did not occur overnight, this has been a development that has found prominence through many years of neglect and mismanagement. Despite the very significant commitment made to education by the president and government in the past few years, especially to UBE, the scale of the problem has grown to such an extent that nothing less than major renewal of all systems and institutions is required. Reforms and investments are essential to break the downward cycle and put the nation on a path towards an educational system which can match its aspirations to become an efficient and competitive economy on the world stage, and a leader of nation within Africa.

The development of socio-economic structures of a country depends on its education system. The academic level of citizens plays an important role in strengthening the social, economic and technological fabric of a nation. Qualitative education delivery is major contributor in the overall progress of any nation. Innovative strategies need to be evolved for tackling new local as well as global issues which are confronting the developing nations in the 21st century. For a developing country like Nigeria, qualitative education should be treated as governing factors for making the best use of its human as well as natural resources. Qualitative education, of course, is responsible for producing learned citizens and good skills to perform in various fields of human endeavours. The product of qualitative education is that which decides the fate of the nation because it deals with the citizens belonging to the most productive age groups.

Qualitative education not only imparts effective and applicable knowledge to the youths, it also helps them in bringing out the best to tackle the growing levels of illiteracy.

Education is not just about getting children to school, it is about equipping them with the skills they need for a better future. Education on its own is not enough, we also need to create skilled jobs for our youths. Education is also more than skilled jobs. It is also a vehicle for transmitting those tangible but powerful forces that bind societies together; forces like respect tolerance and shared values.

Today, education in Nigeria remains chronically underdeveloped. This concomitant neglect of the sector as a potentially important motor of development is damaging. The neglect may not be surprising in the light of the fact that the ruling elite in Nigerian society is one that accords education a second fiddle role to politics and power! And it is a truism that every nation gets the education it is willing to pay for! Beginning from Aristotle, it has been recognized that education and society are interdependent, it is society which sets the goals which education follows. (S.J Cookney, "The Nigerian National Curriculum Conference of 1969", The University of Lagos. In Adeniyi Aderalegbe, ed, Philosophy for Nigeria Education (Lagos Nigeria, Educational Research Council 1972 Pg. Xxxii

In trying to tackle the question "Are more tolerant societies more likely to invest in education?" This paper will be looking at 4 critical positions as it affects educational development in Nigeria and some countries of the world who started out on not too smooth a platform but have written their names today in the educational "Hall of fame" by reason of the involvement of their various societies.

Firstly, we will take a critical look at the various positions of education as put together by various school of thoughts: The role of education and its attendant effect on those who benefitted from it. The second position will find prominence on who a tolerant society is and its roles in the educational development in Nigeria. The third position will x-ray the inherent challenges faced by Nigeria education sector and the way forward. The fourth position will look at the politics in education and conclusion.

Different Positions of Education

Education is an essential element of the empowerment of citizens in any nation. A good quality education designed to meet the needs of its people will build the individuals' capacities and prepare them to seize opportunities in the public domain. The empowerment of the citizenry is crucial to change some of the mundane attitudes and behaviours that has so adversely affected the development of the Nigerian nation. The development of a nation is anchored on the development of its people. When the citizens of a nation make progress, the nation also makes progress.

Education, Keller informs us, has two senses one broad and the other narrow and technical. In its broad sense, education refers to any act or experience that has a formative effect on the mind, character or physical ability of an individual. In this sense, education is a continuous process. We learn every day and throughout life by experience. G. K Keller, Introduction to philosophy of education (London: John Willey and Sons 1964), Pg 20

Education is also seen as a process of development by which humans adapt to their environment. It is a socialization and learning process. Shipment writes: "Education is that part of socialization process that is specifically organized to ensure that learning occurs.(Mr D. Shipman Education and modernization (London Faber&Faber Ltd 1971) P. 34 Still in its broad aspect, Emile Durkhein defines education as the influence exercised by the adult generation on those that are yet ready for social life. (Emile Durkheim, Education and sociology(New York Free Press:1996) P. 12

In his thinking, the main objective of education is to arouse and develop in the individual certain number of physical, intellectual and moral status which are demanded of him or her by society as a whole and the specific milieu i.e environment or social surrounding.

For which he/she is specifically destined. This concept of education springs from Durkheim's idea of man. To him, man is a biological animal or creature who lives in the society. Since he must live within the framework of society, it is necessary that he learns the social way of life. For this reason, Durkheim thinks that education is of prime importance to society. (Ibid, Pg. 16)

In its technical and narrow sense, education is the process by which any society, through schools, colleges, universities and other institutions, deliberately transmits its cultural heritage. i.e its accumulated knowledge values skills from one generation to another (J.F Keller. Op cit.)

Keller also defined education as an attempt to make one a cultural member of a society by developing his or her intellectual capacities. To Peters, education is the systematic training and instruction geared towards the development of ability, character physical and mental powers of the individual through the careful dissemination of knowledge (R.S Peters Philosophy of Education (London: Oxford university press 1980. P1)

Tolerant Societies

A people are said to be tolerant when such a one willingly submits to an issue for the general good of the society, as such will aid the development and progress of her own. To drive home what a tolerance society is, I will capture three prominent societies in Nigeria and two other countries (Singapore & India) that demonstrated high level tolerance that liberated their various societies from the clutches of illiteracy.

One of the outstanding and beneficial heritages our colonial master gave to us was formal western education as the magic wand, the "joker", the password that could unlock the hidden treasures in the science and technology of the western world.

They therefore heavily invested heavily in formal western education. Education was accorded prominence in all ramifications, with the allocation of substantial amount in education budget. A development that generated an all-time attention in the sector. Thus western Nigeria providing the leadership in the early 1950s, primary school education was free in both western and eastern Nigeria. The Northern Nigeria was also not isolated in this drive as a lot of incentives were accorded the education sector to lure children to school. Apart from government the various nation groups in Nigeria- the Igbo state union, the Ibibio state union and the Egbe Omo Oduduwa to mention a few invested in the education of their people. They built, funded primary school and offered scholarship to their children to acquire education abroad. Thus, by 1960 when Nigeria obtained its independence, it had one of the most educated and viral workforces in Africa and the third world.

When Lee Kuan Yew came to power in Singapore in 1959, that country's GDP was $400. The country was bedevilled with racial tension, deep scars from years of Japanese occupation, Malaysian oppression, lack of resources, and embedded corruption.

The country's grief was almost complete when its only access to the hinterland was cut off as a result of separation from Malaysia. Singapore was on its own. A turnaround was a huge bet against the odds. But it was done, regardless. Within the first 11 years of Yew's watch, the country was tackling its worst demons head on. In spite of the oil crisis in the early 1970s that threatened to derail its progress, the pillars of growth and development had been established.

"We had to work against seemingly inseparable odds to make it from poverty to prosperity in three decades" Yew wrote in his famous book, *From third world to first*. The beauty of Singapore's achievement is nothing short of education. President Yew invested in technological development vis-a-vis the support he gave to the development of education. Today, Singapore has zero tolerance illiteracy and corruption, and also has the single honor of being identified as the neatest country in the world.

India became an independent state at midnight on the 15th of August 1947. Jawahrel Nehrul the first prime minister gave a clarion call to the nation outlining the arduous task of nation state that lay ahead of the fledging nation state.

That future, one of ease or resting but of incessant striving so that we may fulfil the pledges we have so often taken and the one we shall take today. The service of India means the service of the millions who suffer. It means the ending of poverty and ignorance and disease and inequality of opportunity. The future beckons to us whether we go and what shall be our endeavours.

Fighting ignorance by expanding educational opportunities to all its citizens and making all of them functionally literate have been high on the nation's developmental agenda in various national plans since 1951. As a result of all these efforts over the last 55 years, the literacy rates have gone up substantially. While only 17% of the population could read and write at the time of independence, more than 65% were literate in 2001. It is also worth noting at this stage at the beginning of the twentieth century, only 5.4% of the total population was literate. So the growth of literacy rate in the post independent India is much more dramatic than the growth in pre independent colonial India clearly pointing to a positive, dynamic influence of a state policy. India's laudable achievement was achieved through various initiatives. e.g Night schools. The consensus had been built that facilitates for educating adults should be supported through a network of night schools. These schools working for about 3 hours everyday between 7pm and 10pm were intended to impart basic literacy skills in about 2 years. Reading, writing and arithmetic formed the core curriculum but there were lessons on health, hygiene and first aid. In the 1960s, another program called "Farmers Functional Literacy Project" (FFLP) was initiated in 1967 to make farmers literate with ultimate aim of boosting farm productivity. The farmers were expected to become aware of the latest advances in farm policies like use of improved variety of seeds and fertilizers. Underlying this program was the belief that literacy is a critical tool for livelihood and income generation and that literacy must be linked up with livelihood concern to make it more sustainable . The central board of workers education took over programs for workers in urban area. This centre called Shramik Vidyapiths (Workers institute) now provides polyvalent education to neo-literate youth and workers in urban as well as rural areas.

Challenges faced in Education Sector

Education plays a dominant role as an effective instrument for large scale achievement and involvement in all spheres. Purposeful education enables the individual to understand and study the real life situation and develop opportunity for creating in the minds of younger generation and provide a strong base for natural and value oriented and nation building progress.(Mayers and Harbison, 2001)

Education is also a supplier of trained manpower. The educational system of a nation determines the type, nature and calibre of manpower to be supplied to the various sectors in the nation. In recent times, the calibre of man power graduated from the tertiary educational institution in Nigeria is an indicator that the educational system is ineffective

This is so because knowledge acquired makes them readily unfit for the labor market. This simply means that there is a mismatch between the skills acquired and labor market requirements.

The international partners over the years have been doing a lot trying to bridge the gap of mismatch through various services they offer towards educational improvement agenda.

According to United Nation's Children Fund (UNICEF) Nigeria has the highest number of out of school children in the world. This is both alarming and scary. About 10.5 million children are out of school in Nigeria. To put things in perspective, 10.5 million is about the population of Libya and Liberia put together. The danger owe harbour therefore is that we may be building a nation of unenlightened, ill informed, the misfits, the vagabonds and ill equipped individuals for the future.

Describing the situation, UNICEF says *"Nigeria's population growth has put pressure on the country's resources, public services and infrastructure. With children under 15 years of age accounting for 45% of the 180 million population the burden on education has become most overwhelming."*

To be sure, little progress has been made even as UNICEF also admits that primary school enrolments has increased in recent years, but net attendance is only about 70% . Still the country's number of out of school children at 10.5 million is the highest in the world. To the discerning, we cannot set for ourselves the goal of becoming the largest economy in Africa and a leading one globally while contending with such grim statistics with regards to early childhood care and education. It is simply unacceptable.

The Nigeria school system has been plagued with critical infrastructural decay, inadequate funding, exam malpractice and cultism, incidences of unqualified teachers. Some of which has culminated into incessant strike actions leading to unstable and unharmonized educational calendars especially within the university system. The entire educational system needs to be reengineered to meet the 21st century demands.

The fundamental source of the present crises is in the Nigeria education system has to do with either a failure to appreciate and therefore come to grips with the truth that education is the indispensable key to sustainable development, human capital being the most crucial factor of production or with the historic lip service that leaders have characteristically paid to that truism. (A. Akindele "Wanted : An urgent overhaul of Nigeria's (higher) educational   system, editorial comments, Newsletter of the social science academy of Nigeria Vol A, No 2 Sept 2001, P.111

Politics in Education

Efficient leadership in a nation's development cannot be underestimated. Thus, practice of healthy politics can be an effective measure in this direction, when asked whether political parties should enter the college campus at the time of elections of the college council the student response was as depicted by the diagram below.

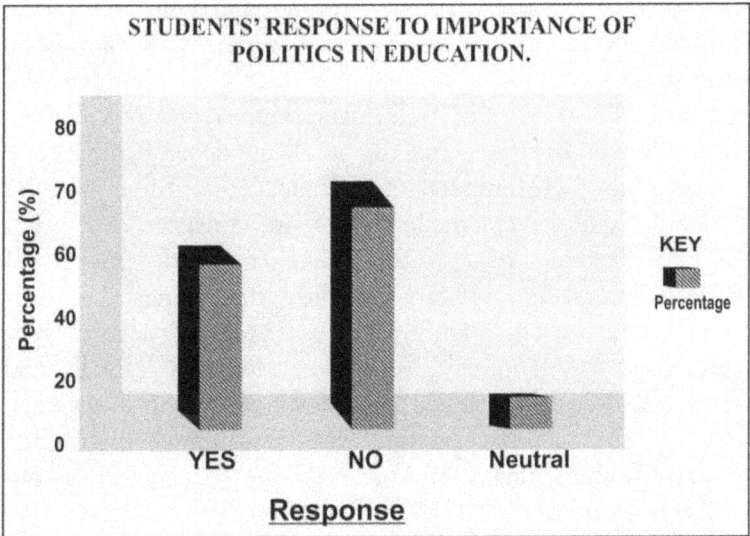

The student's response itself shows their awareness to the condition of Nigeria's current political space. Since there is a growing awareness of politics among student fundamental. Politics education should become mandatory in schools and colleges. This would improve the students' awareness and help develop the essential leadership qualities in them so that those interested in being political leaders may step ahead in the right direction. Jawaharlel Nehra the first prime minister of India dispend an academic atmosphere in the university and should not be polluted by party politics. In his letter to the minister he wrote "If we are to maintain any kind of academic atmosphere or discipline in a university, we must keep out what we call party politics from it"

How true was the statement students involvement in politics though mentioned hitherto in this piece will prepare interested materials for future politics has not helped issues at the long run. The admixture of education and politics have only bred the misfits, the vagabonds, the rude and all such characters that has adorned our political space off late. The comatose state of education that have defied known remedies is not unconnected with the prolonged military rule. This problem cannot be better expressed them in the words of Amuwo that "After almost three decades of repressive military rule in Nigeria, political appointments by Generals and colonials have become the stock in trade of intellectual moonlighting". Members of the academic hired by the military regimes were made to contain, constrict and shrink the intellectual space rather than facilitate intellectual empowerment. The military rule did worse things: The self-worth and moral dignity of the academic sector were threatened (Adekunle Amuwo; Between intellectual responsibility and political commodification of knowledge Nigerian's Academic political scientists under Babaginda military Junta, 1985-1993) African studies review Vol 45, No 2, 2002 , P.113

The Federal Government of Nigeria, under Muhammed Buhari's watch in conjunction with some states in the country initiated the home grown school feeding programme to promote enrolment at the primary school level. Studies from different parts of the world have shown the promise inherent in school feeding programmes and initial feedback suggests that some level of success is recorded here in Nigeria as well. But a realization of the enormity of the task at hand should inform the need to do more and hurriedly too.

Conclusion

We have tried in this paper to make the point whether or not tolerant societies are more likely to invest in education through various positions captured with the response of various nation states in Nigeria whose positive roles generated wide spread educational progress. We also cited the roles played by Singapore and India in advancing educational frontiers of their own. The sacrifices each individual nation did that altered the otherwise gloomy educational landscape in their countries. We have also highlighted on the various positions of education, from different school of thoughts what education means to different people and situations. The paper also discusses the challenges that plagued Nigerian educational system and the need to keep the education sector devoid of politics and the negative aura prolonged military administration in Nigeria enveloped the Nigeria educational sector.

We will end this presentation with a heartfelt appreciation to the Lord Almighty for giving us this wonderful and uniquely outstanding country. We strongly believe that with the brilliant population Nigeria is blessed with, our educational frontiers is destined to be branded among the very best in the world where merit takes precedence over quota system and unnecessary politics. We in Peniel Library and National Action Committee on Read Campaign of the Federal Ministry of Education on whose Mandate the presentation is made commend the organizer of Dr Okwadike Chukwuemka Ezeife's 80th Birthday Anniversary for the opportunity extended to us to do this presentation.

It is a truism that every nation gets the education it is willing to pay for! Let's invest in the education of our children for qualitative service delivery. Quality is never an accident, it is always the result of high intention, sincere effort, intelligent directions and skillful execution, it represents the wise choice of many alternatives (William A. Foster)

References

Adekunle, Amuwo "Between Intellectuals, Responsibility and political commodification of knowledge. Nigeria's Academic Political scientist under Babangida Militart Junta, 1985-1993") African studies Review, Vol 45, No 2, 2002, P.113

A.Akindele,2Wanted. An Urgent overhead of Nigeria's (Higher) Educational system, "Educational System, "Editorial comments, newsletter of the social science academy of Nigeria, Vol. A No 2, Sept 2001, P.11

Emile Durkhein, Education and sociology (New York's Free Press. 1966).P.12

G.K. Kneller, Introduction to philosophy of Education (London: John Willey and sons 1964), Page 20

Ibid, P.16

Mayers and Harbison, 2001, M.D Shipman, Education and modernization (London Fater and Faber LTD, 1971) P.34

P.s-Peters, Philosophy of Education (London Oxford University Press 1980)

J Cookney of 1967, The university of Lagos. In Adeniyi Aderalegbe, ed, philosophy for Nigeria Educational Research council 1972)

J. Cooknet, "The Nigeria National Curriculum Conference of 1967", The university of Lagos. In Adeniyi Aderalegbe, ed, philosophy for Nigeria Education (Lagos Nigeria Educational Research Council, 1972) P. XXXII

31

DEMOCRACY AND SUSTAINABLE NATIONAL DEVELOPMENT IN NIGERIA (2000 – 2014): DISSECTING CUM X-RAYING THE NEXUS

By Chukwudi Ucheagu

Chukwudi studied Philosophy and Humanities. He holds a Bachelor of Science Degree in Political Science from Enugu State University of Science and Technology. He also studied for Masters in Business Administration at the Ambrose Alli University, Ekpoma, and is currently a postgraduate student of Political Economy and Development Studies, University of Abuja.

INTRODUCTION

Democracy is at the crossroads in Nigeria. National Development also has altogether, only materialized in the inscrutable imaginations of Nigeria's national development planners. Indeed, a plethora of studies exist on democracy and development in Nigeria (Achebe 1983).

There is therefore, ostensibly in existence, a humongous volume of panacea on the possibilities of establishing an empirical nexus between democracy and sustainable national development in Nigeria. Furthermore, the most contemporary critical policy ambitions and interventions in the area of democracy and sustainable national development in Nigeria, are inter alia: the National Economic Empowerment and Development Strategy (NEEDS), promoted by the Olusegun Obasanjo Administration (1999-2007); the Seven-point Agenda of the Umaru Yar'Adua Dispensation (2007-2010) and the Transformation Agenda of the current Goodluck Jonathan era, which commenced 2010. In effect, what the above-mentioned development try-outs seriously have in common, is the assumption that democracy and national development are products of policy sentiments. The endpoints of these assumptions have been pedagogic imaginations that are cast in stone, on how some immutable precepts of classical democracy and some modern versions of democratic shenanigans, invariably lead to sustainable national development. In this regard, Ja'afaru Bambale (2011:22) opines that in reality the NEEDS reforms have left much to be desired; Dode (2010:7) contends that the Yar'Adua Administration lacked the political and administrative will to implement the seven-point agenda; while Gyong (2012:106) sees as a major challenge to the success of the Transformation Agenda of President Jonathan, the near absence of a purposeful, trusted, respected and focused leadership in Nigeria.

Indeed, in December 2013, ex-President Obasanjo, generally known to have been responsible for Jonathan's ascendancy to Nigeria's presidency, in an 18-page publicly circulated letter, addressed to President Jonathan, accused the President as a person, of being deficit in purposeful, trustworthy, respectable and focused leadership credentials. Chief Obasanjo, in highly acerbic tones, accused President Jonathan of being bereft of democratic tendencies and credentials. Yet, as pointed out by Campbell (2013), there is irony in Obasanjo's critique, as he more than anyone else was responsible for Jonathan's selection as PDP vice presidential candidate in 2007 and with the death of President Yar'Adua in 2010, Jonathan became the president – and the incumbent in 2011, after emerging victorious in a general election. Truly, since Nigeria's return to the path of democratic governance in 1999, among the greatest tests to the resilience of the nation's new democracy, must be counted the attempt by the then President Obasanjo to extend his stay in office, beyond the constitutionally permitted two terms of four years each.

Thus, reacting then to the defeat at the Nigerian National Assembly, of what was nationally known as Obasanjo's Third Term Agenda, Sango (2006) opined that for the vast majority of the ordinary people across Nigeria, President Obasanjo was synonymous with socio-economic disaster. Curiously, this same Ex-President Obasanjo has returned to advise President Jonathan on democracy and development. Furthermore, on policy ambitions, we highlight that beyond the three policy encapsulations strictly identifiable above with the three democratic leadership epochs in Nigeria, there is yet the fourth of such grandstanding that its initiation or fine-tuning, could be partly claimed by any of the abovementioned Nigerian regimes. The occasioning esoteric ambition goes by the au courant nomenclature of Vision 20:2020. However, there is hardly anything in the contents of Vision 20:2020 in Nigeria, that is new; that cannot be found in extant Nigerian policy documents. In fact, in a burst of curious self-deprecation, Nigerian Vision 20:2020 (2009:7) claims to have encapsulated the key principles and thrusts of the National Economic Empowerment and Development Strategy (NEEDS) and the Seven Point Agenda of the democratic administration (2007-2011); positing to have situated both policies, within a single, long term strategic planning perspective that would take Nigeria to the year 2020. But the fact remains that in its entirety, the contents of Nigerian Vision 20:2020 are already embedded in extant Nigerian development literature; in long term, short term or strategic perspectives.

Truly, in Nigeria's current post-military dispensation, politics without progress or politics as national bazaar, invariably translate to democracy without progress. Parenthetically, democracy without progress is democracy without development. Progress must be person-centered and development, human focused. Progress must not be conceived in terms of official figures that ostensibly indicate growth. Hence, what is to be done requires some re-imaginations. Accordingly, the general objective of this study is to examine the relationship between democracy and sustainable national development in Nigeria and consequently reimagine their nexus. The specific objectives are to: (i) examine the extent to which there is politics without progress in Nigeria (ii) verify the extent to which there is democracy without development in Nigeria and (iii) recommend ways of making Nigeria's democracy, invariably lead to national development. The theoretical framework for the study is the political economy framework. The theory of political economy draws heavily on the subject of economics, political science, law, history and sociology or different closely related branches of economics to explain the politico-economic behavior of a country (Timimi 2010:1).

Thus, it is strictly held in this study that economic development is central to national development. In other words, it is strictly held in the study that the effective interplay of politics and economics lead to national development. The study uses as research methodology, the critical mode of research; which fundamentally, conforms to the study's theoretical framework of political economy.

Democracy: A Conceptual Elucidation

The democratic form of government has fascinated philosophers since the first democracies appeared in ancient Greece about 2500 years ago (Fleck and Hanssen, 2002:2). In the process, a number of scholars have concluded that although the term democracy, is derived from Greek *demokratia,* literally peoplepower, democracy today has nothing to do with power or the people, let alone the power of (all) the people and if it still retains any content whatever, it is merely that of "free elections" and other sorts of occasional voting, for what is becoming an ever-smaller proportion of the potential electorate (Cartledge, 2007:162; citing Dunn 1993; Wood 1995).

Hence, in further situating democracy within the historical context of its ancient Greek origins, Ober (2007:94) argues that to say that an event made democracy possible requires us to define what we mean by democracy. Ober (2007:99) further argues: my preferred alternative is to look at the root meaning of the compound word dêmokratia and the ideals that are exemplified in philo-democratic writing (and parodied by democracy's critics) from the fifth through the fourth century. Dêmokratia means, imprimis, the power of the people: the publicly manifested power of the dêmos to make things happen. It is the authority or dominance of the demos in the polis (Ober, 2007:99). In continuation of his definition of democracy; Ober (2008), posits that the original meaning of democracy is the capacity to do things, not majority rule. This is instructive, within our context of democracy and sustainable national development in Nigeria. This is because, there is this apparent Nigerian orthodoxy that equates democracy to majority rule. However, a basic assumption of democracy is that it should guarantee the welfare of the citizens. In Nigeria however, Ojakorotu and Allen (2009) have demonstrated that democracy neglects the welfare of the citizens.

Hence, any system of government that fails to guarantee the welfare of the citizens will be difficult to market as democracy. It may be more germane to call such a system ceremonial democracy. It does appear however, as if the underpinnings of Nigeria's brand of democracy, fully shows the tendencies of democratic capitalism, otherwise known as capitalist democracy.

The Concept of Sustainable National Development

Sustainable national development in the context of this study is intrinsically related to economic development. It is also important at this juncture to highlight that economic development in this study also highly relates with economic security, which in the final analysis should be human centered.

It is quite distinct from economic development as represented by growth-figures from the officialdom. Hence, by the problem of economic development may be meant the problem of accounting for the observed pattern, across countries and across time, in levels and rates of growth of per capita income (Lucas, Jr, 1988:3). In this study, per capita income still means a measure of the amount of money that is being earned per person in a certain area (http://www.investopedia.com). However, the twin concepts of poverty and inequality, which in their extreme cases translate to destitution, are more in tune with our methodology. Amaefule (2013:1) quotes the World Bank as announcing that over 100 million Nigerians live in destitution.

The World Bank Country Director for Nigeria, Marie-Francoise Marie-Nelly, said this at the bank's Country Programme Portfolio Review in Enugu, Nigeria, on Tuesday, November 12, 2013. According to the World Bank boss, the number of Nigerians living in destitution makes up 8.33 per cent of the total number of people living in destitution all over the world. Marie- Nelly also said that although the World Bank was the largest overseas development agency that provided assistance to Nigeria, the contribution of the organization to the country was very small compared to the budgets of the states and the Federal Government. She said if the World Bank's small assistance could produce so much result because of effective implementation and monitoring, the revenues accruable to the country could do much more if they were similarly utilized (Amaefule, 2013:1). Incidentally, Nigeria's politico-economic class is not enamored by such distracting suggestions as effective implementation and monitoring of the revenues accruable to the country. They are more in love with letter writing, as tool of governance.

Hence, the national concept of business is weird. In its Doing Business 2014 Economy Profile, the World Bank (2013), ranked Nigeria at the 147th position, out of 189 countries. As a matter of fact, Nigeria dropped by -9 points from her 2013 position of 138 out of 185 countries. Thus, both in its literal and metaphoric interpretations, doing business in Nigeria has become traumatic and negates the positive assumptions that might have informed all the extant policy plans in the current democratic dispensations, from NEEDS to every other emotive design. Thus, sustainable national development remains realizable only in the emotive imaginations of policy planners, while destitution increases.

Indeed, it is not yet clear and acceptable to the politico-economic class in Nigeria that sustainable national development is more of a product of attitude than blue prints. Truly, sustainable national development is a function of the attitudes of a contented citizenry. It is not a function of some imported artefacts that malfunction perpetually, in the midst of poverty and inequality, leading to endless alibi of insufficient megawatts that lead to unending darkness, in place of electricity.

Democracy and Sustainable National Development in Nigeria: An Elucidation Using Democratic Capitalism.

The problem of democracy and sustainable national development in Nigeria is fundamentally, a problem of democratic capitalism. Streeck (2011: 3) has characterized democratic capitalism as follows: a political economy ruled by two conflicting principles or regimes of resource allocation: one operating according to marginal productivity or what is revealed as *merit* by a free play of market forces and the other following social need or *entitlement*, as certified by the collective choices of democratic politics.

Governments under democratic capitalism are under pressure to honor both principles simultaneously, although substantively the two almost never agree - or they can afford to neglect one in favor of the other only for a short time until they are punished by the consequences, political in the one case and economic in the other (Streeck, 2011:3). Younkins (1998:1) further highlights that according to Michael Novak, democratic capitalism is an amalgam of three systems: (1) an economy based predominantly on free markets and economic incentives, (2) a democratic polity and (3) a classical liberal moral-cultural system which encourages pluralism. Essentially, capitalism is an economic system characterized by freedom of thought and voluntary action creatively applied to production; it is based on private property rights, economic justice, the profit motive, competition, a division of labor, and requisite social cooperation. Democracy is based on the principles of consent and political equality and may be defined as a political system in which governments are established by majority votes cast in regular, unhindered and uninterrupted elections. It is often argued that capitalism is a necessary but not a sufficient condition of democracy since democracy requires basic economic rights that are separate from the state (Younkins, 1998:2). Here lies the contradictions of democratic capitalism.

Indeed, the above explications read like elucidations on Nigeria's troubled political economy. Nigeria's political economy is managed by an ostensibly inchoate and dubious politico-economic class, whose actual dilemma rather borders on the contradictions of democratic capitalism. Let us illustrate: when this class designs NEEDS and their various

AGENDA and VISIONS; they know that the programmes are outlandish. But they need such bizarre designs in all their multiplier dimensions to gratify and recompense their capitalist partners, whose interests and tastes must be accommodated at all times. They also use such eccentric designs to give a semblance of democratic commitments to salivating but bemused citizens.

Hence, after nearly a decade and half of NEEDS, a Seven-point agenda, a Transformation agenda and a Vision 20: 2020 master plan, a curious position has arisen whereby, ostensibly as part of the agricultural miracles of these fateful experimentations, Nigeria is now the No. 1 producer of cassava on the face of the earth (see Asante-Pok, 2013). However, in all the (local) Nigerian markets, the cost of garri, a food derivative of cassava and a major Nigerian staple, keeps recording unbearable increases (Orewa and Egware, 2012: vanguardngr.com, 2013), an indication that democracy or democratic capitalism has not guaranteed economic security. This is the current position.

Let us turn to the future reality. In essence, the future reality is contemplated with trepidation. Kukah (2012:1) alludes to the future reality as the type that might emanate from a present terminal condition. He goes further to posit that with the nation tottering dangerously on the precipice, with the increasing central role being played by non-state actors and institutions, with the political class treating politics as a national bazaar, it is clear that the matters of the survival of the nation are too serious to be left to the political class which behaves as if there is neither a teacher nor a class (Kukah, 2012:1). It is not highfalutin to suggest that the Nigerian nation is tottering dangerously on the precipice, in an era that Kukah (2013) characterizes as an era of Epistolatocracy (Government by Letter Writing). This is in an apparent reference to the harvest of letters witnessed by the political system in Nigeria, after ex- President Obasanjo wrote to President Jonathan in December 2013, accusing the President of being deficit in democratic tendencies and credentials and above all, questioning the President's moral credentials as a person. Former President Obasanjo's first daughter (Iyabo Obasanjo-Bello), was purportedly the next to write (to her father), probably provoked by her father's letter to President Jonathan; calling her father unprintable names and vowing that the letter was her last communication ever, with an irresponsible father, who had been behaving as if he was the owner of Nigeria. Very many other open political letters were consequently transmitted to the polity, until the climax or anti-climax (depending on the reader's political leaning) came in the form of President Jonathan's reply to former President Obasanjo. In any case, we are more concerned in this study, with the import of President Jonathan's reply to ex-President Obasanjo, than with the contents; being that the contents of the three principal letters (the contentious Iyabo letter inclusive), were never fundamentally about the welfare of Nigerian citizens. According to Momodu (2013:1), none of the letters truthfully addressed the issues of development - the issues of economic security. They were letters reeking with personal animosity and rabid vendetta.

The common motive was simple and easy to decipher: who controls power and Nigeria's commonwealth from 2015, after the general elections? No more, no less (Momodu, 2013:1). Furthermore, Igbokwe (2013), feels as follows: open stealing of the common patrimony, lack of accountability, impunity, intimidation of opposition, weak leadership, insecurity; nepotism and gross abuse of office have been the hallmark of President Jonathan's administration. Ex-President Obasanjo's letter to President Jonathan should be seen as a service to fatherland even though the messenger is defective, and his hands ugly. If Jonathan and his handlers are not managed or called to order, they can rock the boat (Igbokwe, 2013). In essence, the foregoing advances our thesis of a precarious

NIGERIA - DEMOCRACY & STATE OF THE ECONOMY

picture of future reality.

Nigeria's Dilemma in Democracy and Development

Truly, Nigeria needs development, which in the context of this study translates to economic development, which further translates to economic security, which is person-centerd. Indeed, devoid of economic security, economic development becomes an abstraction. Nigeria's vociferous advisers however claim that she needs democracy. We underscore the fact that economics as a science instructs citizens and politicians that markets are better for them than politics and that *real* justice is *market* justice under which everybody is rewarded according to contribution rather than to needs redefined as rights. In the real world, however, it is not all that easy to talk people out of their "irrational" beliefs in social and political rights, as distinguished from the law of the market and the right of property (Streeck, 2011:3/4). Beliefs in social and political rights embolden citizens to demand the dividends of democracy, from their representatives in government. As a matter of fact, democracy is fundamentally about the social and political rights of citizens. Market justice is their antithesis. Market justice is the major impetus for the capitalist side of democratic capitalism. Incidentally, it also supplies fuel to profligacy in the management of state resources in a state like Nigeria. In the process, Nigeria is perceived to be running the costliest democracy in the world. Ejuvbekpokpo (2012) has abundantly demonstrated that excessive cost of governance in Nigeria hampers economic development. Onyisi and Eme (2013) have also sufficiently demonstrated with concrete instances, that under the Jonathan Presidency in Nigeria, cost of governance is rather outrageous. According to Enwegbara (2013), government after government in Nigeria, since the return to democracy in 1999, has talked about reducing the country's high cost of governance.

The irony is that rather than reducing, every new government

313

seems to be increasing it further than it inherited from its predecessor (Enwegbara, 2013). In fact, since Nigeria's return to the path of civilian government in 1999, the market justice theorists have taken the center stage.

A particularly pronounced promoter of market justice theory in the political economy of Nigeria is the internationally reputable World Bank bureaucrat, Dr Ngozi Okonjo-Iweala, who was Minister of Finance and the Coordinating Minister for the Economy, in the Jonathan Administration. Recently, Okonjo-Iweala made the following admission, about the economy of Nigeria:

According to Thisdaylive (2013): The Coordinating Minister for the Economy and Minister of Finance, Dr. Ngozi Okonjo-Iweala, has warned that the Nigerian economy may be in a precarious situation if the private sector does not join hands with government to create jobs and reduce inequality in the country. Okonjo-Iweala who made this known at a breakfast dialogue in Lagos, tagged: "The State of the Nigerian Economy in 2013," organized by the Nigerian Economic Summit Group (NESG), also warned that the politicization of Nigeria's budgeting process would not help the country. The minister, who accused the private sector of creating wealth for a few and not jobs, disclosed that the federal government created a total of 1.6 million jobs in 2012 and another 431, 000 jobs in the first quarter of 2013.

This, she added, showed an improved trend of job creation and increase of 11.69 per cent over the level in the fourth quarter of 2012. The minister, who hailed the government's economic policies, stated that without microeconomic stability there could be no jobs, adding that the government would continue to pursue microeconomic stability so that companies could plan. According to her, the quality of growth in the economy needs to improve; we are not creating enough jobs, the Minister complained (Thisdaylive, 2013). We need to grow faster in job creating sectors at between 10 per cent per annum, to create jobs needed to substantially reduce poverty in the country. The inequality in the country is growing faster and the growth in the economy is not inclusive. If the private sector does not create jobs, the economy will be in danger. Only the top 10% of Nigerians are enjoying most of the growth in the economy unlike what is obtainable in the United States of America. We also very importantly need to take care of regional disparity and carry every region of the country along, Okonjo- Iweala concluded (Thisdaylive, 2013).

The issue of substantiating claims of creating a total of 1.6 million jobs in 2012 and another 431,000 jobs in the first quarter of 2013 in Nigeria by the market justice devotees, whose key player in Nigeria's political economy was Okonjo-Iweala, could be suspended for now; after all, in listening to somebody's dream experiences, the listener is obligated to the dream narrator, over matters of the benefit of the doubt, on the veracity of claims made by the dreamer. The truth remains however, that Okonjo-Iweala's admission of the imminence of danger in the economy is evident of development in reverse gear in the political economy of Nigeria; in tandem with the inherent contradictions of capitalist democracy, as led by market justice. Invariably, Nigeria's dilemma in democracy and development is the dilemma of democratic capitalism. Essentially, if "we, the people", jettison their market justice theory at this point, under the ambition of reinstituting democracy, the people will be accused of torpedoing the process of development. Alternatively, the long-suffering citizens will continue to bear the weight of the contradictions of capitalist democracy. Parenthetically, if the victims of market justice ("we, the people") fail to act, they do grave injustice to democracy, as their social and political rights are trampled upon. This is the dilemma of democracy and development in Nigeria.

Conclusion/Recommendations

In conclusion, we reiterate that democracy is at the crossroads in Nigeria and that development also has only materialized in the unbecoming imaginations of Nigeria's ostensibly eminent development planners; mostly advocates of the market justice worldview. Our findings indeed, highly support the thesis that there is politics without progress in Nigeria.

Furthermore, our findings justify the viewpoint that critically, there is democracy without development in Nigeria. Our concept of development is entirely man-centered as contrary to the highfalutin performance indicators from officialdom. In conclusion, we have postulated in our re-imaginations, that what needs to be done in locating the nexus of democracy and sustainable national development in Nigeria is truly not complicated.

Democracy we imagined, must lead to the creation of new Nigerians / a stock of new human capital and that the core of the brand of democracy that would link democracy with development in Nigeria, has to be essentially deliberative. In essence, in our re-imaginations, we inferred that the location of the elusive nexus between democracy and sustainable national development in Nigeria involves far more than an understanding of theory, since it will only succeed when real people with limited knowledge and conflicting interests can be persuaded to put aside some part of their own private needs in order to contribute to a collective and cooperative enterprise (Brett 2000:20) officially known as the Federal Republic of Nigeria.

References:

Aborisade, S. (2013): "INEC to Spend N93b on 2015 Elections" http://www.punchng.com/news/inec-to-spend-n93bn-on-2015-elec Accessed, 20/12/13.

Achebe, C. (1983): *The Trouble with Nigeria.* Enugu: Fourth Dimension Publishers.

Asante-Pok, A. (2013): *Analysis of Incentives and Disincentives for Cassava in Nigeria.* Technical Notes Series. Rome: Food and Agricultural Organization (FAO) of the United Nations.

Aimurie, I and Agba, G. (2013): "Shale Oil: We Must Diversify Economy Now – Jonathan". http://leadership.ng. Accessed, 20/12/13.

Akwen, G and Gever, D. (2012): "Challenges of Democracy and Development in Nigeria's Niger Delta Region: An Appraisal". *European Scientific Journal* 8(16) 52-67.

Amaefule, A. (2013): "100 Million Nigerians Live in Destitution – World Bank." http://www.punchng.com/news/100-million-nigerians-live-in-Accessed, 20/12/13.

Arthur, J. (1992): *Democracy: Theory and Practice.* New York: International Thomson.

Berger, P. (1986): *The Capitalist Revolution.* New York: Basic Books.

Brett, E. (2000): "Development Theory, Universal Values and Competing Paradigms: Capitalist Trajectories and Social Conflict" Working Paper Series No.00-02, LSE Development Studies Institute, London School of Economics and Political Science

Campbell, J. (2013): "Former Nigerian President Obasanjo's Letter to President Goodluck Jonathan" http://blogs.cfr.org/campbell/2013/12/13/former-nigerian-president-ob Letter-to-president-goodluck-jonathan/. Accessed, 16/12/13.

Campbell, J. (2011): *Nigeria: Dancing on the Brink.* Lanham, Maryland: Council on Foreign Relations (Rowman and Littlefield)

Cartledge, P (2007): "Democracy, Origins of: Contribution to a Debate." In K. Raaflaub, et al (Ed.) *Origin of Democracy in Ancient Greece*, Berkeley/los Angele: University of California Press

Clark, N and Ausukuya, C. (2013): "An Overview of Education in Nigeria" http://wenr.wes.org.Accessed, 30/12/13

OKWADIKE@80

Dode, R. (2010): "Yar'Adua 7-Point Agenda, the MDGS and Sustainable Development in Nigeria". Global *Journal of Human Social Science* 10(4) 1- 8.

Dunn, J. (1993): *Western Political Theory in the Face of the Future.* 2d ed. Cambridge: Cambridge University Press

Ejuvbekpokpo, S. (2012): "Cost of Governance on Economic Development in Nigeria." *Global Journal of Management and Business Research* 12 (13) 18-24.

Enwegbara, B. (2013): "High Cost of Governance in Nigeria." http://www.punchng.com. Accessed, 27/12/13.

Farrar, C. (2007): "Power to the People." In K. Raaflaub, et al (ed.) *Origin of Democracy in Ancient Greece,* Berkeley/los Angele: University of California Press.

Federal Government of Nigeria (2009): Nigeria Vision 20: 2020 Economic Transformation Blueprint

Fleck, R and Hanssen, F. (2002): "The Origins of Democracy: A Model with Application to Ancient Greece" http://www.tsoulouhas.info/PDFsIOworkshop/Greece%207.5.pdf Accessed, 18/12/13.

Gyong, J. (2012): "A Social Analysis of the Transformation Agenda of President Goodluck Ebele Jonathan". *European Scientific Journal* 8 (16) 95-113.http://www.investopedia.com/terms/i/income-per.   Accessed, 29/12/13.

Ibobor, S (2004): "Democracy and National Development" *Multidisciplinary Journal of Research Development* 3(1) 96-101.

Igbokwe, J. (2013): "Obasanjo's Letter: Please Cut the Hand but take the Message." http://olorisupergal.com.Accessed, 27/12/13.

Ja'afaru Bambale, A. (2011): "National Economic Empowerment Development Strategy & Poverty Reduction in Nigeria: A Critique" *Economics and Finance Review* 1(1): 15-24.

Joseph, R. (1987). Democracy and Prebendal Politics in Nigeria: The Rise and Fall of the Second Republic, London: Cambridge University Press.

Joseph, R and Gillies, A. (2010): "Nigeria's Season of Uncertainty" *Current History*.109 (727)179-185.

Kukah, M. (2012): "Nigeria as an Emerging Democracy: Dilemma and Promise."http://www.thenationonlineng.net/2011/index.php/law/. Accessed, 11/11/13.

Kukah, M. (2013): ""In This Era of Epistolatocracy (Government by Letter Writing)" http://saharareporters.com. Accessed, 27/12/13.

Lawal, T. and Olukayode, O. (2012): "Democracy and Development in Nigeria" *International Journal of Development and Sustainability* 1(2) 448– 455.

Lijadu, L. (2013): "Nigeria is Already a Failed State." http://saharareporters.com/article/nigeria-already-failed-state-david-l Accessed, 27/12/13.

Lucas Jr, R. (1988): "On the Mechanics of Economic Development." *Journal of Monetary Economics* 22 (-) 3-42.

Majekodunmi, A. (2012): "Democratization and Development in Nigeria: The Fourth Republic in Perspective". *International Journal of Academic Research in Economics and Management Sciences* 1(5) 62-74.

Momodu, D. (2013): "Beyond the Letter Writers" http://www.thisdaylive.com/articles/beyond-the-letter-writers Accessed, 28/12/13

Muoghalu, K. (2013): "The Human Capital Dimension of Economic Transformation" Lecture Delivered at the Golden Jubilee Ceremony of the 1st Graduates of the University of Nigeria, Nsukka.

Novak, M. (1982): *The Spirit of Democratic Capitalism.* New York: Simon and Schuster.

Novak, M. (1989): *Free Persons and the Common Good.* Lanham, MD:

Madison Books. Nwanegbo, C and Odigbo, J. (2013): "Security and National Development in Nigeria: The Threat of Boko Haram" *International Journal of Humanities and Social Science* 3(4) 285-291.

Ober, J. (2007): "I Besieged that Man." Democracy's Revolutionary Start. In K. Raaflaub, et al (Ed.), *Origin of Democracy in Ancient Greece.* Berkeley/los Angele: University of California Press

Ober, J. (2008): "The Original Meaning of 'Democracy': Capacity to Do Things, not Majority Rule" *Constellations* 15(1) 3-9.

OKWADIKE@80

Ofuebe, C. (2005): *The Scramble for Nigeria: Essays on Administrative and Political Engineering in Nigeria.* Enugu: New Generation Books.

Ogundiya, I. et al, (Eds) (2011): *Assessment of Democratic Trends in Nigeria.* New Delhi: Gyan Publishing House

Ojakorotu, V and Allen, F. (2009): "From "Authoritarian Rule" to "Democracy" in Nigeria: Citizens' Welfare a Myth or Reality" *Journal of Alternative Perspectives in the Social Sciences 1*(2) 152-192.

Okeke, R. (2010): "Legislature-Executive Relationship and the Nigerian National Assembly: 1999-2007." A Ph.D Seminar Paper Presented to the Department of Public Administration and Local Government, University of Nigeria, Nsukka.

Omodia, S. (2013): "Democracy and Development in Africa: The Nigerian Experience". *Mediterranean Journal of Social Sciences* 4(1) 569-573.

Onyisi, T and Eme, O. (2013): "The Presidency and Cost Of Governance In Nigeria: A Case of Jonathan's Administration" *Arabian Journal of Business and Management Review* (OMAN Chapter) 3(2) 1-24

Orewa, S and Egware, R. (2012): "Comparative Analysis of Rural and Urban Market Prices For Garri in Edo State, Nigeria: Implications for Food Security" *Journal of Development and Agricultural Economics* 4 (9) 252-257.

Osaghae, E. (1998): *Crippled Giant: Nigeria since Independence.* Bloomington: Indiana University Press

Oyovbaire, S. (Ed), (1987): *Democratic Experiment in Nigeria: Interpretative Essays.* Benin City: City Omega Publishers

Raaflaub K and Wallace, R (2007): "People's Power and Egalitarian Trends in Archaic Greece." In K. Raaflaub, et al (ed.), Origin *of Democracy in Ancient Greece.* Berkeley/los Angele: University of California Press.

Raaflaub, et al (2007) (Eds): *Origin of Democracy in Ancient Greece.* Berkeley/los Angele: University of California Press

Sango, S. (2006): "Nigeria after the Defeat of "Third Term" Agenda: What Way Forward For the Masses? http://www.socialistworld.net/doc/2335. Accessed, 17/12/13

Soludo, C., et al. (2004): "Nigeria: National Economic Empowerment and

320

Development Strategy (NEEDS)" Abuja: National Planning Commission

Streeck, W. (2011): "The Crisis in Context: Democratic Capitalism and Its Contradictions." MPIfG Discussion Paper 11/15. Max Planck Institute for the Study of Societies, Cologne. http://www.mpifg.de/pu/mpifg_dp/dp11- 15.pdf. Accessed, 19/12/13.

The Nigerian Economic Summit Group 'NESG' (2013): "Shale Oil Revolution: Implications for Nigeria". Policy Paper, 04 July.

Timimi, K. (2010): "Political Economy Theory" http://www.economywatch.com/political-economy/political-economy Accessed, 13/12/13.

United States Embassy in Nigeria (2012): *Nigeria Education Fact Sheet.* http://nigeria.usembassy.gov/. Accessed, 20/12/13.

Usher, D. (1981): *The Economic Prerequisite of Democracy.* New York: Columbia University Press. Vanguardngr.com (2013): "Price of Garri Records 50 % Rise." http://www.vanguardngr.com/2013/05/price-of-gari-records-50-rise/. Accessed, 27/12/13.

Wood, E. (1995): *Democracy against Capitalism: Renewing Historical Materialism* Cambridge: Cambridge University Press

World Bank (2013): *Doing Business 2014: Understanding Regulations for Small and Medium-Size Enterprises* Washington, DC: World Bank Group.

Younkins, E. (1998): "The Conceptual Foundations of Democratic Capitalism" http://www.quebecoislibre.org/younkins16.htm. Accessed, 22/ 12/13.

32

IS NIGERIA BETTER UNITED AND WHAT ARE THE FACTORS CAUSING DIVERGENCE IN NIGERIA?

Eze, Uzoamaka Jennifer
Executive Director: Ada Igbo Women Development Initiative
uzoamakajeze@gmail.com

Abstract

Nigeria is a diverse society that has witnessed various types of conflicts arising from different factors causing its non-cohesive engagement. With over 180 million people living in Nigeria, Nigeria is Africa's most populous country. It is divided into six regions, with two dominant religions, and over 250 ethnic groups and languages among which are three dominant ethnic groups- Igbo, Yoruba and Hausa-Fulani. With thirty six states and the Federal Capital Territory as its basis for state administration, Nigeria yearns for nationhood and rebirth of the concept of its nationhood in recognition of the divergent constituents which formed the foundation of agreement to form a federation true to its name- Federal Republic of Nigeria. There are many factors causing the divergence in Nigeria; for instance culture, politics, ethnic, religion and economy among other factors. This paper looks at these factors that are prominent in causing divergence in Nigeria.

Introduction

It has been difficult to establish and maintain stability and stable political culture based on rule of law and on merit toward building and integrating Nigerians. This is not far from the inadequate and lack of durable political orientations, absence of leadership and national patriotism. In most countries, the educational system was used to strengthen or to establish social understanding and cohesion. Nigerian case is a difference in that institutions for establishing social cohesion have become institutions promoting divergence.

Nigeria is a country divided along its cultural, political, ethnic, religious and economic classes among other divides. This division caused by lack of cohesion and national agreement based on understanding of various complexities challenging its nationhood has generated serious suspicion, distrust, and antagonism among its people. The divisions have caused problems such as lack of national economic growth and development, stable political engagement and patriotism, unity and survival of the unity of the country.

There have been different measures and approaches applied by different Nigerian administrations to unite and preserve the Nigerian nationhood which has been seen to be less effective and replete with bias (not merit) considerations giving rise to more distrust of the system and often times give rise to insecurity, religious violence, ethnic strife, political instability, social intolerance and threats of disintegration.

Nigeria is one of the most diverse countries, with a number of different linguistic and ethnic backgrounds. Nigeria yearns for nationhood and recognizing that the different divergent constituents of linguistic and ethnic backgrounds if better managed would be in a good position to confront these factors causing the country's slow development, crises of insecurity, intolerance, and inequalities which are along geographic and socio-economic lines causing ethnic divisions.

By truly confronting these issues openly and sincerely and imbibing the true essence of nationhood, these factors of divergence would surely become strength to achieving true nationhood based on respect for each other, bridging the gap of various forms of inequality and building social tolerance, equal participation and equal punishment for breaking the law. This paper therefore examines the factors that cause divergence in Nigeria. Let's look at what national cohesion means.

What is National Cohesion?

National cohesion is a "process of unifying a society which tends to make it a harmonious city, based on an order its members regard as equitably harmonious" (Duverger, 1976:177). This means that for Nigeria to attain a harmonious society, its constituents have to adopt an order which all groups have to regard as equitable. It also means to attain that harmonious society, there has to be an agreement based on certain principle of fairness that will develop into patriotic zeal leading to nationhood. Deutsch et al (1966:2) defines it as "the attainment, within a territory of a 'sense of community' and of institutions and practices strong enough and widespread enough to assure, for a long time, dependable expectations of peaceful community." This means that institutions of governance play a vital role in the promotion of national cohesion whereby these institutions are created to ensure a peaceful community, every member of the community is assured of protection promoting sense of community that brings together people rather than divide the people by beating down social differences and work towards building a harmonious community. For this reason, Coleman and Rosberg (1964:9) view national cohesion as the "progressive reduction of cultural and regional tensions {...} in the process of creating a homogeneous political community". A cohesive society is built when every aspect of divide is narrowed and promotion of equal participation through merit and application of rule of law are upheld. This gives utmost sense of community and builds a united nation.

Chukwuemeka Odumegwu-Ojukwu calls it is an 'active nation-building' by "forging out a nation out of our diverse ethnic groups." As this active nation building is not achieved; "Today, the result is that tribalism and ethnicity has become a potent source of friction, rather than diminish in the face of an emergent, virile and modern nation" (Odumegwu-Ojukwu, 1989:182).

Now that we have failed in the active nation building which has given rise to so many frictions, let us look at some of the factors that have made the nation building for national cohesion an upheaval task in today's Nigeria.

The Factors That Cause Divergence in Nigeria

Culture

Culture is "that complex whole which includes knowledge, belief, art, morals, law, custom, and any other capabilities and habits acquired by man as a member of society" (Tyler: 1870 in Avruch: 1998) . It is also "the set of attitudes, values, beliefs, and behaviors shared by a group of people, but different for each individual, communicated from one generation to the next.'(Matsumoto 1996: 16)

Culture by the definitions above is a complex way of life of a people within a given society, which makes them distinctive from other people. The belief system enshrined in the way of life of a people allows them to behave in certain ways when with other people other than a person of shared identity. Hence there is no national accepted culture, seen to be held supreme over ethnic cultural identity and way of life, Nigerians thereby cling to their respective cultures making no effort to beat down these attitudes in other to give way for active nation building.

In other to bridge the gap of national culture, Nigerian leaders tend to emphasize one Nigeria as national identity to improve social cohesion, and active nation building. The challenge then is to make diverse cultural identities an integral part of the national identity.

Politics

By 1949, Nigeria's first president Dr. Nnamdi Azikiwe in his address to Igbo people had complained of political exclusion of the Igbo by the colonist Britain which accompanied by the press of the day, labeled Igbo people as "the most hated in Nigeria" (Azikiwe 1961:243). This situation of exclusion and characterization of an ethnic group gave rise to other agitations of exclusion in the national polity culminating towards the Nigeria's independence which had other political constituents to strive for political domination. The political squabbles of the first republic gave rise to the civil war that pitched Nigerians against each other. Since then, politics is viewed with suspicion and strife until Nigerians came together to take control of their new nation and build a cohesive country using the 1963 constitution as their launching pad. But it did not end the struggle for dominance until the military came to power in 1966. The military's abrogation of the peoples' constitution centralizing governance pitched each political constituent against each other in the fight for the center thereby giving rise to the winner (ethnic or political constituency) takes it all.

However, politics could be used to engender economic growth, development and underdevelopment of a political constituent, depending on who is at the winning end of power play. This struggle for dominance has entrenched suspicion in the polity that Nigeria's national life activities are viewed through the lenses of ethnicity and other means of identity.

The politics of domination and marginalization gave birth to six regional groupings whereby each ethnic group will have a sense of community through rotating leadership and contributing to the nation building. Federal Character or Quota system was introduced to give all regions a fair participation but the lack of merit and equal participation within the quota system gave rise to feelings of favoritism and marginalization. This alienates Nigerians and perpetuates the embrace for one's ethnicity and identity against nation building for national cohesion.

Ethnicity

Ethnicity does not bring about conflict but subjective interpretation of the differences is of consequence. Sithole (1992) as cited in Anyebe (2016) asserts, "that mere difference and an awareness of (ethnicity) is of no consequence, but it is the subjective interpretation of the difference that is of consequence". It implies ethnic identity and awareness in itself is good but the perception of policy and evaluation of events, gives room for one ethnic group to see itself as dominant group based on numerical strength, feeling of superiority and seeing of others as rivals. For this, Teshome (2008) says, "ethnicity could be the basis for the unequal treatment of people and it may be the cause of ethnocentrism and prejudices against members of other ethnic groups".

Anyebe (2016) says, "Ethnicity, in addition, often contains an obscured class component. In this sense, it becomes a tool for the elite members of society to exploit to their advantages". It gives the feeling of conscious identity which often is employed to exploit benefits.

Ethnicity has been created by the privileged few to exploit the sentiments of the group to consolidate power. Sklar (1967) as cited in Osaghae (1994) views ethnicity as "implying the fact that in Africa, ethnic movements may be created and instigated to action by privileged men in a bid to further their own interests".

In Nigeria, political elites have many times used the sentiment of ethnicity to instigate social strife and struggle for the available resources and ultimately for their own interest. The struggle and rivalry has made nation building more difficult.

Religion

Nigeria has roughly equal number of Muslims and Christians (PEW, 2011) While Christian is at 46.3%, Muslim is at 46% as Traditional religion constitutes about 7.4%, others are at about 0.3% (Acs-Italia.org). While Christians dominate the southern part of the country, Muslims dominate the northern part of country. Christianity and lslam constitute the major religions in Nigeria, because they have large followership.

Nigeria has witnessed a number of crisis and conflicts that have deep root cause from religion. The earliest religious riot took place in Kano December 1980. The Bulunkutu riots occurred in Borno state and Kaduna, between October to November (1982) in Jimeta (1984) and Gombe (1985) were an extension of Kano crisis. The colonial policy of Britain and later the sharia debates of 1977/78 are responsible for the spate of violence in Nigeria (Egodi, 2004). The demand for sharia for a long time became a bargaining tool for the political elite. This has since gained a popular appeal among the ordinary Muslims. As sharia debate grew, religious leanings and fanaticism grew.

There has been suspicion and tension which has affected the understanding and integration of Nigerians. This was exacerbated by the President Ibrahim Babangida regime. In 1986, he registered Nigeria which has been seen as a secular state into the Organisation of Islamic Countries (OIC).

To try to recognize the Nigeria's diversity of religious

328

environment and attempt at not elevating or super imposing a particular religion over another, in the 1999 constitution 10, states, "The government of the federation or of a state shall not adopt any religion as state religion". Section 38 of the constitution also states that: "Every person shall be entitled to freedom of thought, conscience and religion, including freedom to change his religion or belief, and freedom {...} to manifest and propagate his religion or belief in worship, teaching, practice and observance".

Efforts have been made over time to actualize and promote a good dialogue for great understanding of the different world views of the two dominant religions which gave rise to balancing of elected officers, observing public prayers by the two religions etc. But these efforts have not been far reaching. Sharia debates persisted and in 2001 it gained recognition in twelve states of northern Nigeria. Christians interpreted sharia implementation as a provocation. This brought about religious violence, which has become a regular feature of Nigerian society. This has led to the rise of Boko Haram which declared, "War on Christians". They said, "The Nigerian state and Christians are our enemies and we will be launching attacks on the Nigerian state and its security apparatus as well as churches until we achieve our goal of establishing an Islamic state..." They declared, "We will create so much effort to have an Islamic state that Christians will not be able to stay" (Acs-Italia.org). With their declarations, there have been spates of killings within the Christian dominated areas in Nigeria.

In recent time, there have been killings of Christians and abduction of Christian girls by the Muslim youths and forceful conversion to Islam. "Ese Oruru, a minor, was allegedly abducted by Dahiru Yunusa in August 2015, taken to Kano State, converted to Islam and married off without her parents' consent" (Vanguard, 2017). The present government of President Muhammadu Buhari has done little or nothing in bridging the tensions. Under him there have been spates of killings in large numbers, taken place in many areas seem to be dominated by Christians. For this, the Christian Association of Nigeria (CAN) wrote, "The recurring decimal of violence and murder of innocent Nigerian citizens on the basis of religious intolerance demands specific and relevant response from all concerned citizens in the country more so when the government in power seems to have adopted an attitude of lukewarm response to the evils being perpetrated in Nigeria in the name of religion. The discrimination against non-Muslims in Nigeria under the Buhari Administration is assuming a dangerous dimension that should not be left to the vagaries of time and circumstance to resolve" (PremiumTimes, 2016). These issues have compounded the problems of nation building. The killings and wounds created will be hard to heal.

Economy

Heritage Foundation defines economic freedom as "the fundamental rights of every human to control his or her own labor and property, where individuals are free to work, produce, consume, and invest, where governments allow labor, capital, and goods to move freely, and refrain from coercion or constraint of liberty beyond the extent necessary to protect and maintain liberty itself." Importance have been accorded to economic freedom which is measured by property rights, freedom from corruption, fiscal freedom, government spending, business freedom, labor freedom, monetary freedom, trade freedom, investment freedom and financial freedom. These give rise to economic growth and development.

For this freedom, there have been agitations in Nigeria over control of resources and free economic environment which will ensure economic growth. The management of resources has been with the federal government which enables political elites to favor their constituencies and sometimes for themselves. The monthly allocation of fund has made several states to feed off from few states which see themselves as cash cow. For this reason, the agitation for resource control, fiscal federalism, economic restructuring etc, took a center stage. Economic freedom will energize the economy and institute competition which will attract investments.

Where government gets foreign aid from other developed countries, there is little effort to improve the economy. In a situation where for political reasons, certain investments are destroyed. As Abuja manages and controls every sector of the Nigerian economy, why would investments be attracted whereby the entire income tax is collected and shared depending on federal allocation criteria which largely are based on land mass? A state which produces more income tax and collect little in allocation, compared to states that produce little and collect large allocation due to large land mass, why would such a state make the effort to attract and promote investments? This has given rise to agitation of restructuring, and or at best outright division.

Conclusion

The factors costing Nigeria's unity and national cohesion are many. The call for restructuring which i believe will help to stop cultural, ethnic, religious and economic struggles will have less tension in its politics. If Nigeria deems to remain united for long, there is great need to decentralize economic and political power to ensure equal participation. Merit rather than cronyism should be elevated. With economic freedom towards individual regional control of their resources and political restructuring along the regional lines enshrined in a constitution decided by the people, instead of divergence, Nigeria will witness, economic growth, social cohesion and maintenance of cultural identities for national unity.

References

Anyebe, A A (2016) Ethnicity and Nation-building: Nigeria's Experience EPRA International Journal of Economic and Business Review volume 4/7

Avruch, K. (1998) Culture and Conflict Resolution. Washington DC: United States Institute of Peace Press.

Coleman, James S. and Rosberg, C.G. Jr. (1964) Political Parties and National Integration in Tropical Africa. Berkeley: University of California Press.

Deutsch, Karl et al (1966) Political Community and the North Atlantic Area, Integrational Political Communities: An Anthology. Gardens City: New Doubleday.

Duverger, Maurice (1976) The Study of Politics. Hong Kong: Nelson Political

Science Library.

Egodi, Uchendu (2004) Religion and Nation Building in Nigeria. Nigerian Heritage Journal of The National Commission for Museums and Monuments volume 13

Matsumoto, D. (1996) Culture and Psychology. Pacific Grove, CA: Brooks/Cole.

Nnamdi Azikiwe (1961) Zik: A Selection from the Speeches of Nnamdi Azikiwe, Cambridge University Press

Teshome W.B. (2008) Ethnicity and Political Parties in Africa: The Case of Ethnic-Based Parties in Ethiopia. The Journal of International Social Research, Volume 1/5.

Osaghae, E.E. (1994) Ethnicity and its Management in Africa Lagos: Malthouse Press Ltd.

Odumegwu-Ojukwu, Emeka (1989) Because I am Involved. Ibadan: Spectrum Books Ltd

Acs-Italia.org, Nigeria. <https://acs-italia.org/wp-content/uploads/Nigeria.pdf>

Constitution of the Federal Republic of Nigeria 1999

Heritage Foundation, Index of Economic Freedom <https://www.heritage.org >

Pew Research Center (2011, January 27) The Future of the Global Muslim Population <http://www.pewforum.org/2011/01/27/the-future-of-the-global-muslim-population/>

Premium Times (2016, July 12) CAN Reacts to Brutal Killing of Female Christian Preacher in Abuja <https://www.premiumtimesng.com/news/top-news/206747-can-reacts-brutal-killing-female-christian-preacher-abuja.html>

Vanguard (2017, January 31) Ese Oruru: Again, Judge's Absence Stalls Yunusa's Trial <https://www.vanguardngr.com/2017/01/ese-oruru-judges-absence-stalls-yunusas-trial/>

THE CONTRIBUTORS

OBIORA OKONKWO, PhD, is the Chairman of The Dome Entertainment and Hospitality Center, Abuja. He holds a Doctorate in Political Science from the Russian Academy of Science, Institute of World Economy and International Relations, Moscow.

NWOSU M. EZE, *MBA, CFA, FCNA, DEd, PhD.* currently heads Audit Division of the National Institute for Legislative and Democratic Studies, National Assembly, Abuja Nigeria. He is Fellow at the Association of National Accountants of Nigeria; the Institute Of Company Accountants, United Kingdom; and the Society of Company and Commercial Accountants, United Kingdom. He is also Member at ICFE, London.

WILFRED ETA EYO, is a consultant reader and library developer, co-ordinator, peniel library (member: National Action Committee, on Read Campaign; (fme) and Reading Association of Nigeria). He has won Reading Association of Nigeria award of excellence for promotion of community litracy.

CHUKWUDI UCHEAGU, is a Philosopher. He holds a Bachelor of Science Degree in Political Science from Enugu State University of Science and Technology. He also holds a Masters in Business Administration at the Ambrose Alli University, Ekpoma, and is currently a postgraduate student of Political Economy and Development Studies, University of Abuja.

LOUIS NWABUEZE EZEILO, PhD Leeds, is a member of the Institute of Chartered Economists of Nigeria, the Economic Network of the Higher Education Academy, United Kingdom and the Research in Development Network (RiDNet) of the University of Leeds, United Kingdom. His interests are highly focused on the issue of poverty and how to create an inclusive environment for a better economic and human development in Nigeria.

EZE, UZOAMAKA JENNIFER, is the Executive Director of Ada Igbo Women Development Initiative. She holds Advanced Degree in Linguistics.

www.ingramcontent.com/pod-product-compliance
Lightning Source LLC
Chambersburg PA
CBHW020524270326
41927CB00006B/436